Facts On File Encyclopedia of

Black Women

IN AMERICA

Social Activism

Encyclopedia of Black Women
in America

Facts On File Encyclopedia of

Black Women

IN AMERICA

Social Activism

Darlene Clark Hine, Editor

Kathleen Thompson, Associate Editor

☑® Facts On File, Inc.

Facts On File Encyclopedia of Black Women in America: Social Activism

Facts On File, Inc.
11 Penn Plaza
New York, NY 10001

Library of Congress Cataloging-in-Publication Data

Facts on File encyclopedia of Black women in America / Darlene Clark
Hine, editor ; Kathleen Thompson, associate editor.
p. cm.
Includes bibliographical references and index.
Contents: v. 1. The early years, 1619–1899—v. 2. Literature—
v. 3. Dance, sports, and visual arts—v. 4. Business and professions—
v. 5. Music—v. 6. Education—v. 7. Religion and community—
v. 8. Law and government—v. 9. Theatre arts and
entertainment—v. 10. Social activisim—v. 11. Science, health,
and medicine.
ISBN 0-8160-3424-9 (set : alk. paper)
ISBN 0-8160-3435-4 (Social Activism)
1. Afro-American women—Biography—Encyclopedias. I. Hine,
Darlene Clark. II. Thompson, Kathleen.
E185.96.F2   1997
920.72′08996073—dc20   96-33268

Text design by Cathy Rincon
Cover design by Smart Graphics

Printed in the United States of America

RRD VCS 10 9 8 7 6 5 4 3 2 1

This book is printed on acid-free paper.

Contents

How to Use This Volume

SCOPE OF THE VOLUME

The *Social Activism* volume includes entries on individuals and organizations in the following subject areas: civil rights, feminism, labor organization, social welfare, and community organization.

RELATED OCCUPATIONS

Professionals in related occupations that are covered in other volumes of this encyclopedia include the following: elected officials (*Law and Government*), teachers (*Education*), lawyers (*Law and Government*), community leaders (*Religion and Community*), clubwomen (*Religion and Community*), and philanthropists (*Religion and Community*).

HOW TO USE THIS VOLUME

The introduction to this volume presents an overview of the history of black women engaged in social activism. Law, health care, churches, and black women's clubs are frequently included in this overview, but more extensive coverage of these areas can be found in other volumes of this encyclopedia. A chronology following the book's main entries lists important events in the history of black women social activists in the United States.

Individuals and organizations are covered in alphabetically arranged entries. If you are looking for an individual or organization that does not have an entry in this volume, please check the alphabetically arranged list of the entries for all eleven volumes of this encyclopedia that appears at the end of this volume, in addition to tables of contents of each of the other volumes in this series.

Names of individuals and organizations for which there are entries in this or other volumes of the encyclopedia are printed in **boldface.** Check the contents list at the end of this book to find the volume where a particular entry can be found.

Facts On File Encyclopedia of

Black Women

IN AMERICA

Introduction

> In every human Breast, God has implanted a
> Principle, which we call Love of Freedom; it is
> impatient of Oppression, and pants for Deliverance.
>
> —**Phillis Wheatley,** Letter to
> Samson Occom February 11, 1774

The history of social activism among African Americans began the first time a slave joined a secret church service or lied to an overseer to protect a neighbor. It includes every act of resistance to the slave owner's mastery and every act of support for members of the slave community. The women who participated in slave revolts in New York in 1708 and 1712 were social activists. **Jenny Slew,** who sued for her freedom in a Massachusetts court in 1765—and won—was a social activist.

However, organized resistance by African Americans to the conditions of their life in this land largely began with the American Revolution and the coming of independence. It was inevitable that the patriots' talk of freedom and justice would waken in the black population the hope that these values could be applied to their lives as well.

Elizabeth Freeman, also known as Mum Bett, went to court in 1780 in search of freedom. She maintained that, since the Massachusetts state constitution declared all men free and equal, slavery was illegal. She was illiterate herself, but she found a lawyer to present her case. Like Jenny Slew, she was granted her freedom. It was a landmark case in American law. Freeman intended it to free all the remaining slaves in the state, but it didn't. As the future would prove again and again, legal action could take the fight for freedom only so far.

Still, in the North, many of those who fought for America's freedom and formed its new government recognized the contradiction between their belief in "inalienable rights" and the existence of the institution of slavery. Beginning with Vermont in 1777, the Northern states gradually eliminated slavery. By 1804, all states north of Maryland had abolished it.

However, being "free" was a seriously limited condition. There were few civil rights or economic opportunities. Most black women did the same jobs as freedwomen that they had done as slaves.

They had no say in government. And they lived in the shadow of slavery, which was growing ever stronger in the South.

The first organization formed specifically to improve the condition of black Americans was the Free African Society. It was established in Philadelphia in 1787. Though it was not a religious group, it led to the founding of the African Methodist Episcopal Church.

Black churches were, from their very beginnings, a part of the movement for rights and freedom. They served as gathering places, as support groups, and as sources of African-American unity. And women were the backbone of the black church. As in the white church, they seldom held positions of leadership. They weren't in the pulpit or sitting at the head of the table at church meetings. But they kept the church going. And there were some, such as **Jarena Lee, Rebecca Cox Jackson,** and **Julia A. J. Foote,** who emerged as independent preachers and leaders.

Lee and Foote both challenged convention by insisting that they, and other women, had rights in the eyes of God that were not being recognized by their brothers in the church. Behind their determination to change things for black women was a certainty that what they believed came from divine inspiration.

Jackson's activism went beyond religious rights. It was to describe Rebecca Cox Jackson that **Alice Walker** coined the term "womanist." In the early decades of the nineteenth century, Jackson traveled from town to town and church to church, preaching her own personal vision of God. But she also spoke of the importance of unity among black people. And she insisted that churches had to deal with the funda-

mental questions of black life—civil rights, families, education, and the possibilities for better jobs. In 1857, she founded a Shaker community that was made up primarily of black women. The community lasted almost up to the twentieth century.

The Free African Society also gave rise to the Female Benevolent Society of St. Thomas. This group was one of hundreds of benevolent societies that were formed by free African Americans in the North before the Civil War. More than a hundred came into being in Philadelphia alone. And more than half of those formed in the new country were women's groups. Among all the benevolent societies, more than two-thirds of the members were women.

These were considerably more than just charitable organizations. They fed the hungry and cared for the sick, but they also founded schools and engaged in antislavery activities. And, by 1830, they were joined by other free black organizations—insurance companies, credit unions, literary societies, moral reform groups, and political protest groups.

All of these groups were dedicated to the survival and advancement of black people. Indeed, in 1827, the Female Literary Society of New York was the main financial support of the first black newspaper, *Freedom's Journal,* which actively campaigned against slavery.

In the South, of course, the situation was very different. Activism, which could be defined as resistance to slavery, took more desperate forms; but it never stopped. It was seldom organized, but it was communal.

Although the first black churches were formed in Southern colonies, they were soon banned. Slave owners feared that the churches would encourage slave rebellions. For the same reason, education was outlawed. Everything in law and custom went against the African American's inborn desire for justice and freedom.

And the slaves resisted. They rebelled within the system of slavery and against it. There was a work ethic that was part of the unspoken code of the slave culture. It specified that, in exchange for slave labor and obedience, the owner would provide food, shelter, and clothing, in addition to acceptable physical and emotional treatment and some freedom in their intimate relations. Slaves who felt that this silent agreement had been violated rebelled against their owners.

Others rebelled against slavery itself. Some ran away. About 10 percent of fugitive slaves in the colonies were women. Some carried out resistance activities on the plantations. They refused to meet work quotas, talked back to authority figures, stole food, met in secret, plotted against masters, and even physically harmed white owners.

In 1777, for example, Jenny, a slave woman to John Lewis, was condemned and executed for conspiracy. The following year, Rachel, a slave of Lockey Collier, was executed for murder. In 1800, Nanny Prosser joined with her husband, Gabriel, and other slaves to plan a revolt near Richmond, Virginia. Between 1819 and 1831, seventeen female slaves in the state of Virginia were found guilty of crimes such as stealing and suspected arson and were transported out of the state. Six were found guilty of capital crimes such as murder, conspiracy, and arson and were executed.

There were also free black women in the South. For them, any kind of activism was enormously dangerous and difficult. They were in as much danger as slave women if they violated Southern law and custom, and they had a great deal more to lose. They lived in a kind of limbo—free in a slave society, black in a white society, women in a male society. Most of their protests were silent, and most of their aid to their slave brothers and sisters was secret.

Still, networks formed that would be the basis of later resistance movements. In the urban areas of the South, free African Americans—most of whom were women—developed close, supportive communities. In the not-too-distant future, those communities would produce important antislavery organizations.

However, at the same time organizations for black advancement in the United States were developing, there were others who believed that the best hope for African Americans in this country was to leave it.

EARLY BLACK NATIONALISM

Black nationalism did not begin with Malcolm X. It didn't begin with Elijah Muhammad or even Marcus Garvey. In the early years of the nineteenth century, there were African Americans who were already thinking and talking about separatism, violent resistance, and, especially, emigrationism—leaving the United States altogether.

In 1829, Robert Alexander Young wrote his "Ethiopian Manifesto" and David Walker his "Appeal to the Colored Citizens of the World." These were two of the earliest documents to discuss ideas that were later identified with black nationalism. Just a few years later, in 1832, **Maria Stewart** stood before a crowd in Boston and called for self-determination for all African-American men and women.

Stewart was controversial from the very beginning. For one thing, she was the first American-born woman of any ethnicity to give a series of public lectures. For another, she called for black independence—economic and otherwise—from all whites, even kindly, liberal ones. This was a radical message for those days, and it reflected the mood of a significant portion of free black Americans.

In 1836, a group of black women forced their way into a courtroom in Boston and rescued two fugitive slave women before they could be returned to the South. That same year, another group of black women did the same in a New York courtroom. Henry Highland Garnet's "Address to the Slaves," in 1843, again called for violent resistance. And separatism grew.

Rebecca Cox Jackson's Shaker community was only one of many all-black settlements that were established in the 1830s and 1840s. Located primarily in the Midwest, these towns provided an opportunity for African Americans to live apart from social pressures and discrimination. They were not merely noble experiments, but pockets of black self-reliance, some of which continue to exist and have an impact on our society to the present day.

In 1849, **Mary Ann Shadd Cary** added her voice to the call for black self-reliance with a pamphlet entitled "Hints to the Colored People of North America." Three years later, she published another pamphlet, and this time she strongly encouraged blacks in the United States to go to Canada. Cary had moved there herself in

1850 after the passage of the Fugitive Slave Law. That law allowed Southern slave owners to pursue escaped slaves into the North.

Cary did not speak only for emigration. She attacked any form of black dependency on whites. She was particularly opposed to the Refugee Home Society, which provided money, clothing, and land to escaped slaves. To Cary's disgust, they acquired these commodities by begging. This went against her firm belief that African Americans must be proud, self-reliant, and free from any hint of inferiority. She also attacked black folk religion, insisting that it kept her people morally and socially undeveloped.

Mary Ann Shadd Cary was not the only black American to emigrate to Canada after the Fugitive Slave Law was passed. Literally thousands left towns all over Ohio and Pennsylvania. Most went north, but some went to Central and South America and to Africa. Several emigration conventions were held. In 1854, women were one-third of the delegates at the National Emigration Convention, and Mary E. Bibb was elected second vice president.

However, as the Civil War neared, there came to be only one issue at the forefront of black activism. That was abolition.

THE ABOLITIONISTS

Not surprisingly, the first public abolitionists were white. The most important word in that sentence is *public*. Of course, all African Americans were against slavery, but what they thought or said, in the colonial period and the early decades of this country, had no public impact. And so, it is not unusual to read historical accounts of the abolition movement that focus primarily on white abolitionists. In *The New York Public Library Book of Chronologies,* for example, a chronology of the important events in the abolition of slavery contains only one black name, that of Nat Turner.

The Society of Friends, or Quakers, took a public stand against slavery from the beginning. Many of its members fell from grace during the early eighteenth century, but by 1750, the church was punishing members who owned slaves. By 1780, Northern Quakers were forcing church members to free their slaves. Many Congregational and Methodist churches joined in this effort.

During this time and for some years after the Revolutionary War, most people who spoke against slavery did not speak for immediate abolition of the institution. They proposed gradual methods of doing away with slavery. States began to outlaw slavery without forcing slave owners to give up their slaves. The children of slaves were born free. Selling slaves was outlawed. At the beginning of the Civil War, when all of the Northern states had outlawed slavery, there were still eighteen slaves living in the North.

What we usually think of as the abolition movement began to grow during the 1820s, when there was no longer any significant number of slaves in the North. But it was not, as some have portrayed it, a Northern phenomenon. By 1827, there were about 130 antislavery societies in this country, and 106 of them were in the South.

For a time, the movement was sidetracked by an effort to transport black Americans back to Africa, and 1,400 people actually were moved to Liberia by the American Colonization Society. However, by 1831, that effort had died a well-deserved death.

Soon, white abolitionist William Lloyd Garrison emerged as a major leader. Black workers in the abolition movement had justifiable complaints about many white abolitionists. Their conviction that slavery was evil did not always lead them to the conclusion that the races were equal. At the same time, it can't be denied that, for their beliefs, abolitionists suffered the hatred of their white neighbors and physical danger from anti-abolitionist mobs. They often did not understand what they were fighting, or what they were fighting *for,* but they put themselves at considerable risk in the battle. Still, the great black abolitionist Frederick Douglass spoke for many when he said that abolition "is emphatically our battle; no one else can fight it for us."

If the abolition movement was long dominated by its white members, it was always dominated by its male members, black and white. That is not to say that black women were inactive. They were simply, as would be true later in the civil rights movement of the twentieth century, not often recognized.

In 1832, a landmark organization dedicated to the elimination of slavery was founded. It was called the Female Anti-Slavery Society of Salem, Massachusetts, and its founders were free black women. The next year, an interracial group, the **Philadelphia Female Anti-Slavery Society,** was founded. Among its charter members were some of the most important women in the abolition movement.

There were forty-two women whose names were on the charter. Nine of them were black. The white women included Lucretia Mott, who would later be a leader in the suffrage movement. The black women included Charlotte **Forten** and her three daughters—Harriet D. Purvis, Sarah Louisa Forten, and Margaretta **Forten**—Grace Douglass, Mary Woods, Lydia White, Margaret Bowser, and Sarah McCrummel. Sarah Mapps Douglass, Grace Douglass' daughter, joined the organization a little later.

The Philadelphia group continued in existence for thirty-six years, until the Civil War and the Emancipation Proclamation had removed its reason for being. At all times, black women were dynamic members of the group.

Also in Philadelphia, black women founded the **Colored Females' Free Produce Society.** Its purpose was to encourage the boycotting of goods produced by slave labor. It was part of a larger Free Produce movement, and it provided the public with the opportunity to buy products, such as cotton and sugar, that had been produced entirely by nonslave workers.

In other parts of the country, as well, black women were in the forefront of the struggle. The great orator **Sojourner Truth** traveled around the country, speaking against slavery and for women's rights. **Harriet Tubman,** in the South, personally rescued more than 200 slaves, guiding them north on the Underground Railroad. **Sarah Parker Remond** toured the Midwest and, later, England, speaking out against slavery.

Mary Ellen Pleasant, later to make her fortune as an entrepreneur in San Francisco, helped finance John Brown's raid on

Harpers Ferry. **Frances E. W. Harper,** later to be the first black woman novelist, began her career writing and lecturing for the Maine Anti-Slavery Society.

Virtually all of these women remained active in the fight for black rights long past the end of the Civil War. And many were in the vanguard of yet another struggle.

WOMEN'S RIGHTS

The United States of America was founded on principles of equality, justice, and freedom . . . for white men. From the first, there were those who challenged the exclusion of black men from these basic human rights. And there were those who challenged the exclusion of women. These people were often, but certainly not always, the same.

The one group that had a personal stake in both struggles was black women. They were denied full participation in citizenship as African Americans, as women, and as African American women. As they fought for self-determination, they faced difficult choices, and still do.

Although the demand for women's rights began even before the founding of this country, it was the abolition movement that brought the issue to the fore. White women as well as black committed themselves to that movement. Both were consistently denied the right to speak, forced to take a back seat to male leaders, and confronted by the reality that they were not considered equals by men who talked eloquently about equality.

In 1840, Lucretia Mott, one of the white founding members of the interracial Philadelphia Female Anti-Slavery Society, was chosen as a delegate to the World's Anti-Slavery Convention in London. When she got there, she and all the other women delegates were refused the right to be seated on the convention floor. They were told they could remain only if they sat in the balcony, silent, behind a curtain.

Lucretia Mott became very angry. Her entire organization, an influential group of black and white women, was being denied representation at the convention. And Lucretia Mott stayed angry. In 1848, with the help of Elizabeth Cady Stanton, she organized the Seneca Falls Convention on Women's Rights. Frederick Douglass was one of those who addressed the gathering.

Black women were active from the early days. Sojourner Truth was on the women's rights lecture circuit, as well as the anti-slavery circuit, as early as 1849. She often spoke on the same platform with white feminists such as Susan B. Anthony.

Sarah Jane Woodson Early was active in the early women's movement, as were Harriet Forten Purvis, Margaretta Forten, and Sarah Remond. **Nancy Gardner Prince** was a participant in the 1854 National Women's Rights Convention.

After the Civil War, there came a crisis for the movement, which had by now focused on suffrage, or the right to vote. The vast majority of suffragists had also been abolitionists. The Thirteenth Amendment to the U.S. Constitution prohibited slavery. When the Fourteenth Amendment was passed, saying that no citizen could be denied the rights guaranteed by the Constitution, black and white suffragists challenged the unwritten assumption that all citizens were male. Just as Susan B. Anthony attempted to vote in New York State, Sojourner Truth tested the law in Michigan

and Mary Ann Shadd Cary in the District of Columbia.

However, there were other women—black and white—who believed that all attempts to gain the vote for women—black or white—should be shelved until it had been guaranteed to black men. This issue of priorities has come up repeatedly for black women, and it is not an easy issue to decide. It definitely split the woman suffrage movement right down the middle in the nineteenth century.

The women who fought to make the Fifteenth Amendment include women as well as black men joined the National Woman Suffrage Association—which claimed among its members Sojourner Truth, Mary Ann Shadd Cary, Susan B. Anthony, and Harriet Forten Purvis. Those who suspended their agitation for woman's suffrage until black male suffrage was won joined the American Woman Suffrage Association—which attracted Frances Harper, Caroline Remond Putnam, and Lottie Rollin, under the presidency of white abolitionist Henry Ward Beecher.

When the Fifteenth Amendment was passed, the right to vote could not be denied to any male citizen on the basis of race, color, or previous condition of servitude. It would take women another fifty years to win the same right.

During that time, relations between black and white women in the suffrage movement deteriorated. By the last decades of the century, there were few white suffragists who had fought next to black women for abolition. Susan B. Anthony, in her seventies and eighties, remembered her African-American allies and recognized publicly the important contributions of **Ida B. Wells-Barnett,** the women of the black women's club movement, and others. But Anthony was in the minority.

Most white suffragists ignored the fact that black men in the South were being deprived of their right to vote by Jim Crow laws, and that black women would be equally deprived, regardless of a constitutional amendment. Others counted on that fact. They secretly and not-so-secretly assured potential Southern supporters that they would not challenge the status quo.

More and more, black women began to wage their war for the vote as part of their own club movement, rather than as part of the mainstream suffrage movement. Their rights as women were, for them, inseparable from their rights as black women. As a result, the black women's club movement became a force for social change that had nothing to do with garden talks and afternoon teas.

The Clubwomen

The club movement had its roots in the women's church groups and in the benevolent societies that grew up in the North before the Civil War. It was grounded in the literary societies that had promoted social improvement and the advancement of the race. It was a product of free, urban society in Northern cities such as Boston and Philadelphia, but eventually it spread around the country.

The members of black women's clubs came from the black middle class. They have been described as the black elite, and they were. However, they were anything but the idle rich. The members of the Bethel Literary and Historical Association in Washington, D.C., for example, were al-

most all teachers. The **Woman's Loyal Union,** in New York, was founded by a teacher and a journalist. The Woman's Era Club of Boston, was founded by a journalist who had also served on the U.S. Sanitation Commission. Some of these women were also the wives of prosperous business and professional men, but a great many were not.

Black women's clubs had a different composition from that of white women's clubs, and they also had different purposes. Behind all of their activities was the desire to advance African-American people. Every time a member gave a talk on English poetry, they believed, it was proof of the intellectual and artistic abilities of the race. Each performance of concert music on the piano was an opportunity for a musician who would never find a public arena.

The clubs founded schools and raised funds for hospitals, orphanages, and homes for the aged just as their white counterparts did. But there was a special consciousness behind their efforts, an awareness that they were serving their own people—and that no one else would.

The clubs also addressed serious social concerns. They confronted segregation in housing and transportation. They were in the forefront of the antilynching movement. And they worked constantly for the rights of women.

In the early 1890s, a crisis arose for black women's clubs. The **World's Columbian Exposition** in Chicago was being organized, and it was being proclaimed the most important and spectacular world's fair ever held. Under pressure from suffragists, the United States Congress had agreed to the establishment of a Woman's Building at the fair. The suffragists, however, were not put in charge of the building. That job went to Mrs. Potter Palmer, the socially prominent wife of one of the fair's financial backers. When she put together her "Board of Lady Managers," suffragists were conspicuously absent—and so were black women.

A group of Chicago women confronted the Lady Managers, but their petition for participation in the building was rejected. According to Palmer, black women were not included in the planning of the building because they had no national organization to represent them. The Colored Women's League, in Washington, D.C., tried to organize a national convention of black women's clubs in time to qualify. But they weren't successful.

In the end, the Lady Managers accepted a proposal from **Fannie Barrier Williams,** wife of a prominent black attorney in Chicago. She was appointed a clerk in charge of exhibit installations, and a New York black women's club put together an exhibit that was accepted.

However, the move toward a national organization of black women had begun. The First National Conference of Colored Women of America met in Boston in 1895. There were 104 delegates representing fourteen states and the District of Columbia. Out of this conference came the National Federation of Afro-American Women.

There was, however, a competing national organization—the National League of Colored Women, headquartered in Washington, D.C. In 1896, the two groups merged to form the **National Association of Colored Women** (NACW). **Mary Church Terrell** was its first president. In the years to come, there would be conflicts within the group. The militant leanings of some members would clash with the steely determination of others to present a respectable, ladylike image of black women. But the club movement continued to function as an important political force. And it was at the forefront of the next great battle black Americans had to fight.

THE ANTILYNCHING MOVEMENT

In 1892, three store owners were lynched in Memphis, Tennessee. One of them was the close friend of a journalist named Ida Bell Wells. Wells was the co-owner of a newspaper called the *Memphis Free Speech.* She had been speaking out in defense of her people and their rights all her life. After the lynching, she spoke out with a vengeance.

She wrote searing editorials. She demanded that African Americans fight back. She ripped apart the myth that black men rape white women, the usual justification for lynching. Her attacks were so brutal—and so effective—that whites destroyed her press and threatened her life.

However, Ida B. Wells had just begun. Unintimidated by white threats, she carried her crusade to New York and then across the nation and to Europe. Behind her at every turn were the black women of America.

Her first book, *Southern Horrors,* was published in 1892. The money to finance it came from a fund-raising event in New York that was called "the greatest demonstration ever attempted by race women for one of their own number." In 1919, the

National Association for the Advancement of Colored People (NAACP), of which Wells was a founder, committed itself to lobbying against lynching.

Mary Talbert, president of the NACW, enlisted women's groups in support of the effort. In 1922, she formed a group called the Anti-Lynching Crusaders. This women's group soon had 900 members and pledged itself to enrolling one million.

Among other things, the Crusaders worked to bring white women into the antilynching movement. During the 1920s, the National Council of Women, under pressure from the Crusaders, voted to endorse the movement. Then, in 1930, an organization called the Association of Southern Women for the Prevention of Lynching was founded by white women. These women rejected their role as the excuse for white male violence against black men.

The movement worked for federal antilynching laws for several decades. In this, it was not successful. However, it did change public opinion. By 1942, a Gallup poll showed that a great majority of white Americans favored such laws.

But the antilynching movement was only a part of a greater war. And that war was being fought on many fronts.

JIM CROW

There are three enemies that African Americans have fought against for their rights—law, custom, and violence. Law has been the most powerful of these enemies, custom the most enduring, and violence—including lynching—the most cruel.

These three forces have worked together, supporting and sanctioning each other. Those who have fought against them have seldom been able to isolate and attack one without finding themselves painfully entangled with the others. This was never more true than in the last decades of the nineteenth century and the first decades of the twentieth.

The South did not placidly accept the end of slavery. During Reconstruction, federal troops moved into the region to protect black citizens and their rights. But when Rutherford B. Hayes withdrew the troops in 1877, the progress that African Americans had made began to unravel. In 1881, the first of the Jim Crow laws was passed in Tennessee.

Named after a figure from minstrel shows, Jim Crow laws were designed to shut African Americans out of the mainstream of American life. They forced black citizens to use separate facilities of all kinds, public and private. These laws went against the Civil Rights Act of 1875, which stated that there could be no discrimination in public places or on means of transportation within the United States. And, at first, that act offered some protection against Jim Crow.

However, in 1896, in the *Plessy* v. *Ferguson* case, the United States Supreme Court declared that separate but equal facilities in interstate railroad transportation were legal. This set a precedent that would be used in court cases concerning everything from public washrooms to public schools. From that ruling until the 1954 *Brown* v. *Board of Education* ruling, "separate but equal" prevailed, and the definition of "equal" was pretty much up to whatever white sheriff, mayor, or school board was in charge.

In 1913, the Supreme Court made this form of discrimination official when it ruled that the Civil Rights Act of 1875 was unconstitutional. The test case was that of Emma Butts, a black woman who sued a steamship company for denying her accommodations equal to those it provided for white passengers. She lost, and so did all other black Americans.

What developed was two separate societies, which were far from equal. There were segregated hospitals, schools, restaurants, and neighborhoods. There were signs all over the South that said "whites only" or "colored only." They hung over water fountains, bathrooms, and doorways. They were posted on vending machines. Black citizens were denied the right to enter amusement parks and swimming pools, concert halls and zoos. In the courtroom, they were sworn in on a different Bible.

There is no way of describing the effect this had on both blacks and whites. It was one of the most profound examples of brainwashing the world has ever known. Those who grew up in this segregated world did not just *believe* that African Americans were inferior, they *knew* it. That knowledge was reinforced a hundred times a day.

But there were countless African Americans, and a large number of whites, who resisted the brainwashing. In the words of **Nannie Helen Burroughs,** "Men and women are not made on trains and on streetcars. If in our homes there is implanted in the hearts of our children, of our young men and of our young women the thought they are what they are, not by

environment, but of themselves, this effort to teach a lesson of inferiority will be futile."

Many black citizens chose to find ways of living outside the segregated society of the United States of America. Some followed Bishop Henry McNeal Turner to Liberia, but most sought those ways within U.S. borders.

There were the pioneers. Many black women and men went west to find freedom. They did not find a society free from racism, but they often made impressive lives for themselves anyway. Annie Neal opened the Mountain View Hotel in 1895 in Oracle, Arizona. For many years, she offered her guests nursing care, a private school, and monthly church services in the middle of the Wild West. **Mary Fields** drove a stagecoach. Elvira Conley did laundry for Wild Bill Hickock before becoming governess to a wealthy family.

There were black towns. Between 1890 and 1916, thirty towns with largely black populations sprang up in Oklahoma Territory alone. The town of Boley, Oklahoma, had two banks, a sawmill, a cotton gin, three newspapers, two hotels, and a college. No one walking down its streets ever faced a "whites only" sign. And there were dozens of such towns in the West, from Kansas to California.

Josephine Allensworth and her husband founded a town near Bakersfield, California, because they were disappointed by the racist climate of Los Angeles. She was president of the school board, established a library for the colony, and sponsored organizations for self-improvement.

Economic independence from the white mainstream was another path chosen by

African Americans around the turn of the century. One of the key figures in this movement was by **Maggie Lena Walker.** Walker was the chief officer of the Independent Order of Saint Luke and president of the Saint Luke Penny Savings Bank. One of her stated goals was to create jobs for African Americans, especially women. She believed that once money entered black hands it should stay in black hands. It made no sense to her that the black American who is constantly oppressed by whites "carries to their bank every dollar he can get his hands upon and then goes back the next day, borrows and then pays the white man to lend him his own money."

Another champion of economic independence from white society was Marcus Garvey. He also proposed cultural independence from that society through identification with Africa and other Africans. **Amy Jacques Garvey,** his second wife, was an important figure in his black nationalist organization, the **Universal Negro Improvement Association** (UNIA). Among her other duties, she was editor of the women's pages in the UNIA newspaper, *Negro World.*

Another prominent Garveyite was **Henrietta Vinton Davis,** one of the founding members of the UNIA. She was a well-known actor before she gave up her career to speak for black liberation. A magnetic speaker, she drew large crowds in the United States and in Central and South America.

These independent women—some of whom could be counted among the early black nationalists—were important to the struggle against racism in this country. There were, however, many more who focused on changing and belonging to mainstream American society. One of their most difficult challenges was finding jobs with adequate pay and reasonable working conditions.

THE LABOR MOVEMENT

Black women are workers. No one has ever been able to deny that. And yet, when the cry has gone out for "workers of the world" to unite, black women were rarely mentioned.

For centuries, most black women have worked outside their homes. What seems to have kept the labor movement from addressing their problems is that they worked *inside* somebody else's home, or perhaps in somebody else's field. But they were not usually able to get jobs in the factories that were the focus of the American labor movement.

So, the actions black women have taken to better their job situations were often outside that movement. There were strikes among black women fieldworkers as early as 1862. More than 3,000 black women were involved in a strike by the Washerwomen's Association of Atlanta in 1881. However, when the American Federation of Labor (AFL) was founded in that same year, black women were not included.

Many black women went into the factories during World War I. But when the war ended and labor shortages no longer existed, this small gain in economic progress was wiped out.

Then, in 1935, the Congress of Industrial Organizations (CIO) separated from the AFL. The new group concentrated more on black workers and on unskilled workers in the South in general. So, during

A strike was usually the only way manual workers could hope to improve their working conditions. These women (and men) represent the range of people employed as laundry workers. (ARCHIVES OF LABOR AND URBAN AFFAIRS, WAYNE STATE UNIVERSITY).

the Depression and World War II, the relatively small number of women in industry became involved in labor activism.

The Food Workers' Industrial Union, a CIO affiliate in St. Louis, was organized by Connie Smith and 3,000 nut pickers, 85 percent of whom were black women. They staged a successful strike in spite of management's efforts to break it by offering more money to striking white women to return to work.

The Southern Tenant Farmers Union (STFU) protested federal agricultural policies. Among the many black women involved in the protest were spokespeople Carrie Dilworth and Henrietta McGee. They made sharecropping and its inequities a national issue.

In the tobacco industry, black women became very important labor activists. They worked mainly as tobacco stemmers, the lowliest job in the plant. In 1938, Louise "Mamma" Harris, a black stemmer, started a series of walkouts at the I. N. Vaughn Company in Richmond, Virginia. The strikes that resulted were supported by white International Ladies Garment Workers Union (ILGWU) women. This was a shock to Southern managers. The strikes led to the formation of the Tobacco Workers Organizing committee, another CIO affiliate.

In 1943, there was a major strike at the R.J. Reynolds company in North Carolina. Among the union activists involved were several black women, including Theodosia Simpson, Velma Hopkins, Viola Brown, Ruby Jones, and Miranda Smith. The strike resulted in Reynolds' agreeing to sit down and talk with Local No. 22 of the Food, Tobacco, Agricultural, and Allied Workers of America (FTA). Later, Miranda Smith became a regional director of the FTA. It was the highest position held by a black woman in the labor movement up to that time.

When World War II began, black women were again hired in the nation's factories. However, wartime labor shortages notwithstanding, black women were the "last hired, first fired" and they were underpaid. The racism of white women periodically erupted into so-called hate strikes against black women workers, which unions did little to counter.

In order to fight discrimination by management, black women had to find a way past discrimination within the labor movement itself. Efforts to segregate workers in organized labor were widespread, particularly in the AFL. "They're trying to have Jim Crow unions," said tobacco stemmer Luanna Cooper in 1943. "They wanted me to join. I told them: I get Jim Crow free. I won't pay for that."

In 1943, the CIO formed the Committee to Abolish Racial Discrimination. That same year, Detroit's United Auto Workers co-sponsored with the NAACP a rally at which 10,000 workers demanded that war industry jobs be opened to black women. Between 1940 and 1945, black union membership rose from 200,000 to 1.25 million.

After the war, black women workers faced severe setbacks. Unions worked with management to eliminate women from the work force. The CIO caved in to anti-Communist hysteria and expelled eleven so-called suspect unions, all with strong records for interracial organizing. The Taft-Hartley Act in 1947 further limited organized labor. Even organized labor's postwar Southern organizing drives—"Operation Dixie"—primarily targeted the all-white textile industry or expected black workers to accept their second-class status.

Miranda Smith clearly linked civil rights and labor activism in her speech to the CIO in 1947. "We want to stop lynching in the South," she said. "We want people to walk the picket lines unafraid." However, the national labor movement was unwilling to endorse the link between civil rights and labor activism or make the fate of black workers a priority.

By 1947, accusations of Communist domination, a House Un-American Activities Committee investigation, and competition with the AFL had severely eroded the power of the FTA's Local 22 in Winston-Salem. Three years later, nonunion forces were victorious at R.J. Reynolds. By 1948, most of the economic advances made by black women during the war had eroded, and by 1950, 41 percent of laboring black women worked as domestics.

Black women were among the labor leaders who tried to resist red-baiting in the National Negro Labor Council (NNLC), formed in 1951. The short-lived NNLC put pressure on industries to comply with the Fair Employment Practices Committee nondiscrimination policies in peacetime. The group also stressed the continuing need for black workers to organize. One-third of its original delegates were black women. Octavia Hawkins, a garment worker active in the Amalgamated Clothing Workers, was the organization's first treasurer.

A series of successful NNLC strikes in the early 1950s opened jobs as stewardesses and cashiers to black women. In these and other organizations, black women and men united to advance their collective interests and to challenge economic racism thoroughly. These efforts were among the forces that led to the modern civil rights movement.

THE NAACP AND BEYOND

In 1908, a truly terrible race riot had devastated the black community in Springfield, Illinois. In reaction to it, socialist journalist William English Walling issued a challenge to his readers in the *Independent* to fight against racism. In response to the challenge, Oswald Garrison Villard—grandson of prominent abolitionist William Lloyd Garrison—asked Americans who believed in democracy to meet together. This invitation is often referred to as "the call." Sixty people signed their names to the call along with Villard's. Of those, one-third were women. The two black women who signed were Ida B. Wells-Barnett (now married to Ferdinand Barnett) and Mary Church Terrell.

The organization that was formed in response to the call had both black and white members. In the beginning, the majority of the officers were white. However, the first field secretary of the NAACP was a black woman named **Kathryn Johnson.** And educators **Mary McLeod Bethune** and Nannie Helen Burroughs were on the board of advisors for more than thirty years.

Still, for the most part, the visible leaders of the national organization were men. Over time, they changed from white men to black men, but they remained men. The irony of this is that the local organizations, the supporting organizations, the grassroots groups that kept the NAACP alive were usually run by women.

The same women who founded black women's clubs and sororities founded local chapters of the NAACP. The same women who raised funds for black churches raised funds for the NAACP. Those who had recruited members for their Parent-Teacher Associations now recruited members for the NAACP.

In recent years, historians have begun to look again at the history of the civil rights movement in this country. The pattern they have detected runs through virtually every major civil rights organization. Women have created and operated the structures by which actions are accomplished. Men have spoken for the group and interacted with white leadership.

This pattern is not rigid. There have been exceptions. Especially on a local level, women have often been spokespeople. And certainly there have been men sitting at tables registering voters. However, when looking at the history of the movement in the United States, it is important to remember that the most visible people are not necessarily those who have had the greatest impact.

In its early years, the NAACP participated in the antilynching movement at the urging of Ida B. Wells and others. Later, the focus of the organization would shift. Of the three enemies black people must fight—law, custom, and violence—the NAACP chose to confront the first. Its officers believed that, in that way, it could win against the others as well.

This strategy put men squarely in the forefront of the NAACP. (In the twenties and thirties, few black women had law degrees.) However, there was one woman who could not be ignored, and who staunchly opposed the strategy.

Ella Josephine Baker had been organizing people for a long time before she connected with the NAACP. In 1930, at the age of twenty-seven, she joined the Young Negroes Cooperative League, in Harlem. She was soon elected national director. This group believed that black people must cooperate economically and otherwise in order to survive. Collective decision making and interdependency were highly valued. Individualism was frowned upon.

She also worked, during this time, with the Women's Day Workers and Industrial League, the Harlem Housewives Cooperative, and the YWCA. By the time she joined the NAACP in 1940, she was an experienced organizer, committed to involving black people of all social, educational, and economic levels. She was not about to see NAACP field offices turned into fund-raising groups for a series of legal cases.

Baker started as a field secretary and later became director of branches. Her fieldwork took her to small black communities throughout the South. Before long, she had contacts everywhere, a network of friends and supporters. However, by 1946 she was fed up. She could no longer work in the NAACP bureaucracy nor believe in the legal strategy. She resigned. However, she remained a volunteer for the organization and was president of the New York branch, the first woman to hold that position.

In 1952, the NAACP went to court with its biggest case so far. It was a direct challenge to the "separate but equal" precedent set by *Plessy* v. *Ferguson*. Thurgood Marshall and his crack team of lawyers presented five cases of discrimination in schooling to the U.S. Supreme Court. The court decided to hear all of them on one day and make a decision. The group of cases was heard under the name *Brown* v. *The Board of Education of Topeka, Kansas*, because that particular case was outside the South. A year after the cases were first presented, the court voted unanimously that, as Chief Justice Earl Warren said, "in the field of public education the doctrine of 'separate but equal' has no place. Separate educational facilities are inherently unequal."

It was a tremendous victory. However, it was all but overshadowed by a tired woman in Montgomery who refused to give up her seat on a bus. Rosa Parks' action sparked a wildfire that spread across the South.

THE MONTGOMERY BUS BOYCOTT

Rosa Parks was not just any tired woman. And her decision to remain seated on that fateful day in December, 1955, did not come out of the blue.

Montgomery, Alabama, had had racially segregated buses since the city bus line began operation in the mid-1930s. It was supported by a city ordinance first enacted in 1900 to segregate streetcars. Montgomery's bus customs were harsher than those in many other Southern cities. Not only were black passengers often required to pay their fare at the front and then reboard through the back door, but also they frequently had to stand over vacant seats reserved for whites. If the forward white section was full, drivers ordered black riders to relinquish their seats in the unreserved middle section for arriving white passengers—and they often did so rudely, with racial slurs.

Black women bore the brunt of the abusive treatment. Because women made up 56 percent of the city's black population, and because the majority of employed women worked as domestics in white homes across town, they rode the buses in much greater numbers than did black men.

For more than a decade before the boycott, individual women defied the injustice of segregated seating. In 1944, for instance, Viola White was arrested on a bus in Montgomery for violating the segregation code and then was beaten and jailed. She was released from jail, but when she died ten years later, the appeal of her conviction had still not been heard.

In 1946, Dr. **Mary Fair Burks,** head of the Alabama State College English Department in Montgomery, founded the **Women's Political Council** (WPC). Its goal was to promote voter registration and civic activism by black women, especially by professional women. The group addressed community problems such as inadequate parks and playgrounds and mistreatment on buses.

In the fall of 1949, a newly hired English professor at Alabama State College, **Jo Ann Gibson Robinson,** joined the WPC. After a painful experience of abuse by a bus driver, she dedicated herself to remedying the bus situation. When she succeeded Burks as council president in the early 1950s she made this issue its prime concern.

Robinson and other WPC activists met regularly with city officials to discuss the segregation policy, without success. In May 1954, four days after the *Brown* v. *Board of Education* decision, Robinson wrote a letter to Mayor W. A. Gayle warning him of a boycott if conditions did not improve. "Please consider this plea," she concluded, "for even now plans are being made to ride less, or not at all, on our buses."

A major turning point in the bus campaign came in March of 1955 with the arrest and trial of fifteen-year-old Claudette Colvin, a junior at Booker T. Washington High School, for refusing to give up her seat in the unreserved midsection of a bus. The Colvin incident roused the black community and made bus seating an issue, for the first time, in the municipal election that month. Robinson acted as the main spokesperson at two meetings the WPC and other black groups held with city commissioners and bus company officials.

One member of the black delegation was Rosa Parks, a longtime civil rights activist and mentor of the National Association for the Advancement of Colored People Youth Council, of which Colvin was a member. The meetings yielded only empty promises from city and bus company officials. When Colvin was convicted, even though the bus company manager admitted that the driver had violated company policy, boycott sentiment grew.

A sizable number of people refused to ride for several days. Robinson pushed for an organized boycott, but civil rights leader E. D. Nixon decided that Colvin, who was pregnant at the time, would not be a fitting symbol around which to mobilize protest. Nor did hers seem a promising test case to challenge bus segregation in federal court. The men "were afraid," Robinson later said. "Women are more daring when it comes to what we face."

In July 1955, the black community was heartened when the U.S. Court of Appeals for the Fourth Circuit in Richmond, Virginia, declared in *Flemming* v. *South Carolina Electric and Gas Company* that bus segregation, even on buses that operated within one state, was unconstitutional. Sarah Mae Flemming, arrested on a Columbia, South Carolina, bus the year before, had sued the bus company for violating her Fourteenth Amendment rights to equal protection. (The ruling was upheld by the U.S. Supreme Court in April 1956, but was not enforceable in Montgomery and the city ignored it.) When, in October 1955, eighteen-year-old Mary Louise Smith was arrested on a Montgomery bus, community leaders again decided not to press the case for federal appeal.

In the early evening of Thursday, December 1, 1955, after a long day of tailoring at Montgomery Fair department store, Rosa Parks was arrested on a city bus when she refused to give up her seat in the unreserved section to a white man. Although Parks had not planned her calm protest, she recalled that she had "a life history of being rebellious against being mistreated because of my color." The time had come "when I

had been pushed as far as I could stand to be pushed. . . . I had decided that I would have to know once and for all what rights I had as a human being and a citizen."

Parks was bailed out of city jail by E. D. Nixon, with whom she had worked for twelve years in the Montgomery NAACP. He was accompanied by Clifford Durr, a prominent local attorney who had served on the Federal Communications Commission under President Franklin D. Roosevelt, and his wife, Virginia Durr. These Southern whites were outspoken opponents of segregation. All four returned to Parks' home, where Nixon persuaded her, against her husband's wishes, to make hers the major test case challenging segregation laws. Parks' virtuous character and high stature in the black community made her the ideal representative of black grievances and goals.

Meanwhile, when Jo Ann Robinson learned of Parks' arrest, she decided to begin the boycott. After phoning Nixon and getting his support, she hastily drafted a flyer that called on all black residents to stay off the buses on Monday, the day of Parks' trial. "Another Negro woman has been arrested and thrown into jail," Robinson wrote, "because she refused to get up out of her seat on the bus for a white person to sit down. . . . Negroes have rights, too, for if Negroes did not ride the buses, they could not operate. . . . The next time it may be you, or your daughter, or mother."

Around midnight Robinson drove to the Alabama State College campus where, risking her job, she and a business department colleague stayed up all night mimeographing 50,000 copies of the flyer. The next day—using distribution routes that the

WPC had mapped out several months earlier—Robinson and two students drove all over town, delivering the bundles. They went to schools, businesses, stores, factories, taverns, beauty parlors, and barbershops.

Having launched the boycott, Robinson, Burks, and other WPC leaders took part in a large planning meeting at Dexter Avenue Baptist Church, whose newly appointed pastor was twenty-six-year-old Dr. Martin Luther King, Jr. At Sunday services the Baptist, African Methodist Episcopal, and other black ministers urged their congregations to join the protest.

The boycott on Monday, December 5, proved a spectacular success. Very few African Americans rode the buses. In the afternoon the leaders formed a new organization, the Montgomery Improvement Association (MIA), to direct the protest. They elected King president. Several women were chosen to serve on the MIA executive committee, including Robinson, Rosa Parks, Irene West, Euretta Adair, and Erna Dungee.

That night a few thousand boycotters, more women than men, gathered at Holt Street Baptist Church. They resolved to continue the mass protest until they won decent treatment. Robinson and the WPC not only began the boycott but mobilized leadership by other women and by the ministers.

Once the boycott started, King and other men took charge and assumed the major leadership positions. In a short time the young preacher was universally recognized as leader in fact as well as name. Yet if King, Nixon, Ralph Abernathy, and other male leaders dominated the policy making, women leaders took responsibility for

much of the hands-on organizing, including the efficient car pool system, that sustained the boycott for over a year.

"We really were the ones who carried out the actions," MIA financial secretary Erna Dungee Allen recalled. For a number of reasons—including sexism, the need to protect their jobs, and deference to a long tradition of community leadership by black ministers—female leaders remained less visible and rarely if ever served as speakers at mass meetings or press conferences. The women "passed the ideas to men to a great extent," Allen remembered. Burks and Robinson "were very vocal and articulate, especially in committee meetings." Yet in the mass meetings, women "let the men have the ideas and carry the ball. They were the power behind the throne."

Numerous women exercised informal leadership, but Robinson's multifaceted role was probably second only to King's in its impact. She chose to keep a low public profile, however, in order not to endanger either her teaching position at Alabama State College, a black institution dependent on the white legislature, or the supportive college president, H. Councill Trenholm. King reported that "more than any other person," the indefatigable Robinson "was active on every level of the protest." Besides her influential role on major committees, she served as a key MIA negotiator since she had had the most experience dealing with white officials. She also edited and produced the monthly MIA newsletter that was sent all over the country.

While Robinson, Irene West, Euretta Adair, Hazel Gregory, Johnnie Carr, and other middle-class women served on committees, managed the MIA office, and played vital leadership roles, dozens of less-educated women supported the boycott. Georgia Gilmore, a self-employed cook, organized a club that sold pies and cakes, and she donated the proceeds at the mass meetings. Inez Ricks formed a rival club, and the meetings were enlivened by a weekly contest over which club raised more money.

The female leadership network was crucial to the boycott's success, but the backbone of the long protest was several thousand working-class women who, in the face of intimidation and threats, rode in the car pools or walked as far as twelve miles a day, even in the rain. "I'm not walking for myself," said an elderly woman refusing a ride. "I'm walking for my children and my grandchildren."

Another woman, Mother Pollard, promised King that she would walk until it was over. "But aren't your feet tired?" he inquired. "My feets is tired," she answered, "but my soul is rested." Many domestic workers had the support or at least the agreement of their white female employers, who in some cases actually drove them to and from work. As role models whose commitment, sacrifice, and ingenuity inspired leaders and followers alike, the women who stayed off the buses were the protest's prime movers and underlying leaders.

Finally, even in court, women were makers of history in Montgomery. While Rosa Parks' appeal was delayed in state court, MIA and NAACP lawyers filed a federal lawsuit in the name of Claudette Colvin, Mary Louise Smith, and two older women whose rights also had been violated on buses. The *Browder* v. *Gayle* lawsuit resulted in the November 1956 U.S. Supreme Court decision striking down Alabama's city and state bus segregation laws.

Montgomery's black citizens called off the boycott when the ruling took effect in December and buses were no longer segregated. With the bus victory bolstering their morale and confidence, many of the women activists turned their attention to other pressing community issues such as school desegregation and voter registration.

LITTLE ROCK NINE

The next major battle came in Little Rock, Arkansas. Though the NAACP had won an important victory with *Brown* v. *The Board of Education* in 1954, little actual integration in the schools happened right away. In 1957, nine young people were scheduled to enter Central High School in Little Rock when Governor Orval Faubus declared that they would not be allowed to do so.

Faubus' move was a campaign strategy. He was up for reelection and facing a strongly segregationist opponent. He had to prove that he was just as much against black civil rights as his opponent. He chose to take a symbolic stand by turning the nine black students away from the schoolhouse door.

However, those nine students were not just any kids off the street. They were carefully chosen for their scholastic achievement, emotional stability, and supportive families. The woman who chose them was **Daisy Bates**, president of the Arkansas NAACP.

Daisy Bates was a civil rights veteran. She and her husband, L. C. Bates, owned and operated a newspaper, the *Arkansas State Press*. They had been reporting civil rights abuses since 1941 and paying the price for it. They had lost advertisers after reporting the murder of a black soldier by a white policeman, for example. But they kept printing the truth and their newspaper survived.

In 1952, the NAACP asked Daisy Bates to become president of the Arkansas state conference of NAACP branches. Starting in 1954, she had personally been taking black children to enroll in all-white schools around Little Rock. Each time, they were rejected. And each time, Bates made sure the incident was reported in the newspapers.

The case of the **Little Rock Nine**—as the nine students at Central High School came to be called—was the end result of all Bates' work. All of their actions were planned and coordinated by Bates. The one mistake she made turned into a historic moment.

Bates had planned that all of the students would enter the school together on the morning of September 22, 1957. But she failed to get the message to one of the nine, Elizabeth Eckford. When Elizabeth arrived alone at the campus, violence broke out. Her courage and poise as the mobs jeered and threatened her, were reported across the country. She became a symbol of the character of black youth.

Bates went to the school the next day with all nine students. This time, they were escorted by police and entered in secrecy. But the violence outside became so intense they were forced to leave. Finally, President Dwight D. Eisenhower was forced to send in the National Guard. It remained on the campus of the school throughout the year.

Bates watched over the Little Rock Nine. She was there whenever they and their parents met with school officials or police. She made it clear again and again that anyone who challenged these students was challenging Daisy Bates and the NAACP.

All but one of the students completed the school year. Harassment by white students never stopped. But the wall of segregation in Southern schools had begun to crumble. And black young people around the country began to move.

SIT-INS, FREEDOM RIDERS, AND ELLA BAKER

In the 1960s, the South was swept by a tidal wave. From a sit-in at a whites-only lunch counter in Greensboro, North Carolina, to demonstrations in Oklahoma and Texas, protest engulfed the Southern states. Most of the protesters were young people, students. Many of them had belonged to the NAACP Youth clubs. Before long, it became clear that, effective as many of their independent demonstrations were, they needed an organization. The NAACP would not do. They also failed to find what they needed in Martin Luther King's Southern Christian Leadership Conference. Then they found **Ella Baker**.

After the Montgomery bus boycott, when King and others formed the SCLC, that group had called on Baker to head up their Crusade for Citizenship. She agreed to take over this voter rights campaign, but she soon found the same problems she had encountered in the NAACP. Much as she admired King, she felt the movement was depending too much on his charismatic personality. "Strong people don't need strong leaders," she said. She also believed that too many decisions were made by a small group of leaders, without enough participation by the mass of black people.

After Greensboro, Baker quit the SCLC. The new student movement was much more the kind of movement she believed was needed. She went to work for the **Young Women's Christian Association** (YWCA) in order to have a base from which to work with the young people. In April of 1960, she called a conference of sit-in leaders at Shaw University. Out of this conference came the **Student Nonviolent Coordinating Committee** (SNCC).

From the beginning, Baker encouraged the students to abide by the principles she had always valued. These were grass-roots democracy, group-centered decision making, and the involvement of all members of the community. SNCC opened its leadership circles to youth, poor people, and women in a way that was unusual in the civil rights movement.

SNCC organizers went into the rural areas of the Deep South, using the contacts that Baker had formed there over the previous two decades. They emphasized direct action over court battles. In 1964, with Baker's participation, SNCC members **Annie Devine,** Victoria Gray, and **Fannie Lou Hamer** were among the founders of the **Mississippi Freedom Democratic Party** (MFDP).

Fannie Lou Hamer was a sharecropper who worked the fields from the time she was six years old until 1962, when she was forty-five. In that year, she tried to register

to vote. As a result, she had to flee her home, narrowly escaping death from gunfire fired into a friend's house. Soon thereafter, she became a member of SNCC. In 1964, she became a fieldworker.

Hamer faced violence again and again as she worked to register black voters. When the idea of the MFDP arose, she was ready. The purpose of the MFDP was to challenge Mississippi's all-white Democratic Party leadership. In the year of its founding, the MFDP registered 80,000 voters in its Freedom Ballot campaign. Those voters elected a delegation to the 1964 Democratic convention, an alternative to the regular delegation that was elected by white voters. Not legally recognized, the Freedom Ballot election was the only one in Mississippi that year that was run in accordance with the U.S. Constitution and the policies of the Democratic Party.

At the 1964 Democratic convention, the group challenged national Democratic Party leaders to seat them instead of the regular Mississippi delegation, whose election was the result of a discriminatory process. In the course of the action that followed, Fannie Lou Hamer stood before the convention and spoke. She told about a people who had been disfranchised. She also told about what happened to civil rights workers and black people who tried to vote. In painful detail, she described the beating she and five others received in jail. That speech became one of the historic documents of the civil rights movement.

The MFDP wasn't seated. At one point, Lyndon Johnson suggested to Hubert Humphrey that, if the Freedom Party were silenced, Humphrey would be the vice-presidential candidate. Hamer asked Humphrey, "Mr. Humphrey, do you mean to tell me that your position is more important to you than four hundred thousand black people's lives?" Finally, Humphrey and Walter Mondale offered the Democratic National Committee's compromise. The offer was for at-large seats for two members of the delegation. It was rejected by Hamer and the others.

However, the MFDP won from the Democratic Party a vow that no delegation would be seated at the 1968 convention which had benefitted from discriminatory practices in its election. That promise was carried out.

Many other women were active in SNCC. **Diane Nash** and **Ruby Doris Smith** were among the Freedom Riders who went to jail in Jackson, Mississippi. Nash later became leader of the direct-action wing of the organization. Smith (later Smith-Robinson) eventually became executive secretary of the organization. Victoria Jackson Gray ran for Congress on the MFDP ticket. There were dozens more black women in positions of leadership, thousands more who worked with dedication.

During Freedom Summer, in 1964, they registered voters at the risk of their lives. They, along with women and men from SCLC and CORE, started on a march from Selma to Montgomery in March of 1965, only to be clubbed and teargassed by police on horseback. Two weeks later, they started out again. Five months later, Lyndon Johnson signed the Voting Rights Act into law.

SNCC, under the guidance of Ella Baker, proved that black women rose to positions of power and responsibility in the civil rights movement when they were given the opportunity. But, in the late 1960s, the movement was moving toward less involvement, not more.

BLACK POWER

During the sixties, the nonviolent civil rights movement was gaining ground in the South, but the North was another story. In the South, the fight was largely against law at that point. Custom would come later. In the North, custom was the primary enemy and, like some mythological serpent, it was a slippery enemy to fight. "There were no obtainable, immediate results," said Bayard Rustin, "for the northern, ghettoized black whose housing is getting worse; who is unable to find work; whose schools are deteriorating; who sees constantly more rats and roaches and garbage in the streets. He needed Malcolm, who brought him an internal victory."

Malcolm X was the first of the advocates of what would soon be called "Black Power." In the approximately ten years before his murder, he connected strongly with Northern black youth by speaking again of black nationalism, self-reliance, and separation from white society. Others began to strike the same chord. Stokely Carmichael, then SNCC chairman, coined the phrase "Black Power."

The Black Panthers built a party around this growing sense of pride and power. Rejecting the nonviolence of the NAACP and Martin Luther King, a new movement emerged. At least in the beginning, it was a movement that, in its view of men and women, harked back to the immediate post-slavery days.

During slavery, enslaved women were not protected by traditional Western assumptions about what was proper for a woman. They were expected to do hard manual labor, when that was necessary, and were given little time to fill the roles of wife and mother. At the same time, enslaved men were deprived of the traditional privileges of men in American society. They could not, most of the time, protect the women they loved. Any aggression on their part was swiftly punished. They were expected to show the "feminine" quality of submission.

When freedom came, there was a strong emphasis in the black community on reestablishing traditional gender roles. As free black communities took form in the early nineteenth century, this message appeared in the sermons of black ministers, in the expectations of family life, and even in the pages of black newspapers.

Women who worked all day as laundresses were expected to come home at night to cook and clean for their families, because that was what a woman was supposed to do for her man. Of course, these expectations applied to white women as well. But, in the case of black women, they were seen as a way of reestablishing the manhood of which black men had been deprived. They were a woman's duty to the race.

In the middle 1960s, after decades of humiliation, many young black men were filled with rage and the determination to assert that they were, indeed, men. They rejected the nonviolence of Martin Luther King and the established civil rights movement. They did not want to appear harmless and nonthreatening. And, again, as after slavery, they asked submission from black women as a means of establishing their own sense of manhood.

Huey P. Newton and Bobby Seale founded the **Black Panther Party** in Oakland, California, on October 15, 1966. The image of the party was intensely masculine. Inspired by this new movement toward manhood and pride, the Panthers were on the road to serious oppression of black women.

However, the times were changing, and the Panthers were not exactly what they seemed. They were, in an important way, "radicalized." Many of the leaders were ready to call into question *everything* white society had taught them, including the treatment of women. While the public image of black men in black leather with big guns was being promoted by the white press, there was something else going on behind the scenes—a struggle.

The three women nearest the top of the organization were **Kathleen Neal Cleaver, Elaine Brown,** and **Ericka Huggins. Angela Davis** was deeply involved in BPP programs with prison inmates. Just as in the nonviolent civil rights movement, the community programs of the BPP were often organized and run by women. These free programs included breakfast for schoolchildren, medical care (such as sickle cell anemia testing), legal aid and advice, transportation to visit relatives in prison and for senior citizens, political education classes, voter registration, petition campaigns for community control of police, and even the distribution of shoes and clothing. And—just as in the nonviolent civil rights movement—most of the leadership was male.

In the late sixties and early seventies, however, women in all parts of the radical community were beginning to rebel against male structures. The women of the BPP were no exception. In 1969, they began to speak out in the *Black Panther* newspaper and at BPP meetings. They also actively sought and won leadership roles.

The male reaction was mixed. Ericka Huggins said years later, "There were some men who could [not] have cared less about what women thought about anything, and there were some men who were on the right page."

There were enough men on the right page so that, when Huey Newton went into exile in Cuba, Elaine Brown became chairperson of the party. Despite the masculine image and the charges of sexism, the Black Panther Party was the first major organization for black rights to be headed by a woman. Another Black Panther woman, Angela Davis, was one of the first women to become a popular hero of the counterculture.

In the 1980s, the Black Panther Party disbanded. However, according to the February 1995 issue of *Essence,* Elaine Brown, with Fredrika Newton and David Hilliard, are planning to open a model school for African-American children in East Oakland. The students will be taught, among other things, not to wait for anyone to lead them, according to Brown. "There ain't no captain of this ship," she says. "Each one of us just has to take an oar."

She sounds a great deal like Ida B. Wells-Barnett. And Ella Baker. And Fannie Lou Hamer. It's a lesson that black women seem to know well.

FEMINISM

When the new wave of feminism appeared in the late 1960s and early 1970s, there were three basic reactions among black women. Some mistrusted the largely white movement and wanted nothing to do with it. Some plunged in, feeling that the principles belonged to every woman. And some created their own structures to define and express feminist beliefs as they applied to black women.

Flo Kennedy was among those who plunged in. A lawyer and civil rights activist, Kennedy first came to prominence at a Montreal antiwar convention. When the organizers would not let Bobby Seale speak because his focus was racism rather than war, Kennedy took over the platform and, as she puts it, "started yelling and hollering." From that time on, Kennedy became a spokesperson for black civil rights, feminism, and gay rights. During the 1970s, she frequently spoke with white feminist Gloria Steinem, just as Sojourner Truth had once shared the platform with Susan B. Anthony. The two had different experiences and different perspectives but were united by their belief in the tenets of feminism. When **Shirley Chisholm** ran for president, Kennedy organized the Feminist Party to support her.

Chisholm was another avowed feminist. She was an early member of the National Organization for Women (NOW), a founding member of the National Women's Political Caucus (NWPC), and a spokesperson for the National Abortion Rights Action League (NARAL).

Among those who created their own black feminist structures were the founders of the National Black Feminist Organization (NBFO), which was formed in 1973. Women in this group came to it from other rights organizations with a variety of perspectives on black women. The NBFO gave them a means to fight the racism and gender discrimination in society without having to fight those forces within their own group.

Some black women felt, however, that the NBFO failed to deal with the issues of poor and working-class women and lesbians. So, in 1977, a radical group of black lesbian feminists calling themselves the **Combahee River Collective** broke away from NBFO. This group was more leftist in orientation. Its members believed that class, as well as race and gender, needed to be taken seriously by any feminist organization.

From the late 1970s to the present, there has been a tendency among all women, black and white, to organize *as women* around specific issues such as abortion, domestic violence, social welfare, rather than the more abstract idea of "equality for women." The leading workers for women's rights are often women who have never defined themselves as feminist, black feminist, or womanist (a term that was coined by writer Alice Walker and is more acceptable to many black women than feminist).

There are other women, however, who defend the term as well as the principles. Writers **bell hooks** and **Michele Wallace**, for example, are among leading feminist thinkers.

Among young black women, the identification with feminism is just as varied. Rapper **Queen Latifah** rejects the title, one that the women of **Salt-N-Pepa** wear proudly, while Yo-Yo (Yolanda Whitaker) even formed the Intelligent Black Women's Coalition, which is "devoted to increasing the self-esteem of *all* women."

NOW AND THE FUTURE

Understanding history requires knowledge. It requires intelligence and insight. But perhaps most of all, it requires perspective.

In a paper delivered in 1993, Lerone Bennett, Jr., described the victories of the civil rights movement of the 1950s and 1960s as the harvest of a crop planted and tended through the first half of this century. Then Bennett went on:

> And when the people had gathered all the fruit it was possible to take from that particular harvest, when they had tried everything, or almost everything, and when every advance revealed a new wall, a new phase began, marked by . . . a reactionary movement that was almost a mirror image of the reactionary movement that ended the Reconstruction period, and an ebbing of radical energies in Black America. And in the wake of these events, certain people, historians among them, have said that the laws of history have been repealed and that Blacks are condemned to live forever in a time of barren fields and bad historical weather. But this is absurd. It is as absurd as saying that crops will never grow again because the fields have yielded as much as they will yield in that season.

If Bennett is right, the present is a time of planting and cultivating, not waiting for a leader. It is a time of creating structures and building organizations and making networks, not hoping for a hero. It is a time for what black women have shown themselves to be masters of—getting things done.

And black women are doing just that. In Chicago, the Reverend **Willie Barrow** is leading Operation PUSH to get guns out of the neighborhoods, to fight domestic violence, to take care of untended children, to fight for higher education. **Elaine Jones** is heading the NAACP–Legal Defense and Educational Fund (a breakaway group from the NAACP). **Romona H. Edelin** is leading the National Urban Coalition. **Mary Frances Berry** is chair of the U.S. Commission on Civil Rights (she was appointed chair by President Clinton), after suing President Ronald Reagan in 1984 to prevent him from removing her as a member of the commission.

The Children's Defense Fund, formed in the late seventies by **Marian Wright Edelman,** is watching out for the health and welfare of children. Women around the country are organizing local groups to fight for welfare rights.

Even the NAACP has turned to a woman, for the first time in its more than eight decades. **Myrlie Evers-Williams** has worked in the movement since the 1960s, when her husband, civil rights worker Medgar Evers, was murdered. She has come into her new position as chairwoman of the NAACP sounding a great deal like those women who came before her. "The NAACP must vigorously pursue and make welcome members from alienated segments of society," she said at her inauguration—planting and tending the seeds, cultivating the crops.

There are also the women who follow in the tradition of Mary McLeod Bethune and **Hallie Q. Brown.** These are women who work for their people through education, business, and the arts. **Camille Cosby** produces television and stage portrayals of black life and, with her husband Bill, will be instrumental in the building of the **National Council of Negro Women**'s Black Women's Center. **Johnnetta Cole** helps educate and inspire a new generation as president of historically black **Spelman College.** Any number of young women rap musicians rap about self-respect and African-American cultural pride.

And who could deny that **Maya Angelou** is in the great tradition of black women activists when she stands at the presidential inauguration and says, "Lift up your eyes/ Upon this day breaking for you./Give birth again/To the dream."

[This introduction incorporates material from the following articles in *Black Women in America: An Historical Encyclopedia:* "Abolition Movement," by Brenda Stevenson; "Antilynching Movement," by Jacquelyn Dowd Hall; "Black Nationalism," by Gayle T. Tate; "Civil Rights Movement," by Dianne M. Pinderhughes; "Jim Crow Laws," by Alferdteen B. Harrison; "Labor Movement," by Ruth Feldstein; "The Left," by Robin D.G. Kelley; "Little Rock Nine," by Benita Ramsey; "Mississippi Freedom Democratic Party," by Chana Kai Lee; "Montgomery Bus Boycott," by Stewart Burns; "National Association for the Advancement of Colored People," by Lisa Beth Hill; and "National Welfare Rights Movement," by Amy Jordan.]

A

Allensworth, Josephine (1855–1939)

Josephine Leavell Allensworth was one of the guiding forces in the creation of the all-black "race colony" of Allensworth, California, in 1908. Due, in part, to her efforts, the community of Allensworth became a beacon of social change and a symbol of racial advancement.

Born in Bowling Green, Kentucky, on May 3, 1855, Josephine Leavell married Allen Allensworth, a Civil War veteran and local Baptist minister on September 20, 1877. During the next decade, Allensworth supported her husband's religious efforts as they ministered to congregations in Kentucky and Ohio. They had two daughters, Eva and Nella. In 1886, Allen Allensworth became the chaplain for the United States Army Twenty-Fourth Infantry (Colored). For twenty years, Josephine worked with her husband addressing the spiritual and educational needs of soldiers in forts throughout the American West.

After retiring from the army in 1906, the Allensworths settled in Los Angeles. Disappointed in the racial climate of the city, Josephine and Allen decided to create a "race colony" so that black people could live "free from the restrictions of race." To Josephine Allensworth, a successful colony would prove that African Americans were worthy of fair and equitable treatment, and it could provide a home for black soldiers, a reward for their years of service. In 1908, the community of Allensworth was estab-lished in rural Tulare County, thirty miles north of Bakersfield, California. By 1912, Allensworth had a population of 100, two general stores, several large farms, and a number of modest businesses.

While much of the credit for the colony must go to the chaplain, Josephine Allensworth exerted great influence over the operation and direction of the enterprise. She served as the president of the school board, created a library system for the colony, and sponsored educational and social organizations like the Women's Improvement Association.

The colony's success was short-lived, due to declining water resources and the death of Allen Allensworth in 1914. While the town continued into the 1950s, the colony's expansion ended by 1925. Josephine Allensworth left the community in 1920 and spent the rest of her life with her daughter Nella in Los Angeles. She died on March 27, 1939, in Los Angeles.

LONNIE BUNCH

Alpha Suffrage Club

The Alpha Suffrage Club, organized in 1913, was a counterforce to the racist activities of the National American Woman Suffrage Association (NAWSA) and state suffrage clubs. **Ida B. Wells-Barnett** and a white colleague, Belle Squire, established the club to place black women in the state and national suffrage arena, to increase political awareness and knowledge among female constituents, and to politicize black women in Chicago, who had gained the vote on June 26, 1913, when Illinois became the first state east of the Mississippi River to enfranchise women. This partial suffrage bill enabled women to vote for all offices not mentioned in the state constitution including presidential electors, mayors, aldermen, municipal court judges, sanitary trustees, and most local officers. Passage of the bill sent women throughout the state on quests to organize and educate female constituents. Most of these efforts were made among white women.

In addition, the strategy of national white women's suffrage groups was to implement a restricted suffrage, one that would not enfranchise black women. Throughout the 1890s until the passage of the Nineteenth Amendment in 1920, NAWSA embraced the state's rights stance, supported restricted female suffrage, and courted white Southern women.

Two hundred black female members joined with officers Ida B. Wells-Barnett (president), Mary Jackson (vice president), Viola Hill (second vice president), Vera Wesley Green (recording secretary), Sadie L. Adams (corresponding secretary), Laura Beasley (treasurer), and K. J. Bills (editor) in building a power base among black women. They implemented a block system to canvass neighborhoods and they organized once-a-week meeting sessions as learning centers on the rights and duties of citizens. Several women worked as clerks in the registration process and provided the necessary civic education.

The club integrated gender obligations with race obligations by holding membership in national, state, and local female and black organizations. Members sent their president, Ida B. Wells-Barnett, to the National American Woman Suffrage Association's suffrage parade on March 3, 1913, in Washington, D.C. Although snubbed by white delegates, Wells-Barnett successfully completed the march. Moreover, she integrated the suffrage movement, both nationally and in Illinois, by joining the Illinois contingent rather than the all-black delegates section that was relegated to the back of the line.

Early political efforts of the Alpha Suffrage Club disturbed some men. In the February 1914 primary election in the predominantly black Second Ward in Chicago, some black men, unaccustomed to female political activity, dismissed their efforts by heckling and suggesting that the women should be at home caring for their children. Despite male skepticism, the club canvassers played a significant role in garnering the sixth highest registration numbers of the thirty-five wards in the city. Encouraged by this showing, black male politicians began using the techniques and voting power of the club by developing a political partnership.

In the February 1915 Republican Party primary, the Suffrage Club headquarters served as a forum for the three black alderman candidates. Oscar DePriest, Louis Anderson, and Charles Griffin presented their political platforms and entertained questions. The club eventually endorsed Oscar DePriest through its newsletter, the *Alpha Suffrage Record,* and pressed each club in the Second Ward to support DePriest. On February 27, 1915, Oscar DePriest won the primary, and in April he became the first black alderman of Chicago.

The organization of the club, the politicization of black women in Chicago, and the acceptance by political leaders that followed the success of DePriest's election strengthened the role of black women in the political arena. Black and white Republican politicians actively sought the support of these women. In return, black women expected them to commit to encouraging black community political involvement, reform efforts, and economic parity.

WANDA HENDRICKS

Associations for the Protection of Negro Women

At the beginning of the twentieth century, urban reformers were concerned about the poor and less fortunate in American society. In particular, New York reformers attempted to uplift the masses by establishing settlement houses, conducting social work among the poor, and writing about the social and economic conditions of black Americans in the North. The Associations for the Protection of Negro Women were among several social welfare organizations established by prominent black and white reformers during the Progressive era.

Frances A. Kellor was the leading organizer of the associations. A social worker, she received a fellowship from the College Settlements Association in 1902 that enabled her to study New York City's employment agencies. Kellor and eight assistants spent two years investigating employment agencies in New York, Chicago, Philadelphia, and Boston. She published the results of the study in her book, *Out of Work* (1904).

Kellor's book exposed the vicious exploitation of black migrant women from the South. There was no protection for black women at the docks or at the train stations. Agents in large Southern cities persuaded women from the rural districts to move to the North. If the young woman or her relatives could not pay her transportation fee, the employment office loaned it to her, and the woman paid it back at high interest rates.

In April 1905, the Inter-Municipal Committee on Household Research began organizing associations for the protection of black women in New York City and Philadelphia. Kellor was secretary and later director of the committee, which was composed of representatives from several New York City organizations concerned with the problems of domestic employment. Officers in the New York City association in 1905 were Frances A. Kellor, Dr. William L. Buckley, Mary E. Dreier, Dr. Verina Morton Jones, and Mary White Ovington. Fred Moore, editor of the *Colored American Magazine* and the *New York Age,* was then president of the state association.

The activities of the Associations for the Protection of Negro Women were divided into travelers' aid, lodging houses, education, employment agencies, finances, and membership. The association placed an agent at the docks and stations to meet the migrant women and take them to lodging houses established to help them until they could find work. Employment agencies also were established in black neighborhoods and a travelers' aid network was established in Baltimore, Washington, Richmond, and Savannah. Sometimes the association paid the fare so that women who could not compete in the industrialized North could return home. Mrs. S. Layten, the Philadelphia agent, asserted that the associations reached only about a third of the women who needed help.

The Associations for the Protection of Negro Women made considerable advances in providing lodging, employment, and other social services for black women living in cities. One, for instance, opened an attractive home for forty women in Philadelphia in the fall of 1905 at 714 South Seventeenth Street. The New York association did not set up a home and, instead, cooperated with the Colored Mission, the **Young Women's Christian Association** in Brooklyn, and the **White Rose Mission.**

In 1906, the associations united to become the National League for the Protection of Colored Women. Kellor was secretary of both the New York association and the National League for the Protection of Colored Women. The National League, like the White Rose Mission, placed travelers' aid agents at all of the major terminals in New York City. Through its local associations, the National League extended its travelers' aid service to Philadelphia, Baltimore, Memphis, and Norfolk.

The National League for the Protection of Colored Women was one of several organizations established to offer services to disadvantaged groups in New York City. The Committee for Improving the Industrial Conditions of Negroes (CIICN) in New York City, also organized in 1906, was dedicated to increasing employment opportunities for black workers and providing vocational training. The motivator of the group was William Lewis Buckley, a former public school principal in New York City. The CIICN joined the National League and other reform agencies in sending workers to the docks to assist migrant black women.

On October 16, 1911, the National League, the CIICN, and the Committee on Urban Conditions among Negroes (which was organized on September 29, 1910, by George E. Haynes) merged to form the National League on Urban Conditions among Negroes (NLUCAN).

FLORIS BARNETT CASH

Avery, Byllye (1937–)

Byllye Y. Avery, the founding president of the National Black Women's Health Project (NBWHP), has been a women's health activist since the early 1970s. As a dreamer and visionary, Avery has combined activism and social responsibility in developing a national forum for the exploration of health issues affecting African-American women. In 1981, as a board member of the National Women's Health Network, Avery moved to Atlanta, Georgia, to pilot a health program that focused on black women. Under Avery's tireless leadership, the NBWHP grew from an "idea whose time had come" to the sponsorship in 1982 of the First National Conference at **Spelman College** in Atlanta, the catalyst to the incorporation of the NBWHP in 1984 as a national organization for and of black women.

Before moving to Atlanta, Avery was involved in providing direct health service as cofounder of the Gainesville Women's Health Center and cofounder of Birthplace, an alternative birthing center in Gainesville, Florida. Prior to her involvement in health care, Avery taught special education to emotionally disturbed students and served as a consultant to the public schools throughout the state of Florida. Avery, a graduate of Talladega College, Talladega, Alabama, received a master of education degree in special education in 1969 from the University of Florida. Since that time, she has received honorary doctorates of humane letters from the State University of New York in Binghamton and the Thomas Jefferson University in Philadelphia.

As a proponent of self-help and as executive director of the NBWHP, Avery transformed the women's health movement by mobilizing thousands of black women to take charge of their lives and join the campaign to improve their health status. In recognition of her commitment to promoting self-help as the key to empowerment of African-American women and her commitment to building an organization devoted to identifying and defining health issues for black women, Avery was awarded a MacArthur Foundation Fellowship for social contributions in 1989.

Since 1990, Byllye Avery, as the founding president of the NBWHP and national messenger of wellness for black women's health, has written and lectured on how the intersection of race, sex, and class affects empowerment and self-help in the women's health movement. As an international consultant, she has assisted in establishing a health agenda for the Geledes Black Women's Institute in São Paulo, Brazil; the Belize Rural Women's Association, Belize; and Caribbean women at the University of the West Indies, St. Michael, Barbados. She has organized "self-health" groups for the World Council of Churches in Kisumu,

Kenya, and in other African countries. In addition, Avery consults on health issues in Southern Africa, Latin America, and the United States as an adviser to the Kellogg Foundation International Leadership Program.

She is the recipient of numerous awards and citations for her selfless labor and outstanding service to women. Her more recent awards are: Community Service Award, Spelman College, 1991; the Ortho Woman of the Twenty-first Century Award, 1991; the Essence Award for Community Service in Science, Health, and Technology, 1989; and the Outstanding Service to Women and Children, Children's Defense Fund, 1988. She has served on the board of the Global Fund for Women, the International Women's Health Coalition, and the Boston Women's Health Book Collective. Her previous board memberships include the New World Foundation (1986–91), Committee for Responsive Philanthropy (1988–89), and the National Women's Health Network (1976–81).

ELEANOR HINTON HOYTT

Ayer, Gertrude (1884–1971)

A keen social critic and educator, Gertrude Ayer was one of the intellectual leaders of the Harlem Renaissance. By combining a sharp intellect with solid common sense, Ayer changed the direction of social services in the twentieth century.

Ayer was born on October 13, 1884, in New York City. Her father was Peter Augustus Johnson, the third black doctor licensed to practice medicine in New York City. A community leader and entrepreneur, her father was also a founder of

A keen social critic and educator, Gertrude Ayer was one of the intellectual leaders of the Harlem Renaissance.

McDonough Memorial Hospital and of the National Urban League and one of the organizers of Pennsylvania Railroad Station. Her mother was Elizabeth Whittle Johnson, an Englishwoman.

Ayer went to school in New York and was elected student government president of her high school. From 1903 to 1905, she attended New York Training School for Teachers and took additional courses at Columbia University, New York University, Hunter College, and the College of the City of New York. She first became a teacher in 1905, at the age of twenty-one. Except for a seven-year break, Ayer continued working in the New York public school system for the next forty-nine years.

Ayer married Cornelius McDougald in 1911 and left teaching to start her family.

During this break, Ayer became active in her father's new organization, the New York Urban League. She became assistant industrial secretary in 1915 and focused on the situation of the black woman worker. She later became head of the Woman's Department in the United States Labor Department Employment Bureau in Harlem. Next she was a counselor at the Henry Street Settlement.

At this time, most settlement houses were the projects of wealthy, privileged women who wished to share their advantages with poorer women. Unfortunately, this usually meant training the poorer women in the skills of the upper class, such as fine needlework or watercolor painting. Ayer herself was from a privileged background and was a member of the black upper class, having first married McDougald, a lawyer, and then A. V. Ayer, a doctor. However, she could see little point in teaching a woman embroidery when she needed more practical skills to make a living.

Ayer decided that what was needed for black advancement was a combination of education and practical, job-related skills. In 1918 the New York Board of Education asked her to bring this new approach to the New York public schools and start a counseling program.

An example of Ayer's respect for working people is found in a 1923 speech she delivered to the National Conference of Social Work in Washington, D.C. She noted that African Americans were migrating from the states with the fewest opportunities and the worst education systems and moving north to more opportunities and better education. She then made the following point:

It is, after all, simply a phase of the big struggle of the modern era—the struggle of the Common Man for the fullest development. The Negro is regarded as the commonest of common men in America, and any consideration of his welfare, in any field of endeavor, is highly in accord with the tendency of the present era— "appreciation of the genius of the common man."

Ayer never lost her appreciation of the genius of common people. She brought this outlook with her when she became an assistant principal in 1924 and when she became the first black female principal of a New York City public school in 1936. Administering a staff of both black and white teachers, she had grocers, butchers, and carpenters lecture to students. Ayer herself never completed her college degree and did not want students to discount people who gained their wisdom in the real world. She also thought the blue-collar exposure was good for the staff. "The informality helps teachers, too. Sometimes they develop a lot of resistance to being a human being."

Ayer belonged to many social service organizations, even after her retirement in 1954. She died in her home in 1971, at the age of eighty-six, having contributed immeasurably to the development of black education in the United States.

ANDRA MEDEA

B

Baker, Ella (1903–1986)

Ella Josephine Baker was a pivotal behind-the-scenes figure in progressive African-American political movements from the 1930s until her death in 1986. She helped to organize black cooperative campaigns in Harlem during the Great Depression; worked as a grass-roots organizer and national leader of the **National Association for the Advancement of Colored People** (NAACP) in the 1940s; and served as the first interim director of the Southern Christian Leadership Conference (SCLC) in the 1950s. She was a colleague and critic of Martin Luther King, Jr., and was one of the founders and chief sources of inspiration for the **Student Nonviolent Coordinating Committee** (SNCC), which was founded in 1960. Ella Baker's life, which spanned more than eighty years, was literally immersed in political activity. She was affiliated with nearly fifty organizations and coalitions over the course of her life and thus left an indelible mark on twentieth-century African-American political history. Her life was first documented in an award-winning film, *Fundi: The Ella Baker Story* (1983), by producer Joanne Grant, and more recently in a children's book by Shyrlee Dallard, as well as in several articles and essays.

Although Ella Baker is best known for her activities in the civil rights organizations of the 1950s and 1960s, that involvement did not mark the beginning of her long political career. In many ways her childhood experiences in the South formed the basis of her early political awakening. Born in Norfolk, Virginia, in 1903, Ella Baker grew up in the small town of Littleton, North Carolina. Her parents, Blake Baker and Georgianna Ross Baker, were both educated children of former slaves. For most of Ella Baker's childhood, her father worked as a waiter on a steamship that traveled between Norfolk and Washington, D.C. Her mother had worked as a schoolteacher before her marriage, after which she engaged in volunteer work for the Baptist Missionary Society, raised three children, and earned extra money by taking in an occasional boarder. Ella had two siblings—a younger sister, Margaret, affectionately known as Maggie, and an older brother, Curtis.

Ella Baker's early life was steeped in Southern black culture. Her most vivid childhood memories were of the strong traditions of self-help, mutual cooperation, and sharing of economic resources that encompassed her entire community. In a similar vein, the concept of extended family and fictive kinships further bonded the small, close-knit community into a network of mutual obligations.

Mitchell Ross, Ella's maternal grandfather, was a very important figure in her early development. An independent and hard-working farmer, Ross was proud that he had purchased a portion of the North

Carolina land he had once lived on as a slave. A minister and recognized community leader, Ross was an ardent proponent of equal rights and black suffrage. He was proud and defiant, and young Ella admired him greatly. Similarly, Baker's maternal grandmother, Josephine Elizabeth, after whom Ella was named, was also a fighter. As a slave she had stubbornly refused to marry a man selected for her by her white mistress, choosing Mitchell Ross instead. Ella Baker also recalled her grandmother as an avid storyteller who passed on the tales of oppression and struggle she had witnessed in the antebellum South. This upbringing, rooted in a tradition of racial pride, resistance to oppression, and a deep sense of community cooperation, formed the core of her strong social conscience.

Because there was no local secondary school, in 1918, when Ella was fifteen years old, her parents sent her to Shaw boarding school in Raleigh, the high school academy of Shaw University. Founded in the mid-nineteenth century by the American Baptist Home Mission Society, Shaw, like most black colleges at that time, was a conservative institution, run by paternalistic Northern white benefactors. The curriculum was "classical," in contrast to the basic vocational training offered at many other black schools of that era. Shaw students studied literature, philosophy, foreign languages, and mathematics. Ella excelled academically at Shaw, graduating as valedictorian of her college class in 1927. However, she never fully accepted the school's conservative philosophy on many issues. She joined with classmates on several occasions to protest the rigid regulations imposed on students and refused to comply with practices she deemed degrading. On one occa-

sion she acted as the spokesperson for a group of female students who petitioned the dean to allow them to wear silk stockings on campus. On another occasion she refused a request by the college president to join other students in singing spirituals for a group of Northern white guests visiting the campus.

After her graduation from Shaw University, Baker migrated to New York City on the eve of the Great Depression, determined to find an outlet for her intellectual curiosity and growing compassion for social justice. She was deeply moved by the

One of the founders and chief source of inspiration for the Student Nonviolent Coordinating Committee, Ella Baker believed firmly in participatory democracy at all levels in organizations. "Strong people don't need strong leaders." (SCHOMBURG CENTER)

abysmal conditions she witnessed on the streets of Harlem during the 1930s; scenes of poverty, hunger, and desperation were ubiquitous. These scenes of suffering, and the growing radical political culture in New York City in the 1930s, had a tremendous impact on Baker's evolving political consciousness. She traveled throughout the city, attending political meetings, rallies, forums, and discussions. This period proved to be a turning point in her life. It was during her first few years in Harlem that Baker began to define the radical perspective that would inform her political activity for the rest of her life.

The first political organization she joined after moving to Harlem was the Young Negroes Cooperative League (YNCL), founded by the iconoclastic writer George Schuyler in December 1930. The expressed purpose of the group was to gain economic power through consumer cooperation. The YNCL was headquartered in New York City and was made up of nearly two dozen affiliate councils scattered throughout the Northeast and Midwest. Affiliates were organized into buying clubs, cooperative grocery stores, and cooperative distribution networks. In 1931 Baker was elected to serve as the group's first national director.

Baker and many of her idealistic young comrades felt the cooperative movement was much more than a survival strategy to ameliorate the suffering of a handful of black participants; it was also a proving ground for the principles of communalism and cooperation and an alternative to the cutthroat mode of competition that many felt had led to the 1929 stock market crash and the ensuing social disaster. Cooperative ventures would, they hoped, demonstrate, on a small scale, the efficiency of collective economic planning and simultaneously promote the values of interdependency, group decision making, and the sharing of economic resources. The league was also an organization structured around democratic principles, emphasizing nonhierarchical leadership, the full inclusion of women, and the importance of grass-roots involvement and empowerment. As sociologist Charles Payne points out, this egalitarian vision echoed the treasured memories Baker had of her childhood in the South. In many respects the YNCL experiment foreshadowed a very similar youth organization with which Baker would be closely affiliated some thirty years later—the Student Nonviolent Coordinating Committee.

Another important experience that helped to shape Baker's evolving political consciousness during the Depression was her employment with the Workers Education Project (WEP) of the Works Progress Administration (WPA), a program designed to equip workers with basic literacy skills and to educate them about topics of concern to members of the work force. Classes ranged from instruction in basic arithmetic for sharecroppers to English courses for foreign-born workers. The WEP, like many WPA projects, became a gathering place for a variety of left-wing activists living in New York during the 1930s. The staff engaged in constant debates about political theory, world affairs, and revolution. The WEP also had very close ties to the Congress of Industrial Organizations and the growing trade union movement, and Baker worked closely with a number of militant trade unionists. Given their radical political orientation, Baker and her coworkers were not satisfied to limit curriculum to labor and consumer issues alone. Rather, they sought to link these topics to broader world issues, ranging from the rise of fascism in Europe to colonialism in Africa. While the YNCL was Baker's formal introduction to progressive politics, the WEP was where many of her ideas were forged and molded into a more concrete, radical political analysis.

During the 1930s, Baker also began to grapple with the issue of women's equality and her own identity as an African-American woman. She supported and worked with various women's groups, such as the Women's Day Workers and Industrial League, a union for domestic workers; the Harlem Housewives Cooperative; and the Harlem YWCA. Baker refused to be relegated to a separate "woman's sphere," either personally or politically. She often participated, without reservation, in meetings where she was the only woman present, and many of her closest political allies over the years were men. Similarly, in her personal life Baker refused to comply with prevailing social norms about women's place or women's behavior. When she married her longtime friend, T. J. Roberts, in the late 1930s, the marriage was anything but conventional, which typified her rebellious spirit. Baker never assumed her husband's name, an unusual act of independence in those days. Also, even though she was married for over a decade, she never framed her identity as a woman around that of her husband and apparently never allowed domestic obligations to interfere with her principal passion, which was politics.

While in Harlem in the 1930s, Baker also worked as a reporter and editor for a variety of publications, including the *West Indian News* and the *National News,* a short-lived publication run by her close friend George Schuyler. In 1935 she coauthored an investigative article that exposed the plight of African-American domestic workers in New York during the Depression, which was published in the *Crisis,* the magazine of the NAACP. Among her political friends and associates in Harlem during this period were labor leader A. Philip Randolph, Lester Granger of the National Urban League, Communist Party lawyer Conrad Lynn, and George Schuyler.

The next important phase of Baker's political career, which further solidified her evolving views of political struggle and social change, was the beginning of her involvement in the NAACP in 1940. Throughout her relationship with the NAACP, first as a field secretary and later as director of branches (1943–46), Baker fought to democratize the organization and to move it away from legalism as a primary strategy for combating discrimination. She was a staunch advocate of campaigns and strategies that she felt could involve and engage the masses of the NAACP's membership and of linking strategies for racial equality.

Through her fieldwork for the NAACP, Baker established a vast network of contacts in grass-roots African-American communities throughout the South. It was this network of relationships and contacts that formed the foundation for much of the civil rights activity of the 1950s and 1960s. For example, when Baker conducted outreach for the SCLC's Crusade for Citizenship in

1957 and when SNCC volunteers engaged in voter registration and desegregation campaigns in the early 1960s, Baker's web of contacts in the South proved to be an indispensable resource.

Baker remained on the staff of the NAACP until 1946, when, fed up with the top-down bureaucratic structure of the organization and its legalistic strategy for social change, she resigned as director of branches. Another factor that influenced her resignation was the added responsibilities she assumed when she took custody of her nine-year-old niece, Jackie. Baker continued to work with the NAACP in a volunteer capacity as the president of the New York branch, the first woman to hold that post. In that role Baker was a leader of school reform campaigns that sought the desegregation of New York City schools and greater parent involvement in school decision making. She headed a coalition called Parents against Discrimination in Education, which held numerous forums and rallies throughout the city and eventually met with the mayor of the city in 1957 to express its concerns. It was also during the 1950s that Baker became associated with the Liberal party and ran unsuccessfully as its candidate for the New York City Council in 1951. During the late 1950s, she spoke out against McCarthyism and the growing anti-Communist sentiments in the nation.

In January 1956, Baker and two of her closest political allies in New York, Stanley Levison and Bayard Rustin, founded the Northern-based organization In Friendship, to help raise funds for the growing Southern civil rights struggle. Baker served as executive secretary of the group, staffing its office, handling correspondence, and do-

ing outreach to other organizations and individuals. A. Philip Randolph served briefly as nominal head of the coalition, and the noted Socialist Party leader Norman Thomas was a prominent member of the group. In Friendship sponsored several major fund-raisers to aid the Montgomery Improvement Association, which had coordinated the historic Montgomery bus boycott of 1955–56, as well as a number of black sharecroppers who had been evicted from their farms as retribution for their civil rights activities. In Friendship eventually faded out of existence with the founding in 1957 of the Southern Christian Leadership Conference, formed as a regional coalition in order to sustain and build upon the momentum of the successful Montgomery boycott.

Upon the urging of her friends Rustin and Levison, both of them advisers to Martin Luther King, Jr., in January 1958 Baker agreed to move to Atlanta to coordinate the Crusade for Citizenship, a voter rights campaign launched by the fledgling SCLC. In this new organizational context, Baker took up the fight she had waged within the NAACP some ten years earlier to decentralize decision making and to create accessible channels through which local grass-roots people could participate more fully. Although she respected King, SCLC's president, she also felt that the increasing reliance on his public persona and charisma to mobilize people was dangerously channeling the movement's energies in the wrong direction. Baker's message was simply that "strong people don't need strong leaders." Baker eventually felt that as a woman, a noncleric, and a staunch egalitarian, she never received the respect and recognition she deserved from the male ministers who ran the organization from the top down.

Consequently, when the student-led desegregation sit-in campaign erupted in Greensboro, North Carolina, on February 1, 1960, Baker, already dissatisfied with the leadership of the SCLC, immediately shifted her attention to what would prove to be the cutting edge of the growing black freedom movement. Just as she had sought to extend the gains of the Montgomery boycott through her work with the SCLC, Baker once again strove to maximize the momentum of this new upsurge in mass direct action among African-American youth. After leaving the SCLC, Baker took a paid position in the regional student office of the YWCA in order to remain close to and assist with the growth of the embryonic student civil rights movement and to use the YWCA as a base of operation to generate resources and recruit student members for a new organization.

Anticipating that the activity would either fizzle out or be co-opted by more moderate African-American leaders, Baker moved quickly to help create a launching pad for a new independent youth organization that would be militant in its tactics and egalitarian in its structure. She called a conference of sit-in leaders in April 1960 at her alma mater, Shaw University. This gathering led to the formation of the Student Nonviolent Coordinating Committee in October of that year. The founding of SNCC as an independent organization represented an alternative to the more politically moderate and hierarchical civil rights organizations that predated it. From its inception SNCC was based upon the principles of grass-roots democracy and decentralized, group-centered leadership.

SNCC's fluid, localized structure offered women, poor people, and youth—three forces Ella Baker saw as the backbone of the movement—an important entry point into leadership circles and the ability to contribute to the organization, initiate projects, and influence strategy. SNCC distinguished itself from other civil rights organizations by its aggressive use of mass direct-action tactics and the willingness of its organizers to go into rural regions of the Deep South, where racism and vigilante violence were most intense. Perhaps more than any other organization with which she was affiliated, SNCC embodied the principles and politics Baker had fought for most of her adult life. She served as an adult adviser, role model, and intellectual mentor to many of the young SNCC leaders throughout the existence of the organization.

In 1964, SNCC leaders, including Baker, helped to launch the **Mississippi Freedom Democratic Party** (MFDP), a grass-roots political party to challenge the hegemony of the segregated, all-white, Mississippi Democratic Party. Baker went to Washington, D.C., to manage the national office of the MFDP. In the summer of 1964, at the Democratic Party convention in Atlantic City, New Jersey, MFDP delegates confronted Democratic Party leaders, urging them to refuse to seat the all-white Mississippi delegation on the grounds that the state Democratic Party had discriminated against Mississippi's black electorate, and to seat the openly elected MFDP delegates instead. The MFDP was ultimately not seated, but its actions were the impetus for subsequent reforms in the Democratic Party structure that prohibited discriminatory practices in local primaries.

During the early 1960s, Baker also worked briefly for white antiracist activists Carl and Anne Braden as a staff consultant to the Southern Conference Education Fund (SCEF), an interracial group that worked for racial and social justice in the South. While working for SCEF, she traveled around the country speaking on the importance of linking the fight for civil liberties with the fight for civil rights and thereby helping to forge coalition efforts between white liberals and black civil rights organizers.

Baker's influence on political movements of the 1960s extended beyond the bounds of the organizations with which she was directly affiliated. Former SNCC members and others who were inspired by her teachings went on to work in organizations ranging from the antiwar group Students for a Democratic Society (SDS), to the **Black Panther Party,** to mainstream electoral politics, and to the women's liberation movement of the 1970s. Throughout the 1970s and 1980s, despite failing health, Baker continued to serve as an adviser to dozens of organizations, activists, and politicians throughout the country. Although Baker's specific ideological imprint upon the civil rights organizations of the 1950s and 1960s is her most significant contribution to the African-American liberation struggle of the twentieth century, one overriding theme stands out in bold relief as we survey the long and rich history that characterizes her political life. Ella Baker was, above all, a bridge connecting young people to their elders, Northerners to Southerners, black people to white people, and intellectuals to common folk in a web of organizational and personal relationships. Moreover, she was a historical bridge

connecting the social movements of the 1950s and 1960s to the legacy of black resistance and social protest in the decades that followed.

BARBARA RANSBY

Barrow, Willie B. (1904–)

With respect and affection Willie B. Barrow has been dubbed "Little Warrior," "Little Ball of Fire" and "Little Lady with the Big Voice." A minister, she has practiced what she preaches—that one must look after not only people's spiritual needs but their rights and physical well-being, too. The capital letters in the name of the Chicago-based operation she heads, Operation PUSH, now stand for People United to Serve Humanity. But her constant, heartfelt dedication to its cause well might seem to justify, by her example, its original words—People United to Save Humanity.

Born on December 7, 1904, in rural Burton, Texas, she was the second youngest of pastor Nelson Taplin's seven children. She studied at the Warner Pacific School of Theology in Portland, Oregon, where she organized the first black Church of God. She also met her future husband, Clyde Barrow, in Portland, in a Kaiser Company shipyard in which both were welders.

Her civic activities, meanwhile, grew. In 1943 she was a member of the National Urban League, and two years later she joined the **National Council of Negro Women.**

The Barrows began to have difficulty finding work in California and, in 1945, they moved to Chicago. She studied briefly at the Moody Bible Institute and then at the Central Conservatory of Music. She also worked for the Langley Avenue

Church of God, then was a Montgomery Ward file clerk, a Woolworth's salesperson, and, by 1947, an Armour & Company meatpacker.

Her quest for education took her to the University of Monrovia in Liberia on Africa's west coast, where she earned a Doctor of Divinity degree. This attained, she spent much of the decade to follow back in Chicago as a fieldworker for Martin Luther King's Southern Christian Leadership Conference (SCLC), at a salary of twenty-five dollars a week.

In the mid-1950s she gave birth to a son, Keith Errol Barrow, who, after studying psychology at New York University, became a recording artist. The couple also has a second child, Patricia.

An organizer of the momentous March on Washington in 1963, she went on to help set up chapters in the nationwide Poor People's Campaign. Though Operation Push was not founded until 1971 and Barrow not aboard until a few years later, she had become associated with its founder, the Rev. Jesse Jackson, by 1969. That same year, she was named Chicago's Woman of the Year.

Becoming known as a reliable Jackson "lieutenant," she targeted hunger as her special interest. For the state of Illinois, she coordinated the Coalition Against Hunger and led a Special Hunger Task Force, meanwhile serving SCLC as Special Projects Director of Operation Breadbasket. Creating more jobs for African Americans was another goal and, moving toward it, she helped organize a 1973 boycott against the A&P grocery chain.

In the mid-1970s Barrow became PUSH's first woman national vice-president and in 1984 was national deputy campaign

and road manager during Jackson's run for the U.S. presidency. She played the same role in 1988. In 1983, Barrow's son, Keith, died after a battle with AIDS.

Taking over Jackson's post as PUSH president intermittently after 1984, she headed the organization full time between 1986 and 1989 and again, as chairman of the board, in 1993.

In the 1990s she has increased her focus upon such black community problems as the influx of guns, the plight of untended children, "gangster rap" music lyrics, domestic violence, and the need for more opportunities in higher education. She is especially concerned with the failure of families. "That's why society is in such critical shape," she said in an interview for the *Chicago Tribune*. "Sisters and brothers aren't speaking to each other; mothers and fathers are falling out and never falling back in. This year what I'm saying to people on college campuses, in churches, and at gatherings where I speak is for families to unite, to come home, to come together, to forgive."

GARY HOUSTON

Bates, Daisy (1920–)

Daisy Lee Gatson, journalist, civil rights activist, and major force in the integration of the Little Rock, Arkansas, public schools, was born in 1920 in Huttig, a small town located in the lumbering region of southeast Arkansas. She was raised by her adoptive parents, Orlee and Susie Smith; she never knew her real parents. In the autobiographical sections of *The Long Shadow of Little Rock* (1962), she revealed that as a child she was told that her mother had been ravished and murdered, allegedly

In 1957, it took the commitment and planning of the NAACP's Daisy Bates—and 1,000 paratroopers—to get nine black children into Little Rock's Central High School. She is shown here in New York City in the 1960s supporting "sit-in" students in the South. (BENITA RAMSEY)

by three white men; and her father was forced to flee Huttig for fear of reprisals from whites should he attempt to prosecute the suspects. The Smiths were childless friends of her real parents and agreed to adopt her.

Gatson's relationship with the Smiths was warm and supportive, and she was raised as a somewhat spoiled and willful only child. She was indulged by her loving mother and hard-working, though extremely sensitive father, with whom she enjoyed a close relationship. Daisy Lee Gat-

son attended the segregated public schools in Huttig, where the black students were forced to use the worn-out textbooks handed down from the white schools. For Gatson the poor physical condition of the school buildings and facilities for black children symbolized the inadequacy and injustice of Arkansas' Jim Crow educational system.

When Daisy Gatson was fifteen years old and still in high school, she was introduced to Lucius Christopher Bates, an insurance agent and close friend of her father. L. C. Bates was born in Mississippi, attended segregated county schools, and went on to Wilberforce College, the African Methodist Episcopal (AME) church-supported school in Ohio, and majored in journalism. Upon graduation, he worked on the *Kansas City Call* in Missouri, but soon lost this position due to the hard times created by the Depression. Mr. Bates turned to selling insurance and was quite successful, but he wanted to return to journalism.

Orlee Smith passed away in 1941. Shortly afterward, L. C. Bates proposed to Daisy Lee Gatson, and she accepted. They were married that year and eventually settled in Little Rock. L. C. soon convinced his wife to join him in a newspaper venture, and the Bateses used their savings to lease a newspaper plant from a church group and to begin a weekly newspaper, the Arkansas *State Press*. Within the first few months the paper reached a circulation of 10,000, and Daisy Bates enrolled in business administration and public relations courses at Shorter College, an AME school in Little Rock, to learn more about running a business. Initially, the paper was quite successful and attracted a large number of advertisers from the local business community.

With the outbreak of World War II, nearby Camp Robinson was reopened at the request of local businessmen and politicians and was used to train black soldiers. Soon large numbers of African-American servicemen filled the streets of Little Rock on weekends. Incidents of police brutality involving African Americans were regularly exposed by the *State Press,* and at times the investigative reporting by the courageous newspaper publishers angered white businessmen in Little Rock, who threatened to withdraw their advertisements. In March 1942, after the *State Press* reported the gruesome details of the killing of a black soldier by a Little Rock policeman, many advertisements were withdrawn and the Bateses had to double their efforts, working twelve to sixteen hours a day, to keep their enterprise afloat. Gradually, circulation began to increase and within a year the newspaper reached 20,000 readers.

The *State Press* gained a reputation as the independent "voice of the people" and worked for the improvement of the social and economic circumstances of African Americans throughout the state. In Little Rock, the *State Press* continued to expose police brutality, and eventually it was successful in forcing some changes. Black policemen were hired to patrol the black neighborhoods, and the state of race relations improved noticeably. By the end of World War II, Daisy Bates believed that Little Rock had gained "a reputation as a liberal southern city."

The *State Press* continually had supported the programs and activities of the **National Association for the Advancement of Colored People** (NAACP) and, in 1952,

Daisy Bates accepted the position of president of the Arkansas state conference of NAACP branches. With the U.S. Supreme Court's *Brown* v. *Board of Education* decision on May 17, 1954, the NAACP overturned the legal basis for public school segregation. In Little Rock, public school officials wanted to move slowly on school integration, and Daisy Bates led the black community's campaign against this policy of gradualism. With assistance and advice from officials in the NAACP national headquarters, Daisy Bates began taking African-American children to be enrolled in all-white public schools. When the children were denied admission, each incident was recorded and later reported in the local newspapers. Under increasing pressure from black parents and the NAACP, the superintendent of the Little Rock Public School District, Virgil Blossom, announced a plan to begin the desegregation process with Central High School in September 1957.

White opponents in Little Rock were outraged and brought litigation to hold or delay the implementation of the plan, all to no avail. In the summer of 1957, Governor Orval Faubus announced his opposition to public school integration and on September 2, the first day of school, ordered units of the Arkansas National Guard to Central High School to prevent the possibility of disorder and violence. NAACP lawyers Wiley Branton and Thurgood Marshall obtained an injunction from the federal courts against the governor's action, but the troops were not removed.

The nine African-American teenagers who were chosen to participate in the integration of Central High School came to be known as the Little Rock Nine. Their activities were planned and coordinated by Daisy Bates, who stood with the children during the ordeal. Violence erupted around Central High School and throughout the city when Elizabeth Eckford, one of the nine students, mistakenly went to the school alone on the morning of September 22, 1957. Her grace under pressure while she was jeered and taunted by white mobs as she tried to enter the school came to symbolize the strength and determination of an entire generation of African-American students.

On the following day, when the police escorted Daisy Bates and the children into the school in secrecy, mob action escalated and they had to be removed because the chief of police could no longer guarantee their safety. The violence continued, and the police chief requested the assistance of the U.S. Justice Department. The next day, President Dwight D. Eisenhower federalized all Arkansas National Guard units and sent in 1,000 paratroopers from the 101st Airborne Division to carry out the orders of the federal courts. The following day, September 25, 1957, the paratroopers, under the leadership of Major General Edwin A. Walker, escorted Daisy Bates and the nine students into Central High School. The paratroopers were withdrawn to nearby Camp Robinson on September 30, but Arkansas National Guard units were to remain on patrol at Central High throughout the school year.

On October 31, 1957, the Little Rock city council ordered the arrest of Daisy Bates and other members of the Arkansas NAACP for failure to supply the city clerk's office with information about the NAACP's membership, contributors, and expenditures. At the trial in December 1957, Daisy Bates was convicted and fined $100, plus court costs. The conviction was eventually overturned by the U.S. Supreme Court. Meanwhile, Daisy Bates kept in close contact with the black students at Central High School, and she always accompanied them and their parents to meetings with school officials when incidents occurred. Eventually, white school officials and students learned that anyone who bothered "Daisy Bates' children" would also have to deal with Daisy Bates personally. Her vigilance in the protection and support of her children earned for Daisy Bates the resentment and enmity of most Arkansas whites, and a secure place for herself in twentieth-century African-American history.

The *State Press* was forced to close in 1959, but Daisy Bates remained active on the lecture circuit, in voter registration campaigns, and in community revitalization programs. In 1985, however, the Bateses again began to publish the Arkansas *State Press*, and it continues to serve the important social, economic, and political needs of African Americans in Little Rock. Despite some recent illness, Daisy Bates remains active in a variety of community organizations and is sought by the press, politicians, and the people to provide her unique perspectives on the contemporary problems facing the African-American community.

V. P. FRANKLIN

Black Panther Party

Throughout U.S. history black women have always participated in political movements within their communities. Although their roles have not been highlighted by the media in the past, black women have organized as well as participated in the daily functions of various organizations. The Black Panther Party (BPP) was no exception to this rule.

Huey P. Newton and Bobby Seale founded the Black Panther Party in Oakland, California, on October 15, 1966. The organization was established by men, and the predominantly male leadership was the focus of media coverage. Nevertheless, women played significant roles within the organization from 1967 until it ceased to function in the early 1980s. Female BPP members held party leadership positions at local levels as well as national levels, delivered speeches at rallies, and participated in the BPP community survival programs (free food, clothing, and health services, among other necessities).

Women who joined the Black Panther Party participated for a variety of reasons. Some women joined to develop their skills in political organization, other women joined to support spouses or significant others who were affiliated with the party, and still others joined to endorse the party's goals.

The three most prominent women at the top of the organization's hierarchy were **Kathleen Neal Cleaver, Elaine Brown,** and **Ericka Huggins.** Cleaver was the first woman to hold a national leadership position; she was the communications secretary from 1967 to 1971. Elaine Brown held many positions in the BPP before she became the first and only female chairperson of the party, from 1974 to 1977. Ericka Huggins directed the BPP-initiated Oakland Community School from 1973 to 1981.

The community programs of the BPP, often directed and staffed by female members, included free breakfast for schoolchildren; free medical care, such as sickle cell anemia testing; free transportation to visit relatives in prison and for senior citizens; free shoes and clothing; political education classes; voter registration; petition campaigns for community control of police; and legal aid and advice, among other programs.

Although in doctrine the BPP internal structure allowed for no differential treatment on account of sex, once women joined the party they confronted gender-based discrimination and gender-specific tasks. From 1967 until the party folded, many women encountered sexism, and male chauvinism was an issue within the Panther community. A letter from Eldridge Cleaver to Ericka Huggins appeared in the July 5, 1969, issue of the *Black Panther* (the official party newspaper) addressing the issue: "Women are our other half, they're not our stronger half, they're not our weaker half, but they are our other half and that we sell ourselves out, we sell our children out and we sell our women out when we treat them in any other manner." Despite Cleaver's comments, sexism still continued in the BPP, and beginning in 1969, female members began to voice their displeasure with their treatment in the *Black Panther* and at BPP meetings. They also increased their participation in leadership roles and community activities.

Male chauvinism was not the only issue BPP women faced. Questions of female sexuality and motherhood plagued some women. They complained of being pressured into engaging in sexual activity. Reproduction and birth control were also issues. Many confronted the difficulties of rearing a child and being a full-time political activist. Moreover, mothers who were in the Panthers risked being incarcerated and separated from their children.

Two former female BPP members who experienced the hardships of being a mother and being a full-time political activist are Assata Shakur (formerly JoAnne Chesimard) and Akua Njere (formerly Deborah Johnson). Shakur became pregnant while incarcerated and was separated from her daughter immediately after birth. Shakur's mother raised the child while Shakur was incarcerated. Shakur was emotionally affected by the separation from her daughter and the possible negative effects that such a separation might have on their relationship.

Njere is the mother of the son of Fred Hampton, slain BPP chairman of the Illinois chapter. Like Shakur, she was also contemplative about the relationship that would develop between her son and herself. For a short period after her son's birth, Njere's mother cared for Fred Hampton, Jr. Meanwhile, Njere attempted to continue full-time participation in the BPP. Njere soon decided that she needed more time to care for her son. Such constraints caused Njere to even consider leaving the Party to avoid jeopardizing her relationship with her son.

The pressures that female members of the BPP faced sometimes caused them to rescind their membership. Since police surveillance and harassment were equally problematic for women and men, female members faced both internal and external pressures. Nevertheless, there were female members who remained politically active in the party.

During its active reign the Black Panther Party leaders instituted many programs that had a lasting effect on black society and society-at-large. Unquestionably, the female Panther members were an integral part of the creation of this legacy. From their involvement in the community service programs to their national leadership positions, the female Panther members maintained day-to-day functions of the party.

The decline of the BPP was the result of numerous activities and attitude clashes. The intensity of undercover FBI involvement and local police harassment helped to weaken and curtail public interest in the party's activities and members' involvement. The national leadership had also fallen apart over the course of ten years. Throughout this decline, however, large numbers of women sustained the organization's community programs until 1981, when the final Oakland-based program closed.

ANGELA D. BROWN

Blackwell, Unita (1933–)

Unita Blackwell is one of the "extraordinary ordinary" grass-roots leaders of the civil rights movement. Born on March 18, 1933, in Lula, Mississippi, this daughter of sharecroppers rose from poverty in a state that denied Black Americans every basic freedom and became the first black woman mayor in the history of Mississippi. Elected in 1976 in the town of Mayersville, where she had once been denied the right to vote, Blackwell still stands at the forefront of social and economic change in the state.

Blackwell was drawn into the civil rights movement while a young mother in the early 1960s. When civil rights organizers from outside the state launched voter registration drives in rural Mississippi, she was among the first to step forward. Working with the **Student Nonviolent Coordinating Committee** (SNCC), whose goal was to develop indigenous leadership, Blackwell registered voters and organized boycotts and citizen participation drives throughout the state; she was arrested and jailed over seventy times. Blackwell initiated several civil rights legislative challenges; among these was the landmark school desegregation suit *Blackwell* v. *Issaquena County Board of Education* (1965–66), which set a historical precedent nationwide in the continuing legal battle for school desegregation. As a founding member of the **Mississippi Freedom Democratic Party** (MFDP), she was among the delegates to the historic 1964 Democratic National Convention in Atlantic City, New Jersey, where the radically progressive third party challenged the seating of the traditionally all-white Mississippi delegation.

Blackwell's interests in economic development and housing led to cooperative ventures with the **National Council of Negro Women** and the establishment of homeownership opportunities for low-income families in the state. Her most successful effort was the incorporation of Mayersville in 1976. Nationally, Blackwell emerged as a prominent speaker on issues involving rural housing and development. As president of the first United States–China People's Friendship Association, she traveled to the Republic of China and exchanged ideas on development. In 1979, she participated in President Jimmy Carter's Energy Summit at Camp David. Blackwell later obtained a master's degree in regional planning from the University of Massachusetts-Amherst. She was enrolled there based on her abilities, experience, and skills because she had not graduated from high school. She was elected chairperson of the National Conference of Black Mayors in 1989.

Though Unita Blackwell formally received only an eighth-grade education, her philosophy of life, "to educate by doing and being," epitomizes her relentless commitment to social change. Her life and work, as well as the works of other black women activists such as **Fannie Lou Hamer** and **Annie Devine,** have been a wellspring for principled social action. In 1992 Blackwell received the prestigious MacArthur Foundation Fellowship.

VICKI CRAWFORD

Bolden, Dorothy (1923–)

Using the knowledge of her years doing domestic work and her experiences as a community activist, in 1968 Dorothy Lee Bolden organized the National Domestic Workers Union, which successfully improved the wages and working conditions of domestic workers in Atlanta and served as an ongoing model for those in other cities.

Dorothy Lee Bolden was born on October 13, 1923, in Atlanta, the daughter of Raymond Bolden, a chauffeur, and Georgia Mae Patterson, a cook who had migrated to Atlanta from Madison, Georgia. She received her formal education through the ninth grade at E. P. Johnson Elementary School and David T. Howard High School in Atlanta.

At age three, Bolden was blinded after a fall that damaged her optical nerve. Her sight returned between the ages of seven and nine, and during this period, her work life began. She took her first job in 1930 washing diapers after school for $1.25 per week. At age twelve, she cleaned house for $1.50 per week for a Jewish family that, according to Bolden, was kosher and hung her bread "outside the door in a sugar sack" on holidays.

In 1941, Bolden married Frank Smith, whom she referred to later as "just a good-looking man coming." Within a short period of time, the couple divorced and Bolden married Abram Thompson. Bolden is the mother of six children.

Over the years Bolden was employed in a variety of jobs. She worked at the Greyhound bus station, Linen Supply Company, Railroad Express, and Sears Roebuck. She would regularly quit these jobs after a brief tenure and do domestic work, then take on another job with a company in order to pay into Social Security. According to Bolden, "I would quit when I got ready and take a domestic job because of the excitement of going." She worked as a maid from 1930 until 1968. At one time in her career, she was jailed for allegedly talking back to an employer. According to Bolden, "They said I was 'mental' because I talked back. No one had ever talked as nasty to me as she did. I was in jail for five days."

In the 1960s, Bolden was involved in the civil rights movement with her neighbor, Dr. Martin Luther King, Jr. In 1964, when the Atlanta School Board decided to move the eighth grade out of her community to a condemned school building downtown, she organized a boycott and protest demanding equal and quality education. As a result of these efforts, the board built a modern school in her neighborhood.

Well aware of the working conditions and problems facing fellow workers in private households, in 1964 she began plans for an organization that would work to improve the wages and working conditions of maids. The legal minimum wage set by the U.S. government at the time was $1.25 per hour, but African-American maids in Atlanta were earning $3.50 to $5.00 a day for twelve to thirteen hours of work.

The organizing techniques Bolden learned during the skirmish with the school board were to serve her well when she attempted to organize Atlanta's maids. As a result of her community involvement, Bolden was well known to many Atlanta citizens. Further, during bus rides with other maids over the years, she had heard their complaints about "no money, no respect, and long hours." She was also encouraged by King in her organizing efforts.

In 1968, Bolden asked representatives of organized labor for support and direction. They advised her to assemble a meeting of at least ten women. Within a few months, after several hundred women gathered, organized labor responded. Instead of affiliating with the AFL-CIO, the group decided to create a new union, the National Domestic Workers Union. In September 1968, Bolden was elected president.

Under Bolden's charismatic leadership, the group received a charter, and membership increased. As a result of the group's efforts, wages increased and working conditions improved; maids received $13.50 to $15.00 per day plus carfare. Members were taught to work out their problems with their employers. In time the organization gained clout because of its cohesiveness, evangelical spirit, and community involvement. As president, Bolden was recognized as a major community leader.

During the 1970s, Bolden was consulted by presidents Richard Nixon, Gerald Ford, and Jimmy Carter on issues regarding workers, and she received many local, state, and national appointments. From 1972 to 1976, she served as a member of the advisory committee in the Department of Health, Education and Welfare to Secretary Elliot L. Richardson. In 1975, she was appointed to the Georgia Commission on the Status of Women by Governor George Busbee. She also spent considerable energy organizing domestic workers in other cities.

In 1980, negative publicity surrounding a federal grand jury investigation of the National Domestic Workers Emergency Assistance Fund served to undermine the growth of the organization. An audit of the organization's books revealed that more money had been spent than was allocated by grants funding the group. The investigation found, however, that Bolden had supplemented federal funds with personal monies in order to carry out the organization's programs.

The main goals of the National Domestic Workers Union have been to develop training programs for maids and create a nonprofit employee service to provide job placement and counseling for its members. As president of the group, Bolden spends her days providing social services to her clients and placing eligible applicants in domestic jobs. According to Bolden, "God put me here to help other people."

DOROTHY COWSER YANCY

Boynton, Amelia (1911–)

Amelia Boynton (Amelia Platts Boynton Billups Robinson) was perhaps the most important local leader of the civil rights movement in Alabama's western Black Belt. Primarily through her efforts, the Dallas County Voters League sponsored and sustained the voting rights demonstrations in Selma organized by the **Student Nonviolent Coordinating Committee** (SNCC) in 1963 and 1964. When those demonstrations were halted by a state court injunction, Boynton personally induced Martin Luther King, Jr., to come to Selma in 1965 to revive them and thereafter played a central role in generating local support for King's initiatives. As a result, it would probably not be too much to call her the mother of the Voting Rights Act.

Amelia Boynton was born Amelia Platts on August 18, 1911, the daughter of George G. and Anna Eliza (Hicks) Platts of Savannah, Georgia, where George Platts worked as a carpenter and operated a woodyard. She graduated from Tuskegee Institute in 1927 and in 1930 went to Selma as the county's black home demonstration agent for the U.S. Department of Agriculture. In Selma she worked with Samuel William ("S.W.") Boynton, the county's black agricultural agent, and soon became an enthusiastic assistant in his vigorous efforts to secure economic and political advancement for Dallas County's impoverished black tenant farmers and sharecroppers. In 1936, Boynton left his wife to marry Amelia. The two became leading figures in the Dallas County branch of the **National Association for the Advancement of Colored People** (NAACP) and in the black Dallas County Voters League. As a result, they fell under intense pressure from white segregationists. Amelia's marriage had forced her to give up her position as a home demonstration agent, and she had opened an employment agency. In 1952, S. W. Boynton resigned his government job, and together they entered the real estate and insurance business, hoping that if neither of them held a public position the harassment might decline; but, in fact, particularly after they testified at a hearing of the U.S. Civil Rights Commission in Montgomery in 1958, segregationist pressure greatly increased. At the end of 1961, S. W. Boynton was hospitalized with a heart condition, and he remained in the hospital until his death on May 13, 1963, whereupon Amelia Boynton immediately took up his cause. Throughout the 1960s she remained one of the most active and uncompromising black leaders in Alabama. She was an unsuccessful candidate for the Democratic nomination for a seat in the U.S. House of Representatives in 1964, running against the incumbent, Kenneth Roberts. She also was the candidate of the Black National Democratic Party of Alabama for probate judge of Dallas County in 1972 and for state senator in 1974, in both cases also unsuccessfully.

In 1970, she married Robert W. Billups, who died in a boating accident in 1975. In 1976, she married James Robinson and moved to his home in Tuskegee, where she continues to reside. Robinson died in 1988. In recent years Boynton has become a devoted follower of Lyndon La Rouche, whose Schiller Institute in Washington, D.C., published a second, revised and expanded edition of her autobiography,

Bridge across Jordan, originally published in 1979.

Amelia and S. W. Boynton had two sons, S. William Boynton, Jr., and Bruce C. Boynton. Bruce Boynton, a graduate of Howard University law school, is Dallas County Attorney. In 1960, he was the appellant in the U.S. Supreme Court decision *Boynton* v. *Virginia,* which forbade racial segregation in bus terminal facilities. William Boynton, Jr., is a postal employee and restaurant manager in Philadelphia.

J. MILLS THORNTON, III

Brooks, Elizabeth (1867–1951)

Elizabeth Carter Brooks was one of the moving forces in the black community of New England through her role in black women's clubs. In an era when black women were discouraged from political participation, the club system became a way for black women to practice active democracy and influence the fate of their communities.

Brooks was born in 1867 in New Bedford, Massachusetts. Her mother was a former slave who had been sent north to gain an education. Brooks was brought up in New Bedford and attended the public schools. After graduating from New Bedford High School, she taught at the Howard Colored Orphanage in Brooklyn in the 1880s. She attended the Swain School of Design and was elected the first secretary of the Brooklyn Literary Union in 1883.

Brooks returned to New Bedford and became the first black woman to graduate from the Harrington Normal School. She then became the first black teacher in the New Bedford public school system. She continued teaching until her retirement in

1929. In time, a public school was named in her honor.

Brooks was active in women's clubs from an early age. At that time, clubs were an instrumental force in the community, not just social organizations. In many ways, women's clubs operated as a kind of shadow government. Since black women were not welcome to run for public office, they organized groups and voted their leaders into office. They formed committees, made decisions, raised funds, and carried out major projects needed by the community. In short, they accomplished many of the goals that a government seeks for its citizens.

An example of these projects was the way that Brooks founded the New Bedford Home for the Aged. This institution later became the special project of the Women's Loyal Union. Brooks began thinking of organizing a home for the elderly while still at Harrington Normal. She made her dream a reality in 1897. The institution welcomed the poor, accommodating both black and white elderly. Since the home had no funding, Brooks personally paid its rent for its first six months. The home was able to move to a permanent structure ten years later in 1907. Brooks was president of both the New Bedford Home for the Aged and its supporting organization, the Women's Loyal Union, until she left New Bedford in 1930.

Brooks also helped organize larger federations of black women's clubs. She was recording secretary for the National Federation of Afro-American Women in 1895, and the first recording secretary of the **National Association of Colored Women** (NACW) in 1896. She was vice-president-at-large of the NACW in 1906, becoming president in 1908. Under her leadership the organization sponsored scholarships at **Mary McLeod Bethune**'s Normal and Industrial School for Girls at Daytona Beach, Florida. This school later became **Bethune-Cookman College.**

In 1896, Brooks was among the founders of the New England Federation of Women's Clubs, which later became known as the Northeastern Federation of Women's Clubs. Brooks was president of the Federation for twenty-seven years. In that time, she oversaw the sponsorship of community centers, scholarship funds, day care centers, and other services needed by the community.

Brooks was also an early member of the **National Association for the Advancement of Colored People** (NAACP), joining soon after it was created. She founded the New Bedford branch and later served as president of the New England Regional Conference. In 1948 she was honored as president emeritus of the Bedford NAACP and the New England Regional Conference.

During World War I, Brooks joined other black leaders in patriotic war work. She joined the War Work Council of the National Board of the YWCA, and later went to Washington, D.C. to oversee the construction of the Phillis Wheatley YWCA.

In 1930, Brooks married William Sampson Brooks, a bishop of the African Methodist Episcopal Church. William Brooks was bishop of Texas, and so Brooks moved to his home in San Antonio. When he died four years later, Brooks returned to New Bedford, where she continued to be active in organizational affairs.

In one of her later contributions to the black community, Brooks bought the home of Sergeant William H. Carney in 1939. Sergeant Carney was a Civil War hero and the first black awarded the Congressional Medal of Honor. The home became a memorial and was maintained by yet another club, the Martha Briggs Educational Club.

Using her organizational powers within women's clubs, Brooks was a tireless force for good within her community. Described toward the end of her life as "a woman of good deeds," Brooks spent a lifetime of leadership in her community.

ANDRA MEDEA

Brown, Elaine (1943–)

The image of the **Black Panther Party** (BPP) most often perpetuated is a masculine one, but women were central to all aspects of the BPP's development. One of these women, Elaine Brown, held the BPP's highest position, chairperson, during the difficult and transitional years of the early 1970s.

Elaine Brown was born March 3, 1943, in Philadelphia, Pennsylvania, and grew up singing in the junior and adult choirs at the Jones Tabernacle African Methodist Episcopal Church in North Philadelphia. Brown, raised by her mother and grandmother, attended the Philadelphia High School for Girls and upon graduation entered Temple University as a prelaw candidate. Brown later attended the Philadelphia Conservatory of Music, the University of California at Los Angeles, and Mills College in Oakland, California.

When Brown left Temple University in 1965, she moved to Los Angeles, California. In 1967, she began to volunteer as a piano teacher for children in the Jordon Downs projects in Watts. This experience

contributed to her ultimate decision to serve the black community via the Black Panther Party (BPP).

Brown was involved in several political organizations key to the black movement before joining the BPP in April 1968. She began a Black Student Union newsletter at the University of California at Los Angeles and helped to organize the Southern California College Black Student Alliance.

Elaine Brown became BPP deputy minister of information of the Los Angeles chapter in 1969, and was elevated to minister of information in 1971. By 1974 Brown was chairperson of the BPP, the highest leadership position within the BPP ever held by a woman. Under Elaine Brown's leadership the BPP became an influential political force in Oakland. Strong BPP voter registration activities helped Oakland's first black mayor, Lionel Wilson, to be elected in 1977.

In 1973 and 1976, Brown campaigned unsuccessfully for an Oakland City Council position. In each of her campaigns for city government positions Brown's platform was based on establishing social programs for black and poor people and forging a link between the lawmaking bodies and the community. Perhaps the height of Elaine Brown's political involvement in national politics came in April 1976 when she was chosen as a delegate to the Democratic Party's national convention.

Brown was a board member of several political organizations while she was chairperson of the BPP. She was executive director and chairperson of the board of the Executive Opportunities Corporation (EOC), a nonprofit corporation that operated the Oakland Community School and the Community Learning Center. In addition, Brown was a member of the board of directors of the Oakland Community Housing Corporation, whose responsibility it was to allocate funds for replacement housing for the poor.

Elaine Brown left the BPP in November 1977. During the early 1970s she gave birth to her daughter, Ericka. In 1977, they moved to Los Angeles, where Brown focused on her singing and songwriting career. She had already released two albums: *Seize the Time* in 1969 and *Until We're Free* in 1973, the latter recorded on the Motown label. Several songs on each album were based on Brown's experiences while a member of the BPP.

More recently Elaine Brown has worked as a paralegal and as a freelance writer for *Essence*. She published her autobiography, *A Taste of Power: A Black Woman's Story,* in 1993.

ANGELA D. BROWN

Brown, Linda Carol (1943–)

Linda Brown was born in 1943, the daughter of Oliver and Leola Brown. In 1950 her father joined in the **National Association for the Advancement of Colored People**'s (NAACP) test case to integrate the schools of Topeka, Kansas. In September 1950, Oliver Brown, a welder for the Atchison, Topeka and Santa Fe railroad and a lay minister, attempted to enroll his seven-year-old daughter, Linda, in the school closest to their home, the all-white Sumner School. In the lawsuit that followed, Oliver Brown, on behalf of his daughter Linda, became the "named plaintiff" in *Brown* v. *Board of Education* (1954), the landmark case that held unconstitutional laws enforcing segregation in public schools. In the

U.S. Supreme Court, Thurgood Marshall successfully argued this case on behalf of the NAACP.

Because she was a child, Linda Brown took no part in the case; she did not even testify in court. But Oliver Brown did testify, explaining that his daughter had to travel an hour and twenty minutes to school each day, walking across a hazardous railroad yard before reaching her bus stop. Her school was more than a mile from her home, but the Sumner School, which her white playmates attended, was only seven blocks away. Because the decision was not handed down until after Linda had completed grammar school, Linda Brown did not attend integrated schools until junior high, but her younger sister, Cheryl, began school at the previously segregated Sumner School.

As an adult, Linda Brown Smith, a divorced mother of two, was a more active plaintiff. In 1979, she filed suit to reopen the Brown litigation on behalf of her two children, who were attending schools that were segregated, not by statute but because of housing patterns and a combination of two child-placement policies. In response to the Supreme Court's decision in *Brown,* Topeka began to assign children to the schools nearest their homes, but in 1978 the city modified this procedure by implementing a so-called open enrollment policy, which allowed parents to register their children in virtually any school if they did not like their neighborhood school, and by 1979 residential housing patterns had led to segregated schools. (Ironically, had either, or both, systems been in place in 1954, Linda Brown would have attended the Sumner School, and no desegregation case would have been initiated in Topeka.)

The new case was not argued until 1986, by which time Linda Brown Smith had remarried and become Linda Brown Buckner. She was now litigating not on behalf of her children but on behalf of her grandson, who was attending the predominantly black neighborhood school. In 1987, a federal judge in Topeka threw out the new suit, but in 1989 the Tenth Circuit Court of Appeals reversed that ruling, finding "persuasive evidence that the school system has not met its duty to desegregate" and ruling that the city had failed to "actively strive to dismantle the system that existed" prior to the 1954 *Brown* decision. However, in 1992, in a case ironically called *Board of Education* v. *Brown,* the U.S. Supreme Court ordered the court of appeals to reassess its ruling. At the time of this writing, the litigation has not been concluded.

Linda Brown Buckner is a Head Start teacher and community activist who has lectured on desegregation and taken part in various symposia on the original *Brown* case. She co-founded, with her two sisters, Terry Brown Tyler and Cheryl Brown Henderson, the Brown Foundation for Educational Equity, Excellence, and Research, which was organized to provide scholarships to minority students planning a career in education.

PAUL FINKELMAN

Burks, Mary Fair (d. 1991)

Mary Fair Burks, an English professor and scholar of African-American literature, was the founder and first president of the **Women's Political Council,** the grass-roots organization that initiated and helped lead the

Mary Fair Burks founded and was first president of the Women's Political Council, the grass-roots organization that initiated and helped lead the Montgomery, Alabama, bus boycott of 1955–56.

year-long Montgomery, Alabama, bus boycott (1955–56).

As an adolescent growing up in Montgomery during the 1930s, she defied the Jim Crow system by insisting on using white-only elevators, rest rooms, and other facilities in what she later called "my own private guerrilla warfare." At eighteen she earned her B.A. in English literature at Alabama State College in Montgomery. A year later, after receiving an M.A. in the same field from the University of Michigan, she returned to Montgomery to teach English at the Alabama State Laboratory High School and then taught at the college. She married the high school principal, a former professor of hers. In the late 1940s Burks became head of the Alabama State College English Department. She later earned her doctorate in education at Columbia University.

In 1949, Burks created the Women's Political Council, an organization of black professional women, to address racial problems in Montgomery. The council was "the outgrowth of scars I suffered as a result of racism," she recalled, the immediate impetus having been a personal experience of racist treatment by city police. Although it focused initially on voter registration and citizenship education programs, in the early 1950s the council began to lobby city officials about the mistreatment of black passengers on city buses. In December 1955, after the arrest of **Rosa Parks**, the council launched the bus boycott that it had long discussed. Burks, **Jo Ann Robinson,** and other council leaders played a crucial role in sustaining the boycott until segregated seating was abolished by Federal Court decisions a year later.

In 1960, Burks resigned from Alabama State College after several professors were fired for civil rights activity. She accepted a position at the University of Maryland, Eastern Shore, where she taught literature until her retirement in 1986. Her wide-ranging literary scholarship included articles on contemporary black writers such as Toni Morrison. She won teaching awards and numerous professional honors and fellowships, and she did postgraduate study at Harvard University, Oxford University, the Sorbonne, and other leading universities. A longtime resident of Salisbury, Maryland, she continued her civic activism in such areas as coordinating hospital volunteers, serving on the Maryland Arts Council, and founding two African-American historical societies.

Burks died on July 21, 1991. Her only child, Nathaniel W. Burks, is a physician in San Diego, California.

STEWART BURNS

C

Clark, Septima (1898–1987)

From the Sea Islands of South Carolina to urban and rural areas throughout the Southeast, Septima Poinsette Clark's citizenship schools galvanized local citizens who transformed the social, political, economic, and cultural issues of the United States. She was born on May 3, 1898, in Charleston, South Carolina, the daughter of Peter Poinsette, who was born a slave on the Joel Poinsette Plantation, and Victoria Warren Anderson Poinsette, who was born free in Charleston and spent her early years in Haiti. Her mother boasted that her Haitian upbringing better prepared her for the racist United States society. Her mother's dignified and assertive attitude and her father's gentle and nonviolent composure gave Clark the characteristics to work in the South during the civil rights era. She stressed, "When I went to Mississippi and Texas and places like that, I had a feeling that his non-violence helped me to work with people and her haughtiness helped me to stay. We had a lot of harassment from the KKK and the White Citizen's Council in Tuscaloosa, Alabama and Grenada and Natchez, Mississippi."

Clark's parents instilled in their eight children the importance of education. She attended Avery Institute in Charleston. The liberal arts school was founded in 1865 through the joint effort of philanthropist Charles Avery and the American Missionary Association. In 1916, she completed the twelfth grade at Avery, took the state examination, and received the Licentiate of Instruction that enabled her to teach in rural areas. African Americans were not allowed to teach in the public schools of Charleston. Her first teaching job was on John's Island, South Carolina, where she remained until 1919. It was here that her dedication to service and citizenship education commenced. John's Island had dismal economic, social, and health conditions in 1916. Septima Poinsette lived in an attic room with no inside toilet. Workers signed contracts and were employed in tasks on large plantations. Women carried their children to the fields and placed them in boxes at the end of the row where they were working. A "sugar tit"—lard and sugar—was placed in the babies' mouths to squelch crying. A health problem began as a result of the flies and mosquitoes that bit the babies, often causing malaria. Poinsette observed that many babies failed to "reach the second summer." These conditions motivated her to assist in bringing health reforms to the Sea Islands. Conducting workshops on health issues was a segment of citizenship education.

Her work on John's Island prepared her for confronting unequal teachers' salaries and unequal teaching facilities. Her school, the Promiseland School, was made of logs with clay in the cracks. It had no glass windows, only a shutter that was closed when the wind was high. The chimney heated the children who sat in the front. The benches were without backs, and the children learned to read and write kneeling on the floor. The building was creosoted black. It had two teachers and 132 children; Poinsette was a teaching principal. Together the teachers received $60. Across the road in a whitewashed building was a white teacher with three students. She was paid $85. The discrepancy cemented Poinsette's resolve to become a provocateur

for the equalization of teachers' salaries.

Septima Poinsette [Clark] taught at Avery Institute from 1919 to 1921. While there, she joined nationally renowned artist Edwin Harelston and former Reconstruction congressman Thomas E. Miller in their drive to collect 10,000 signatures to demonstrate to the South Carolina legislature that all African Americans in South Carolina, regardless of their economic status, believed that black teachers should be al-

Septima Poinsette Clark's citizenship schools emphasized citizenship training, literacy, and domestic empowerment. Clark is seen here, at center, with Rosa Parks (left) and Leona McCauley (right), the mother of Rosa Parks, at Highlander Folk School in December 1956. (HIGHLANDER FOLK SCHOOL)

lowed to teach in Charleston's public schools. An affirmative law was passed in 1920. Clark was only twenty-two years old, but she felt this to be her first effort to establish for Negro citizens what she firmly believed to be their God given rights. She was now known as an advocate for equal rights.

Septima P. Clark faced housing discrimination following the death of her husband, Nerie Clark, who succumbed to kidney failure in December 1925. They had married in May 1920 and had two children. The first, a daughter, died within a month of her birth. Their second child was Nerie Clark, Jr. Following her husband's death, Clark lived in Hickory, North Carolina; Payton, Ohio; and John's Island, South Carolina (1927–29), until settling in Columbia, South Carolina, where she remained until 1946. In 1935, she sent her son to Hickory, North Carolina, to live with his paternal grandparents because she was not financially able to support him and most boardinghouses did not allow children. A positive result of the separation was that she had the freedom to pursue her studies, receiving her B.A. from Benedict College in 1942 and her M.A. from Hampton Institute in 1945. In 1937, she studied at Atlanta University with the eminent scholar W. E. B. DuBois. DuBois' lectures on racism and segregation helped Clark understand the link between protest and education and assured her that dedication to the eradication of segregation was a noble pursuit. His endeavors toward excellence and scholarly research enhanced her documentation of events as well as her commitment to writing. This became very vivid as she reported the successes of citizenship schools throughout the South.

While living in Columbia, Clark worked to converge the social and political reforms of African-American organizations. Unity was strength. She affiliated with the Federated Women's Club of South Carolina, the Columbia **Young Women's Christian Association** (black component), the Palmetto Education Association, and the **National Association for the Advancement of Colored People** (NAACP). She strongly endorsed the overall mission of the South Carolina Conference of Branches of the NAACP: "To insure the political, educational, social and economic equality of minority group citizens to remove all barriers of racial discrimination through democratic processes."

In Columbia she taught in the elementary department of Booker T. Washington School. On the same corridor was civil rights leader **Modjeska M. Simkins,** who taught algebra in the mathematics department. They and others joined Booker T. Washington principal J. Andrew Simmons, South Carolina NAACP attorney Harold Bloulware, and NAACP counsel Thurgood Marshall in preparing a court case for the equalization of teachers' salaries. Clark openly worked against some of the people who were directing the system for which she worked. One man, C. A. Johnson, Superintendent of Negro Schools, thought that it was foolish for teachers to bring the salary issue to the courts. Equalization of teachers' salaries became a law in 1945 as a result of the Viola Duvall class action suit. Federal District Judge J. Waties Waring rendered the decision. Clark returned to Charleston in 1947 in order to aid her ailing mother. She taught school and actively participated in civil rights activities, serving as membership chairperson of the local NAACP.

The South Carolina NAACP in the 1940s was a major force in eradicating unjust laws in the Palmetto State. Because of its challenge to the status quo, the association suffered the wrath of relentless politicians. In 1945, it had been successful in the Viola Duvall case. The same year it had been instrumental in the case of *John H. Wrighten* v. *University of South Carolina.* Wrighten's denial of entry to the University of South Carolina law school prompted the establishment of a law school at South Carolina State College. In 1947, in *Elmore* v. *Rice,* the South Carolina NAACP helped break the "whites only" membership barrier to the Democratic Party, which denied African Americans the right to vote in primary elections. *Briggs* v. *Elliott* (Clarendon County, S.C.) was one of the test cases that led to *Brown* v. *Board of Education,* outlawing segregation in public schools. The South Carolina NAACP had become more radical and confrontational.

On April 19, 1956, the South Carolina legislature passed a law stipulating that no city employee could affiliate with any civil rights organization. The law was an attempt to minimize the effectiveness of the NAACP. Septima P. Clark was dismissed from her teaching job when she refused to quit the NAACP and to stop her activities to protest the "affiliation statute." She was fifty-eight years old and had been teaching for forty years. She lost not only her job but also her retirement benefits. From 1956 to 1976 she confronted the system that dismissed her until she received

annual stipends to restore her retirement monies.

Myles Horton, director of **Highlander Folk School** in Monteagle, Tennessee, recruited her as director of workshops. Clark had attended workshops at Highlander and was inspired by its humanistic, biracial approach to solving the nation's problems. She mobilized Highlander to support the social programs of people such as Esau Jenkins of John's Island, South Carolina, and **Rosa Parks** of Montgomery, Alabama. Rosa Parks was sent a scholarship to attend workshops at Highlander. She gained knowledge of civil disobedience, which sparked her defiance of segregation statutes in Montgomery, Alabama, leading to the Montgomery bus boycott of 1955. With the assistance of Myles Horton and the expertise of Septima Clark and **Bernice Robinson,** who later directed citizenship schools on John's Island, Jenkins opened a night school for adults in 1956 that became the prototype for citizenship schools that emerged throughout the South.

Literacy training and democratic empowerment were among the goals of the citizenship schools. Between 1956 and 1961, Clark traveled throughout the South, working in citizenship education, teaching people to write their names, balance checkbooks, vote in elections, and write letters. Millions of people were direct recipients. Seven hundred teachers working in the schools and thousands of people were registered to vote. Septima P. Clark helped transform the Southern political system.

In 1961 she joined the Southern Christian Leadership Conference (SCLC) as director of education and teaching. This position paralleled her work at Highlander, focusing on citizenship training, voting, and literacy. At sixty-three years of age, the "grand lady of civil rights" traveled throughout the South, directing citizenship schools. She faced the wrath of the KKK and the White Citizen's Council, observed beatings, harassment, shootings, and killings. She stood her ground and never lost sight of her mission—social, economic, educational, and political parity for all citizens. By 1963 she was concerned that many states were dissolving their citizenship schools because of the lack of follow-up. Many, she felt, preferred the dramatic impact of direct action over the daily routine that came with genuine citizenship education. She observed that follow-up and dedicated service were essential for the continuation of her life's quest of citizenship education. Clark maintained, nonetheless, that citizenship schools had a powerful impact not only in the quest for civil rights but for women's rights as well.

In her later years Clark revealed that women such as **Ella Baker** and Rosa Parks had never received their rightful place in the civil rights movement. Even Clark's position on the executive board of the SCLC was questioned because she was a woman. She credited Martin Luther King, Jr., with being one of the few civil rights leaders who viewed women as equal to men. A great amount of work was done by women, but they seldom received the notoriety.

The citizenship schools of the SCLC enhanced social and political progress in eleven Deep South states. After departing from the SCLC, Clark conducted workshops for the American Field Service, raised money for scholarships, organized day care facilities, and remained a spokesperson for civil rights. In 1975, she was elected to the Charleston School Board. In 1978, the College of Charleston awarded her an honorary doctorate of humane letters. In 1979, President Jimmy Carter presented her with a Living Legacy Award. A section of the Charleston Highway is named in her honor. In 1982, she received the Order of the Palmetto, South Carolina's highest award.

Clark's book *Ready from Within: Septima Clark and the Civil Rights Movement* won an American Book Award in 1987.

Septima Poinsette Clark, political activist, educational reformer, proponent of citizenship education, and civil rights crusader, died December 15, 1987, in Charleston, South Carolina.

GRACE JORDAN McFADDEN

Cleaver, Kathleen (1945–)

Kathleen Cleaver held one of the highest positions in the **Black Panther Party** in the 1960s and worked to build an international base for the party; today she teaches law.

Kathleen Neal Cleaver was born May 13, 1945, in Dallas, Texas, the first child of Dr. Ernest Neal and Juette Johnson Neal. At the time of her birth her father was on the faculty at Wiley College. Shortly thereafter her father joined the foreign service and Cleaver spent her childhood and teen years abroad, spending time in New Delhi, the Philippines, Liberia, and Sierra Leone.

An honor student, she graduated in 1963 from the George School, a Quaker boarding school, outside of Philadelphia. Cleaver entered **Oberlin College,** transferred to Barnard College, and dropped out in 1966 to join the **Student Nonviolent Coordinating Committee** (SNCC).

Cleaver began her work in the New York office then moved to the organization's headquarters in Atlanta in January 1967, where she was secretary of SNCC's campus program. While organizing a black students' conference in Nashville in the spring of 1967, she met Eldridge Cleaver, then Black Panther Party (BPP) minister of information. They married on December 27, 1967.

Kathleen Cleaver left SNCC in November 1967 to join the BPP in San Francisco, an organization more radical and confrontational than SNCC. She became a member of the party's central committee, the highest decision-making body, and served as national communications secretary.

Cleaver was the first woman included in the central committee. She delivered speeches across the country and organized the "Free Huey" campaigns (rousing support for the jailed minister of defense of the BPP, Huey Newton) in 1968. She campaigned, unsuccessfully, on the Peace and Freedom party independent ticket in the 1968 election.

In June 1969, Kathleen Cleaver joined her husband in exile in Algeria, where they established an international branch of the BPP. Shortly after her arrival she gave birth to a son, Maceo. A second child, a daughter, Jojuyounghi, was born in 1970 in North Korea.

The international branch of the BPP was expelled from the national organization in 1971. Kathleen Cleaver and a new group of former Panthers initiated the Revolutionary People's Communications Network, which she promoted both nationally and abroad.

In 1975, Kathleen Cleaver returned to the United States after her husband surrendered to U.S. authorities. She lived in California with her family until 1981. Later that year she and her children moved to New Haven, Connecticut, where, in 1984, she completed a bachelor's degree in history at Yale University and graduated summa cum laude and Phi Beta Kappa. In 1988 she graduated from Yale Law School and joined the New York City law firm of Cravath, Swaine and Moore.

Cleaver divorced Eldridge Cleaver and, in 1991, moved to Philadelphia, Pennsylvania, where she became a law clerk in the Third District Court of Appeals. Since 1992, Cleaver has taught at Emory University Law School in Atlanta, Georgia.

In 1995 and 1996, Cleaver was a fellow at the Bunting Institute of Radcliffe College and the W. E. B. DuBois Institute at Harvard, while on leave from Emory. She is completing her autobiography, *Memories of Love and War.*

ANGELA D. BROWN

Combahee River Collective

In 1974, it took a great deal of courage for black women to assert that they were black feminists. Most African Americans considered the mere act of addressing sexual political issues to be divisive—an attack upon the black community and especially upon black men. It was in January 1974, however, that the first meeting of the Combahee River Collective took place in Roxbury, Massachusetts.

The Collective began as the Boston chapter of the National Black Feminist Organization, which had held its founding conference in New York City in November 1973. In the summer of 1975, Collective members decided to become an independent organization. They took the name of the river in South Carolina where **Harriet Tubman,** during the Civil War, had led the only military campaign in U.S. history that was planned by a woman and that resulted in the freeing of more than 750 slaves.

Like many feminist groups during that period, the Collective's first objective was consciousness raising. By early 1975, meetings were being held at the Cambridge Women's Center and were open to any black woman who wanted to attend. Black women who believed that sexual oppression did indeed affect black women and that sexism as well as racism, class oppression, and homophobia needed to be confronted directly through political action were usually isolated from each other at the same time that they were likely to be ostracized for their views by other members of the black community. Throughout its existence, the Collective served the important function of connecting black feminists to each other, both locally in the Boston area and, eventually, nationally.

During the process of consciousness raising, Collective members began to define black women's issues from a black feminist multi-issued perspective. They also had the opportunity to share, examine, and heal some of the specific pain they faced as a result of being black women in a white male-dominated society.

By the time the Collective decided to become an autonomous organization, it also had made a commitment to radical political activism. In *The Combahee River Collective Statement,* written in 1977, members stated: "The most general statement of our politics at the present time would be that we are actively committed to struggling against racial, sexual, hetero-

sexual, and class oppression, and see as our particular task the development of integrated analysis and practice based upon the fact that the major systems of oppression are interlocking." The Collective also defined itself as anticapitalist, socialist, and revolutionary.

During the six years of its existence, members worked on a variety of issues that affected black women, including sterilization abuse, reproductive freedom, and violence against women. The Collective also worked with women in prison, actively supported the growth of black women's art and culture, and was in the forefront of confronting racism in the women's movement. The Collective often worked in coalition with other women of color, with white feminists, and with progressive men. Membership in the Collective was open to black women of all sexual orientations. Black lesbians, however, often provided the Collective's leadership during an era when many heterosexual black women were reluctant to address feminist issues or did not want to work with open lesbians. One of the Collective's major achievements was to initiate a series of seven black feminist retreats beginning in 1977. The retreats, held in various locations on the East Coast, provided an opportunity for black feminist activists from other cities to meet each other and to engage in critical political dialogue.

The Collective's ability to integrate the politics of race, sex, and class and to build links among various communities culminated in 1979. After twelve black women were murdered in Boston during a four-month period, Collective members wrote and distributed tens of thousands of copies of a pamphlet, originally entitled "Twelve

Black Women: Why Did They Die?" that analyzed the murders as sexual as well as racial violence. They also played a crucial role in the many groups and coalitions that arose in response to the murders.

The Combahee River Collective made a major contribution to the growth of black feminism in the United States. It was one of the earliest groups to assert the legitimacy of black women's opposition to sexual exploitation and oppression. Its widely circulated *Combahee River Collective Statement* helped to lay the foundation for feminists of color organizing in the 1980s and 1990s. The Collective also played a key role in raising the issue of homophobia in the black community and in initiating communication among black women of different sexual orientations. The Collective's historical legacy continues in the contemporary organizing efforts of radical women of color.

BARBARA SMITH

Cosby, Camille (1945–)

In the past, when a show business marriage was also a business partnership, the manager was usually the husband. And it was often assumed that he was the "manipulative, exploitative brains of the oufit," while his wife was the talented but impractical puppet. In the case of Camille and Bill Cosby, no such dark thoughts seem to enter anyone's mind. And that is not solely because they underestimate the power of a woman.

Chief executive and check-signer of Cosby Enterprises, Camille Olivia Hanks Cosby is a Washington, D.C., native and the eldest of Guy and Catherine Hanks' four children. She was born in 1945, her

Camille Cosby is an extremely active and dedicated philanthropist. Among the many organizations she has supported (both with donations and with fund-raising) are Operation PUSH, the NAACP, the United Negro College Fund, and the National Council of Negro Women. (MICHELE AGINS/NYT PICTURES)

father an army colonel, her family middle-class, her schooling parochial, and her surroundings genteel. Her parents encouraged her to study music.

She was a University of Maryland psychology major when she went on a blind date with William Henry Cosby, at twenty-six a high school dropout from Philadelphia's projects. He took her to a nightclub where he performed stand-up comedy. On their second date, he proposed. Guy Hanks thought his nineteen-year-old daughter was too young, and he did not want her studies discontinued, but the pair married on January 25, 1964.

Leaving the university, Camille Cosby traveled to the cities where her husband performed. Ten months after their wedding, and very quickly after a *Tonight Show* spot, Bill became the first African American to costar in a television action series, NBC's popular *I Spy*. It premiered in the fall of 1965 and lasted nearly three seasons. The Cosbys moved to California, still little acquainted with matters of money but suddenly awash in it.

Their inexperience ended, however, after Bill's manager was found to have mishandled the new star's earnings. The couple was determined, from then on, to manage the money themselves. They set up a Los Angeles office for their family business, and Camille began to manage his career.

In the years to follow, they had five children whose names started with "E"—Ericka, Erin, Ennis (tragically killed in January 1997), Ensa, and Evan—because "E," said Bill, is for "excellence." His name, as he became a superstar of screens large and small, went on NBC's *The Bill Cosby Show* (1969–71), ABC's *Cos* (1976) and NBC's enormously successful *The Cosby Show* (1984–92), which has correctly been taken to mirror the Cosbys' relationship.

Camille Cosby meanwhile became an active philanthropist. She helped raise $337,000 for the Reverend Jesse Jackson's Operation PUSH and similarly aided the **NAACP**, the Student Christian Leadership Conference and, her longest involvement, the United Negro College Fund. Cosby Enterprises also gave large sums to the **National Council of Negro Women** and the Harlem Hospital Center for Women and Children.

Talking to black college presidents around the country, she discovered that support for their institutions was flagging, in part because too often the children of alumni were entering nonblack schools. "It was a real eye-opener," Cosby told *Jet* magazine. "I was stunned to know that the graduates of these institutions were not supporting them and that was because, perhaps, we as a people had bought into the idea that 'White is better.' "

The Cosbys set out to reverse the trend. In 1986, they gave $1.3 million to Fisk University and the same amount, the next year, to be split among Central State University, **Howard University**, Florida Agricultural and Mechanical University, and Shaw University. In 1988 a $1.5 million Cosby donation went to Meharry Medical College and **Bethune-Cookman College.**

Camille was the 1989 commencement speaker at Atlanta's **Spelman College,** which received the couple's largest endowment—$20 million, earmarked for professorships in the fine arts, social sciences, and humanities, but mainly for building the Camille Olivia Hanks Cosby Academic Center.

The more general trend she has sought to reverse is the negative stereotyping of blacks by diverse media. To that end, her dedication has affected television, as she produced the series *A Different World*. It has also touched the American theater. In 1995, she produced the play *Having Our Say* on Broadway. It was based on the book of the same title, which tells the life stories of the Delaney sisters, two black women over one hundred years old, who led fascinating lives. For many years Cosby has been at work on a film about Winnie Mandela.

A thing "deferred," or put off until later, is a bad thing in Camille Cosby's vocabulary, as it was in Langston Hughes'. The people portrayed in *No Dreams Deferred,* a 1994 television documentary she produced, face a world that seems intent upon stunting their aspirations. Cosby's friend, Harvard psychiatrist Alvin Poussaint, has said a woman such as she often has only "deferred power," because she is wife to a famous man. But Cosby's power, like determination, skills, and intelligence, are very real.

The wife of Bill Cosby might have been content, during their lasting marriage, with a life of ease and wealth. That Camille Cosby has not been so content attests not to the marriage's shortcomings but to a rare vitality any couple would covet. Author Bill Cosby has given witness to this in his bestsellers on domestic life, *Fatherhood* (1986) and *Love and Marriage* (1989).

And what about the one thing Camille Cosby did defer in her life, her education? Her 1994 book, *Television's Imageable Influences: The Self-Perceptions of Young African-Americans,* was based on her doctoral dissertation for the University of Massachusetts School of Education. She admits she will probably not put the Ph.D. to use. "But psychologically," she says, "it will make me feel great."

GARY HOUSTON

Cotton, Dorothy (1931–)

One of the few women officers of the Southern Christian Leadership Conference (SCLC), Dorothy Cotton spearheaded efforts during the civil rights movement to create educational programs in the South.

Dorothy Lee Foreman was born in 1931 in Goldsboro, North Carolina. After her mother's death in 1934, she and her three sisters, Effie Mae, Dazzelle, and Annie Margaret, were raised by their father, Claude Daniel Foreman, a tobacco factory worker. Cotton remained with her father until leaving to attend Shaw University in Raleigh, where she supported herself by working as housekeeper for the university president. When her employer took the presidency of Virginia State College in Petersburg, Virginia, Foreman transferred to that institution and graduated with a degree in English and library science. Shortly after graduation she married a college acquaintance, George Cotton. She then enrolled at Boston University, where she received her master's degree in speech therapy in 1960.

While completing work for her master's, Cotton became active in the civil rights movement that was spreading throughout the South. Her involvement in protest activities began after she joined the Gillfield Baptist Church in Petersburg and became a protégé of the church's minister, the Rev. Wyatt T. Walker, who also chaired the local chapter of the **National Association for the Advancement of Colored People** (NAACP). Cotton helped Walker organize a protest against the segregation policies of the Petersburg Public Library and also participated in sit-ins at a local segregated lunch counter. As a member of the Petersburg Improvement Association, Cotton taught student sit-in protesters about direct-action tactics.

In 1960, Martin Luther King, Jr., recruited Walker to become SCLC's executive director, and in September of that year Cotton moved to Atlanta to join Walker's administrative team. During the next few years she worked closely with King and other SCLC leaders, including Ralph Abernathy and Andrew Young, to orchestrate the organization's expanding protest activities, from the Freedom Rides of 1961 and voter registration drives to the Poor People's Campaign of 1968. In 1963, she became a director of SCLC's Citizenship Education Program, a **Highlander Folk School** program taken over by SCLC when Tennessee authorities halted the school's operations. The SCLC program sought to increase literacy among black Southerners in order to encourage them to register to vote and to participate in the political life of their communities. The program also trained local leaders in the tenets of nonviolent protest. Using the text of the U.S. Constitution, the Bill of Rights, and the Fourteenth Amendment, Cotton taught black Southerners not only how to read but also to understand the rights embodied in citizenship. She traveled across the South with Young and **Septima Clark** of the Highlander Folk School, recruiting participants for the training program. A talented singer, Cotton also led programs featuring freedom songs from the Southern struggle.

Although Cotton was a laywoman among the male clergymen who predominated in SCLC leadership, her role was not limited. She became one of King's closest confidants and her presence in SCLC's inner circle put her at the forefront of the Southern civil rights movement as a planner, coordinator, and demonstration leader.

After King's assassination in 1968, Cotton continued her work at SCLC, watching the organization suffer internal turmoil until she left in 1972. A year later she became director of the federal Child Development/Head Start program in Jefferson County, Alabama. From 1975 to 1978, she worked at the Atlanta Bureau of Human Services. In 1978, she accepted the invitation of former movement associate John Lewis to become southeastern regional director for ACTION, the federal agency for volunteer programs. After leaving ACTION in 1981, she worked briefly at the Martin Luther King, Jr., Center for Non-Violent Social Change in Atlanta. After more than two decades of intense involvement in civil rights activities, Cotton left Atlanta in 1982 for Cornell University, where she served as director of student activities. In May 1991, she left Cornell to conduct seminars on leadership development and social change.

CLAYBORNE CARSON/STEPHANIE BROOKINS

D

Davis, Angela (1944–)

Shouts of "Free Angela" echoed across the early 1970s, and a California college professor became an icon of the counterculture. She was fierce, brilliant, and uncompromising.

Angela Davis was born on January 26, 1944, in Birmingham, Alabama, the youngest child of B. Frank and Sallye E. Davis. Her mother was a schoolteacher, and her father had been one until, because teachers' salaries were so low, he gave it up to buy a gas station. The family was comfortable financially, living in a middle-class area in Birmingham. Davis' mother taught her reading, writing, and arithmetic before she entered school.

Not all of Davis' classmates were so economically advantaged as she was. Early on she saw children who had no warm clothing or money for lunch and became highly conscious of social differences. In the segregated schools Davis attended, there were teachers who went out of their way to teach black history and instill a sense of black heritage, but there were also school buildings near to falling down and textbooks long out of date. She became aware of the messages black children were being sent by their teachers and others around them. If their parents were poor, the system told them, it was because they did not work hard enough, were not bright enough, did not have enough determina-

tion. Davis ferociously resented these messages and believed they were undermining a whole generation.

As Davis became angrier and more dissatisfied with the life around her, she found support at home. Her mother had been politically active since college, and her grandmother worked to instill a sense of outrage over the injustices suffered by African Americans. While still in elementary school, Davis participated with her mother in civil rights demonstrations. In high school she was one of the organizers of interracial study groups that were disbanded by the police. At the age of fifteen, Davis moved to New York to attend a progressive private school, the Elizabeth Irwin High School. Her tuition was paid by a scholarship from the American Friends Service Committee and she lived with the family of Episcopal minister William Howard Melish.

Elizabeth Irwin High School was the proverbial "hotbed of radicals." Many of the teachers had been blacklisted from the public schools for their leftist political beliefs. Davis was ripe for radicalizing herself and soon joined Advance, a Marxist-Leninist group. She also worked hard to overcome the quality of her early education before she entered Brandeis University in Waltham, Massachusetts. At Brandeis, Davis excelled academically. She spent her junior year at the Sorbonne. In Paris, Davis met with political activity on an intense level. Among her fellow students were Algerians who were involved in the struggle against French colonialism.

In 1963, four girls whom Davis had known were killed when a Birmingham church was bombed, and her radicalism developed deeply personal roots. Then, in her senior year, she began to study under the philosopher Herbert Marcuse. Marcuse's analysis of modern history and his belief in the responsibility of the individual to rebel had a profound effect on Davis. She graduated from Brandeis in 1965 with a degree in French and went on to study philosophy in Europe. In Frankfurt, at Goethe University, she became a member of a socialist student group that was demonstrating against the Vietnam War. By 1967, she had resolved to return to the United States, to study again under Marcuse, who was now at the University of California at San Diego. She became active again in the civil rights movement.

In 1967, she went to Los Angeles for a workshop sponsored by the **Student Nonviolent Coordinating Committee** (SNCC). There she met Kendra and Franklin Alexander, who were active in SNCC, the **Black Panthers,** and the Communist Party. The next year, she moved to Los Angeles to work with the Alexanders. However, various aspects of these radical groups disturbed her, especially the sexism. Finally, she made a choice that would drastically change her life: she joined the Communist Party. In 1969, she made a pilgrimage to Cuba.

Having completed her master's degree and "all-but-the-dissertation" on her doctorate in philosophy, Davis was hired in 1969 to teach philosophy at the University of California at Los Angeles. She was a popular teacher, but that did not help her when her membership in the Communist Party was revealed. The students and administration of the university stood behind her, but the California Board of Regents and Governor Ronald Reagan fired her.

Davis challenged the dismissal in court and won. She was reinstated, but her classes were monitored, and the Board of Regents was determined to find a way to get rid of her.

Davis became more and more involved in work with the Black Panthers, especially with prison inmates, whom she considered prisoners of class war. Then two Marxist inmates of Soledad Prison organized a revolutionary cell in the prison. One of the inmates, W. L. Nolen, was killed by a guard while involved in a fistfight with two other prisoners. The other, George Jackson, was indicted for murder when a white guard was found murdered. Davis became fervently involved in the cause of the "Soledad Brothers." Her speeches in their defense were enough, along with her lack of a doctorate, for the Board of Regents to deny her a new contract.

That was only the beginning. George Jackson, with whom Davis had developed a strong emotional involvement, was killed by guards during an alleged escape attempt—after all charges against him had been dropped. His brother, Jonathan, went to the Marin County Courthouse, where a San Quentin inmate was on trial for stabbing another prisoner, took hostages, and tried to make a getaway. Before he could do so, two prisoners, a judge, and Jackson himself were killed.

Jackson had taken the guns he used in the rescue attempt from Davis' home.

Though the guns had been purchased by Davis because of threats on her life, and though they were registered, a federal warrant was issued for her arrest. She did not wait to be served with the warrant; she went underground. On August 18, 1970, the brilliant middle-class professor of philosophy whose crime consisted of owning guns used in a crime was placed on the Federal Bureau of Investigation's ten-most-wanted list. She was charged by California with kidnapping, conspiracy, and murder. After two months, she was found in New York, extradited to California, and put in jail without bail.

The "Free Angela" movement erupted. The slogan appeared on urban walls, on bumper stickers, and in newspapers. Her face appeared on posters and on T-shirts. Singer **Aretha Franklin** offered to pay her bail, saying, "I'm going to set Angela free . . . not because I believe in communism but because she's a black woman who wants freedom for all black people." On February 23, 1972, she was released on $102,000 bail and, at her trial she was acquitted of all charges. Ronald Reagan and the Board of Regents voted that she would never again teach at a university supported by the state of California.

The defense committee set up for Angela Davis was renamed the National Alliance against Racism and Political Repression, with Davis as cochair. Its purpose was to help in the defense of political cases. The majority of those defended have been blacks and Hispanics.

In recent years, Davis has written and lectured extensively and remained politically active, running for vice president of the United States in 1980 and 1984 on the Communist Party ticket. Her books include *If They Come in the Morning* (1971), *Women, Race, and Class* (1983), *Women, Culture, and Politics* (1989), and the best-selling *Angela Davis: An Autobiography* (1974, 1988).

KATHLEEN THOMPSON

Davis, Henrietta Vinton (1860–1941)

Marcus Garvey described Henrietta Vinton Davis as the "greatest woman of the Negro race today." One of the most illustrious black actresses of the turn of the century in the United States, she became famous internationally as a leader in the Garvey movement.

Born in Baltimore in 1860, Davis was the daughter of Mansfield Vinton Davis, a musician, and Mary Ann Johnson Davis. She taught school in Maryland and Louisiana and in 1878 became the first black woman to be employed in the Office of the Recorder of Deeds in Washington, D.C., where she worked as an assistant to Frederick Douglass. Douglass encouraged her commitment to a dramatic career and introduced her debut performance in Washington, D.C., in April 1883. Over the next decade she traveled widely as an elocutionist, attracting audiences with her rendering of works by Shakespeare, Dunbar, and others. In 1884, she married Thomas Symmons, a Detroit theatrical producer who became her manager, but the marriage and business relationship dissolved by 1893 after he was arrested for domestic violence. After years of performing without winning a place in an established Shakespearean company—despite glowing reviews of her talent—Davis established her own company in Chicago in 1893. She produced works by William Edgar Easton (*Dessa-*

lines, Christophe) and collaborated with New York journalist John E. Bruce in the writing of *Our Old Kentucky Home,* a Civil War drama. She traveled to the Caribbean on tour with singer Nonie Bailey Hardy in 1912–13 and managed the Covent Garden Theater in Kingston, Jamaica.

Her experience and connections in Jamaica, along with her friendship with Garvey supporters John E. Bruce and Florence Bruce, attracted her to the **Universal Negro**

Marcus Garvey called her the "greatest woman of the Negro race today" when Henrietta Vinton put the power of her reputation as a highly acclaimed actress behind the Universal Negro Improvement Association in 1917. (SCHOMBURG CENTER)

Improvement Association (UNIA) as the young Marcus Garvey began to reformulate it in Harlem in 1917 and 1918. The then obscure Garvey relied on her to draw huge crowds in cities where she had gained a reputation as an actress. She became the UNIA international organizer and was indispensable in building the movement, touring tirelessly with Garvey in the early years and chairing key mass meetings at Carnegie Hall, Madison Square Garden, and the UNIA's Liberty Hall. She was one of the founding directors of the UNIA's Black Star Line, and later, an organizer for the Black Cross Navigation and Trading Company, traveling on organizational tours of the Caribbean aboard UNIA ships. Long the only woman among the slate of central UNIA officers, she became Fourth Assistant President General in 1922. She was the only woman in the UNIA delegation that met with President C.D.B. King in Liberia in 1924 and in the committee that delivered petitions to President Coolidge later the same year. During Garvey's incarceration (1925–27), she handled UNIA affairs in British Honduras, and after Garvey's release and deportation, she was his senior administrator in Jamaica, directing UNIA affairs there in his absences. In August 1929, she became secretary general of Garvey's splinter group, the UNIA of the World, and continued to chair meetings, direct pageants, and assist in the organization's administration and with Garvey's *Blackman* newspaper. She became increasingly alienated from Garvey and by 1932 had become the First Assistant President General of the competing UNIA Incorporated, headquartered in New York. In 1934, Davis became the first (and only) woman to be elected President General of that rival organization. She died in Washington, D.C., November 23, 1941, after a long illness.

Davis succeeded grandly in converting her experience as an actress-elocutionist into a powerful political career as an orator and organizer. Her renunciation of the racial discrimination she experienced as an actress fueled the fervor with which she dedicated herself to nationalist politics, especially to the hope of freedom and self-actualization for black people through the redemption of Africa. Her long years of personal dedication to Garvey, however, ended in disillusionment, illness, and relative poverty, and despite her many achievements and popularity, little note was made of her death at the time.

BARBARA BAIR

Devine, Annie (c. 1912–)

Veteran civil rights activists agree that there would not have been a movement in Madison County, Mississippi, had it not been for the work of Annie Belle Robinson Devine.

Raised in the rural town of Canton, Annie Devine grew up during the most oppressive years in the segregated South. When the civil rights movement gained momentum in the early 1960s, all of Mississippi was dead set against change; any efforts to challenge the status quo were met by violence and intimidation. At the request

of **Anne Moody,** who later wrote *Coming of Age in Mississippi* (1968), Annie Devine attended a meeting of the Congress of Racial Equality (CORE). This was the turning point of her life. At fifty, she committed herself to the black freedom struggle, joining the cadre of fearless local leaders who risked their lives for social change.

As a churchwoman, independent insurance agent, and mother, Devine was highly respected in Canton. As an older adult in the community, Devine propelled civil rights organizing throughout the state. Working through CORE, she made an invaluable contribution in launching voter registration and in the political education of Mississippi's black voters. In 1964, along with her close friends **Fannie Lou Hamer** and Victoria Gray, she helped to organize the **Mississippi Freedom Democratic Party** (MFDP). As an alternative to the illegally elected, all-white state Democratic Party, the MFDP challenged the seating of the state delegation to the 1964 Democratic National Convention in Atlantic City, New Jersey. In a history-making precedent, Annie Devine was among the sixty-eight elected representatives to champion the cause of justice.

Annie Devine continues to live in Canton, where her lifetime commitment to social change is still being realized through community leadership and activism.

VICKI CRAWFORD

E

Edelin, Ramona (1945–)

As a standard-bearer of African-American scholarship and culture, Ramona Hoage Edelin has excelled as both an organizer and educator. Whether teaching college, founding an Afro-American studies department, or serving as president and chief executive officer of the National Urban Coalition, Edelin has always been on the cutting edge of cultural relevance.

Born in Los Angeles on September 4, 1945, Edelin was the only child of Annette Lewis Hoage and George Hoage. Her mother, later Annette Lewis Phinazee, was the first woman to receive a degree in library science from Columbia University. She went on to serve as teacher and librarian in a variety of colleges and universities. As a result, young Ramona grew up in the academic world. Her family moved first to South Carolina State College at Orangeburg, then to Atlanta University in Georgia, and later to Southern Illinois University at Carbondale. She attended the laboratory school of Atlanta University (Oglethorpe Elementary), then Lincoln Junior High School at Carbondale. She graduated in 1963 from Stockbridge School, a high school in Stockbridge, Massachusetts.

Edelin went on to Fisk University, where she collected distinctions throughout her undergraduate career. As a sophomore in 1964, she received the Sarah McKim Maloney Award. Later she was part of a select number of undergraduates chosen to pursue intensive studies at Harvard University. She graduated from Fisk in 1967 with a B.A., magna cum laude, in philosophy.

She then married Kenneth Edelin, a doctor, and followed him to England, where he was stationed in the U.S. armed services. While there, she attended the University of East Anglia in Norwich, England, earning an M.A. in philosophy. After graduation she taught at the European Division of the University of Maryland, lecturing in logic. After Edelin returned to the United States, she studied philosophy at Boston University, earning her Ph.D. in 1981. Her dissertation was on W. E. B. DuBois, who continued to influence her thinking and strategy.

While pursuing her Ph.D. at Boston University, Edelin taught at Northeastern University, also in Boston. In 1972, she became acting chairperson of Afro-American studies. In 1974, she became full chair of the department. She taught philosophy at nearby Emerson College from 1974 to 1975 and was visiting professor of Afro-American studies at Brandeis University for the same period.

In 1977, Edelin joined the National Urban Coalition in Washington, D.C. This was an organization founded in response to the riots of the 1960s, in order to foster a national urban agenda. Edelin began as executive assistant to the president and, by 1979, became director of operations. In 1981, she became vice-president of operations. The next year she was promoted to vice-president of program and policy and, by 1982, became chief executive officer.

As CEO of the National Urban Coalition, Edelin has emphasized two special programs. The first was "Say YES to a Youngster's Future." This was a family learning project designed to expose children and teenagers to the fields needed for high technology, including science, math, and computers. The other program was the Leadership Strategy Series. This series of meetings and conferences assembled leaders from politics, business, education, and community groups to decide on strategy for public policy.

Edelin has been particularly identified with what she has called the "cultural offensive." By this she means the need for African Americans to establish full cultural integrity as a necessary step on their path to economic and political power.

In 1989, Edelin was chairperson of the African American Summit, another step toward establishing a unified national agenda for African Americans. Partly for her work there she received the Southern Christian Leadership Conference (SCLC) Leadership Award for Progressive Leadership in 1989. Edelin continues to influence national thought with her weekly column, "On the Cultural Offensive," along with her work at the Coalition.

ANDRA MEDEA

Edelman, Marian Wright (1939–)

In the past, legally protecting children meant little more than limiting the number of hours they could spend running a loom or working in a field. Marian Wright Edel-

Known as "the children's crusader," Marian Wright Edelman is director of the Children's Defense Fund. She has been a powerful voice in the struggle to improve the world for future generations. (RICK REINHARD)

man was one of those who changed that, redefining and defending the rights of children everywhere.

Marian Wright was born on June 6, 1939, in Bennettsville, South Carolina. Her parents, Arthur Jerome Wright and Maggie Leola Bowen Wright, instilled in their five children the belief that serving their community was one of life's highest duties. Marian went to Marlboro Training High School and then on to **Spelman College** in Atlanta, Georgia. Traveling overseas while still a student changed Edelman's perspective on the world. "After a year's freedom as a person," she said, "I wasn't prepared to go back to a segregated existence."

Wright was back in the United States for her senior year. It was 1960, and civil rights demonstrations were beginning all over the South. When she participated in a sit-in in Atlanta, she was among fourteen students who were arrested. Soon she had decided to forgo graduate studies in Russian and become a lawyer. She graduated as valedictorian from Spelman and entered Yale University Law School as a John Hay Whitney Fellow. Her civil rights activities continued. She went to Mississippi to work on voter registration in 1963 and, after graduation, returned as one of the first two National Association for the Advancement of Colored People Legal Defense and Education interns. She opened a law office, became the first black woman to pass the bar in Mississippi, got demonstrating students out of jail, and was put in jail herself. She also became involved in several school desegregation cases and served on the board of the Child Development Group of Mississippi, which represented one of the largest Head Start programs in the country.

In 1968, Wright went to Washington, D.C., on a Field Foundation grant and started the Washington Research Project. Her goal was to find out how new and existing laws could be made to work for the poor. Shortly after Robert Kennedy was shot, Wright married Peter Edelman, who had been a legislative assistant to Kennedy; she and Edelman had met in Mississippi. Though she moved with her husband to Boston in 1971 and became director of the Harvard University Center for Law and Education, Marian Wright Edelman regularly flew back to Washington so that she could remain at the helm of the Washing-

ton Research Project, which developed into the Children's Defense Fund (CDF). The CDF quickly became the nation's most effective advocate for children, and Edelman, as its dedicated director, became known as "the children's crusader." One of the CDF's largest campaigns was mounted against teenage pregnancy, but the Fund has also been active in all areas of children's health, child care, youth employment, social service, child welfare, and adoption.

In 1979, Edelman returned with her husband to Washington, D.C. In 1980, she became chair of the board of trustees of Spelman. She was the first black and the second woman to hold that position. She has also served on the boards of a wide variety of organizations that are involved in children's welfare, including the Carnegie Council on Children, the March of Dimes, and the United Nations International Children's Emergency Fund (UNICEF) Com-

The Children's Defense Fund, the nation's most effective advocate for children, is active in the areas of children's health, child care, employment, social service, child welfare, and adoption. This is the fund's logo. (CHILDREN'S DEFENSE FUND)

mittee. Her activities are not limited to her work for children. She was also the first black woman elected to the Yale University Corporation and has served on the boards of a large number of influential political organizations.

Edelman has been called an unusual and effective lobbyist and has communicated her message eloquently and with passion in many arenas. Her books include *Children Out of School in America* (1974), *Portrait of Inequality: Black and White Children in America* (1980), and the best-selling *The Measure of Our Success: A Letter to My Children and Yours* (1992).

Edelman's Children's Defense Fund, beginning in 1992, coordinated the Black Community Crusade for Children, "a long-term action campaign to alleviate the black child and family crisis."

Marian Wright Edelman received a Mac-Arthur Foundation Fellowship in 1985 and has received honorary degrees from more than thirty universities. She has been throughout her career a powerful voice in the struggle to improve the world for generations to come.

KATHLEEN THOMPSON

Evers-Williams, Myrlie (1933–)

When Myrlie Evers-Williams was elected chairperson of the NAACP's (**National Association for the Advancement of Colored People**) board of directors in February 1995, one could almost hear a collective sigh of relief from many of the group's supporters. In a period when race relations had grown increasingly tense, the nation's oldest civil rights organization had fallen on hard times. Beset by reports of financial impropriety and mismanagement and amid

rising concern that the eighty-seven-year-old organization was out of step with the times, the NAACP was ripe for a "draft Myrlie for chair" movement.

Evers-Williams was the ideal candidate. Her twenty-five years of experience in corporate and public sectors (a former commissioner of the Los Angeles Board of Public Works, she had managed a $400 million budget) were valuable administrative and fund-raising assets. But many of those who rallied around her were paying tribute to Myrlie Evers-Williams' personal integrity, and to her impeccable civil rights credentials that were earned during dangerous times in pre–civil rights Mississippi. Her election reflected the hope of the NAACP's members and friends that Evers-Williams would not only help to restore faith in the organization but also get it on track. Hazel Dukes, her friend and sister board member, calls her "the steel magnolia" in recognition of the determination that has marked her life.

Myrlie Louise Beasley was born in Vicksburg, Mississippi, on March 17, 1933. Her parents separated in her infancy, and her childhood was spent with her grandmother, a collection of aunts and her great-great-grandmother, a former slave.

She was blocked from attending white Southern schools, enrolling instead at Alcorn A&M College. She met Medgar Evers on her first day, then later dropped out to marry him, on December 24, 1951. The couple moved to Mound Bayou, Mississippi, an all-black town in the Mississippi Delta. Medgar became an insurance agent for Magnolia Mutual Insurance, one of the few black-owned businesses in Mississippi with good jobs to offer. The Everses had three children: Darrell Kenyatta, born in

"You can kill a man but you can't kill an idea," said Myrlie Evers-Williams, *explaining her determination to continue the work begun by her husband, slain civil rights leader Medgar Evers. Here, she accepts a veterans' award on behalf of her late husband; at left is Mrs. Malcolm Peabody of Massachusetts; at center is Ralph Bunche of the United Nations.* (NATIONAL ARCHIVES)

1953, and named after the leader of the Mau-Mau liberation movement in Kenya; Reena Denise, born in 1954; and James Van Dyke, born in 1960.

In 1954, Evers was appointed the state's first NAACP field secretary. Despite threats and harassment, he traveled the state, organizing campaigns against racist violence and for voting rights and access to public accommodations. Myrlie Evers ran the of-

fice, researched his speeches, and acted as hostess and chauffeur, while caring for their young children. She also had to contend with much of the abuse that was directed at her husband. As a result, she says, "He began to see me as his partner, and it sometimes surprised him. I had grown into this assertive woman."

After Medgar Evers was assassinated in July 1963, a nearly penniless Myrlie Evers moved—in the midst of her grief and rage—to form a new life. To help ease her financial burden, the NAACP hired her to give a series of speeches that catapulted the once shy woman into the public eye. Evers moved her young family to California. She went back to school and earned her degree in sociology from Pomona College. Then, in 1970, at the urging of local Democrats, she ran for Congress. Despite the fact that she didn't win, the campaign was a personal turning point: "That was the first time I let go of the security blanket of being Medgar's widow. I ran as Myrlie Evers, not Mrs. Medgar Evers."

Although she spurned the mantle of public widow, Myrlie Evers never let go of her determination to see her husband's murderer brought to justice. In 1964, Byron De La Beckwith, who had bragged about the killing, was tried twice, and each time the all-white jury deadlocked. But she never gave up on her quest to see him convicted.

During the 1970s, Evers worked in advertising and community affairs, and she met and fell in love with Walter Williams, a retired longshoreman and union activist. When they married in 1976, she says, "There were many people who thought I should not remarry, that I should be an eternal widow. But Walter gave me tremendous love and was strong enough to deal with Medgar's presence in my life." With her new husband's support, she continued her quest for justice, staying in touch with law officials in Mississippi to keep the case alive, searching for information. Her perseverance paid off when in 1989 a new witness challenged De La Beckwith's alibi.

After the state informed her it could not proceed because the transcripts of the first trials had been lost, her preparedness saved the day: she provided a copy that she had held in safekeeping since 1964. Finally, in 1994, a tearfully jubilant Myrlie Evers-Williams witnessed De La Beckwith's conviction.

It was a bittersweet victory for her, muted by grief for a murdered first husband and, within a few months, by the knowledge that her second husband was ill and dying. The "draft Myrlie movement" couldn't have come at a more difficult time. It was only after her husband urged her on that she declared her candidacy. He died two weeks after she was elected. And once again in the midst of mourning, Evers-Williams went on the road to speak out for the NAACP.

Evers-Williams remembers when the NAACP was at its most vital, and is determined to see it once again become a source of hope, strategies, and solutions. Readily admitting that "we're using stale methods to approach many of the same issues—education, employment, protection under the law, other effects of racism—that Medgar and I worked on in my day," she is determined to create a more relevant progressive agenda. "I do not intend to stay in this position for a lifetime, but I want to leave knowing that we have found a way to attract people who didn't go through the fire in the 1950s and 1960s to join the NAACP. I want to leave this organization healthy, knowing it can make a real difference in their lives."

JILL PETTY

[This entry is reprinted from the January/February 1996 issue of *Ms.* The original title is "Woman of the Year: Myrlie Evers-Williams." It is reprinted by permission of *Ms.* magazine, (c) 1996.]

F

Foster, Autherine Lucy (1929–)

Her ambition to have the best education she could get led her into a nightmare and into history. Autherine Juanita Lucy was born on October 5, 1929, in Shiloh, Alabama, the daughter of Minnie Hosea Lucy and Milton Cornelius Lucy, a farmer. One of ten children, she went to the public schools of Shiloh through junior high school. She also helped her family work in the cotton fields and raise watermelon, sweet potatoes, and peanuts. For high school, she went to Linden Academy, graduating in 1947.

Lucy's undergraduate college years were spent at Selma University in Selma, Alabama, and at all-black Miles College in Fairfield, Alabama, where she met Hugh L. Foster, whom she would later marry. She graduated from Miles with a B.A. in English in 1952. The next decision Lucy made changed her life drastically. She decided to go to graduate school at the University of Alabama. She was not naive; she knew that getting into the school would be a struggle and she prepared for it. With a friend who shared her ambition, she approached the **National Association for the Advancement of Colored People** (NAACP) for help. Thurgood Marshall, Constance Baker Motley, and Arthur Shores were assigned to be her attorneys. While they started laying the groundwork for her case, she worked as a secretary, among other jobs. Court action began in July 1953.

"If I graduated from the University of Alabama," she said in a recent interview, explaining her determination, "I would have had people coming and calling me for a job. I did expect to find isolation . . . I thought I could survive that. But I did not expect it to go as far as it did."

Perhaps no one expected things to go that far. On June 29, 1955, the NAACP secured a court order restraining the university from rejecting Lucy and her friend based upon race. The University of Alabama was thereby forced to admit them. Two days later, the court amended the order to apply to all other African-American students seeking admission to the university. On February 3, 1956, twenty-six-year-old Lucy enrolled as a graduate student in library science. (Her friend had reconsidered the situation.)

That is when the nightmare began. On the third day of classes, Autherine Lucy faced mobs of students, townspeople, and even groups from out of state. "There were students behind me saying, 'Let's kill her! Let's kill her!' " she said. The mobs threw eggs at her and tried to block her way. A police escort was needed to get her to her classes, and even from within the classroom, she could hear the crowds chanting.

That evening, Lucy was suspended from the university. The university's board stated that the action was taken for her safety and that of the other students. The NAACP lawyers did not accept the suspension, however. They filed a contempt of court suit against the university, accusing the administrators of acting in support of the white mob. Unfortunately, they were unable to support these charges and were forced to withdraw them. The suit was used as justification for expelling Lucy from the school.

In the days and months that followed, Lucy was invited to study at several European universities at no charge, but she declined. "I didn't know whom to hate," she said. "It felt somewhat like you were not really a human being. But had it not been for some at the university, my life might not have been spared at all."

For some time after her expulsion, Lucy could not find work as a teacher. She was simply too controversial. In the spring of 1956, she moved to Texas and married her college sweetheart, the Reverend Hugh Foster. They had five children, and eventually she was hired as a teacher. The Fosters lived in Texas for seventeen years, re-

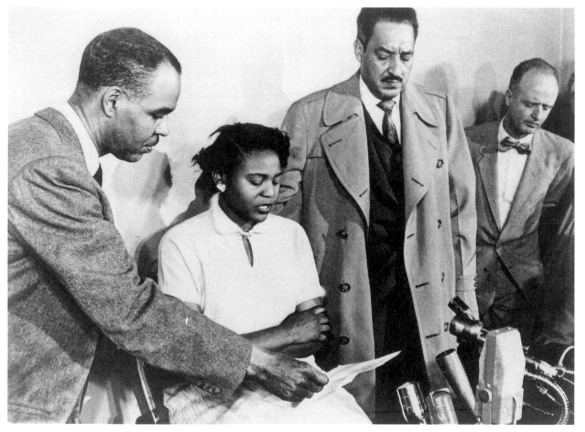

After three and a half years of court action and the efforts of attorneys, including Thurgood Marshall (right), the NAACP succeeded in forcing the University of Alabama to enroll Autherine Lucy as its first black student in 1956. NAACP executive secretary Roy Wilkins is at left. (LIBRARY OF CONGRESS)

Autherine Lucy, left, became the first black student at the University of Alabama in 1956. Thirty-six years after she was threatened and assaulted by rioters—and subsequently expelled—she received a master's degree from the school, alongside her daughter, Grazia Foster, who earned a bachelor's degree the same year. (MIKE CLEMMER)

turning in 1974 to Alabama, where she worked as a substitute teacher. During this time, she maintained her interest in civil rights, speaking periodically at meetings.

Then, in 1988, two professors at the University of Alabama invited her to speak to a class, telling students about her experience more than thirty years before. One of the questions she was asked was, "Did you ever try to re-enroll?" Foster said that she hadn't, but that she might consider it. Several faculty members heard about her statement and began working to get the university to overturn her expulsion. In April of that year, the board officially did so.

A year later, Autherine Lucy Foster entered the University of Alabama to earn a master's degree in elementary education. Her daughter, Grazia, enrolled at about the same time, as an undergraduate majoring in corporate finance. In the spring of 1992, they both received degrees.

TIYA MILES

G

Garvey, Amy Ashwood (1897–1969)

Amy Ashwood Garvey sometimes claimed to have cofounded Marcus Garvey's **Universal Negro Improvement Association (UNIA)**, the most successful Pan-African mass movement ever. What can be asserted with more confidence is that she may have been the first member, apart from Garvey himself.

Born in 1897 in Port Antonio, Jamaica, Amy Ashwood was seventeen years old when she met Marcus Garvey after his return to Jamaica, just days earlier, from four years of wandering in Latin America and Europe. The UNIA was formed shortly after their meeting.

Amy Ashwood became "lady secretary" of the new association, whose objectives included the uplift of the African race locally and internationally. She also became romantically involved with Garvey, and within the next year or so, they became engaged. Throughout the UNIA's first year, Amy accompanied Garvey on organizational trips around the island and figured prominently in the association's activities. She took part in UNIA-sponsored debates, read poetry at UNIA literary events, helped feed the poor, and visited the sick.

Sometime before Garvey left Jamaica for the United States in 1916, Amy left for Panama. In 1918, she joined Garvey in New York. By this time the UNIA was poised for its spectacular take-off into Pan-African acclaim. Amy plunged once more into the work of the association. She traveled across the country with Marcus, helped with the UNIA's new organ, the *Negro World,* and in 1919 became an official of the newly launched Black Star Line Steamship Corporation. In October 1919, she apparently helped save Garvey's life (the facts are disputed) from a would-be assassin's bullet.

Amy and Marcus were married on Christmas Day 1919, in the presence of several thousand UNIA members and well-wishers. The marriage was on the rocks within a few months. Marcus accused his wife of infidelity, excessive drinking, and financial dishonesty; she accused him of infidelity and lack of political correctness. Several suits for annulment, divorce, separation, alimony, and bigamy were brought by one or the other party over the next six years. In the midst of these suits and countersuits, Marcus obtained a divorce in Missouri in 1922 and almost immediately married Amy Jacques. Jacques had been a close friend and roommate of Ashwood's and had been chief bridesmaid at Ashwood and Garvey's wedding. As Garvey's private secretary, she had accompanied the newlyweds on their honeymoon to Canada.

An excellent public speaker and, to a certain degree, a good organizer, Amy Ashwood Garvey had a deep interest in Pan-African affairs, quite independent of Garvey's. These characteristics shaped the rest of her life.

Amy Ashwood Garvey sometimes claimed to have cofounded Marcus Garvey's Universal Negro Improvement Association; in any case, she was certainly its first member, apart from Garvey himself. After her divorce from Garvey in 1922, she maintained a deep and active interest in Pan-Africanism. (SCHOMBURG CENTER)

In London in 1924, she worked with several prominent West Africans in founding a Nigerian Progress Union. Back in the United States in 1926, she collaborated with the Trinidad-born calypsonian Sam Manning on the musical comedies *Brown Sugar, Hey Hey,* and *Black Magic.* She and Manning took a musical revue on tour in the Caribbean in 1929.

Between 1935 and 1938, Amy again found herself at the center of Pan-African activity. Her restaurant in the West End of London became the gathering place for such famous Pan-Africanists as George Padmore and C. L. R. James of Trinidad and Jomo Kenyatta of Kenya. She was an active participant in their political activities.

In Jamaica in the early 1940s, she founded a short-lived political party and attempted to establish a school of domestic science. By now her peripatetic lifestyle was firmly established, and her endless wanderings would continue to the end of her life. In New York in 1944, she was active in the campaign to elect Adam Clayton Pow-

Married to Marcus Garvey in 1922, Amy Jacques Garvey carried on his work with the UNIA during his imprisonment. Her writings on Garvey helped to stimulate a rebirth of interest in Garveyism. She is shown here studying a bust of Garvey in Jamaica, West Indies, in 1956. (SCHOMBURG CENTER)

ell, Jr., to the U.S. Congress. She also came under Federal Bureau of Investigation surveillance for her association with left-wing activists and others such as Paul Robeson suspected of Communist leanings.

She found herself at the center of Pan-African activity once more in 1945 when, together with the elder statesman of the movement, W. E. B. DuBois, she chaired the opening session of the famous Fifth Pan-African Conference in Manchester, England. George Padmore and Kwame Nkrumah of Ghana were the organizers.

She lived in West Africa from 1946 to 1949. In Liberia she became a close friend of President W. V. S. Tubman. In Ghana she was able to trace her ancestry back to the Ashanti, in a manner remarkably similar to that recounted by Alex Haley in *Roots* decades later.

During the 1950s, her time was divided among England, the Caribbean, and West Africa again. Her interest in women's issues, developing for a long time, now competed with Pan-Africanism for the focus of her attention. She lectured to women's groups and encouraged women to organize in a 1953 tour of the Caribbean. In London in this period, she organized a community center and was active in the aftermath of the Notting Hill race riots of 1958.

Amy spent the early 1960s in West Africa, where she tried her hand at a series of unsuccessful business ventures in Ghana and Liberia. The rest of the decade was spent in England, Trinidad, the United States, and Jamaica. In 1964 when Garvey's body was returned to Jamaica amid much pomp and ceremony—he had died in England in 1940—she participated officially in the ceremonies in London marking the occasion. In the United States in 1967,

she was feted by the Black Power generation, who had rediscovered Garvey and were in the process of elevating him to fame and honor once more.

She died in Jamaica in 1969, still dreaming of new business ventures and political activities.

Amy Ashwood Garvey was an engaging woman who was able to engender fierce loyalty in the few friends she made. Her encounter with Garvey was both a blessing and a curse. Garvey and the UNIA presented her with a moment of great glory. The encounter also condemned her to live in the shadow of the man and his organization for the rest of her life. Whether indulging in recrimination over her years with Garvey or basking in the reverence bestowed upon her in later years as wife of the fallen hero, she could not and would not divorce herself from the defining experience of her life.

TONY MARTIN

Garvey, Amy Jacques (1896–1973)

Journalist, Pan-Africanist, and historian, Amy Euphemia Jacques Garvey was a key figure in the **Universal Negro Improvement Association** (UNIA). She was the second wife of Marcus Mosiah Garvey, founder of the UNIA. Amy Jacques was born in Kingston, Jamaica, December 31, 1896, and educated at Wolmers Girls' School. Her parents, Charlotte and George Samuel Jacques, were also formally educated and owned valued property; the Jacques family's heritage was rooted in the Jamaican middle class. Plagued by ill health due to recurring bouts with malaria, Amy Jacques sought a cooler climate and in 1917 migrated to the United States. She became affiliated with the UNIA in 1918 and served as Marcus Garvey's private secretary and office manager at the UNIA headquarters in New York. She married Marcus Garvey, July 27, 1922, in Baltimore, Maryland.

During Marcus Garvey's incarceration for alleged mail fraud, Amy Jacques Garvey's three-tiered (writer, spokesperson, and archivist) activist nature evolved. She served as the editor of the women's page, "Our Women and What They Think," in the *Negro World,* the UNIA's weekly newspaper published in New York. Amy Jacques Garvey's editorials demonstrated her political commitment to the doctrines of Pan-Africanism and also her belief that women should be active within their communities even, to some extent, at the sacrifice of self. As the liaison between Marcus Garvey and UNIA officials, and secretary-treasurer of both the Marcus Garvey Freedom and Protection Fund and the Marcus Garvey Committee of Justice, Amy Jacques Garvey traveled across the United States and spoke on Marcus Garvey's behalf in the campaign to secure his release from prison. Amy Jacques Garvey's uncompromising attitude toward organizational efficiency made her a controversial figure within the UNIA. Nonetheless, she was able to keep meticulous records on Marcus Garvey and the UNIA in the midst of this flurry.

Upon Marcus Garvey's release from Tombs Atlanta Penitentiary on November 26, 1927, and his subsequent deportation from the United States, he and Amy returned to Jamaica. There, Amy gave birth to her two children, Marcus Garvey, Jr. (1930) and Julius Winston Garvey (1933). After Marcus Garvey's death on June 19, 1940, Amy Jacques Garvey continued to serve the UNIA. Her books *The Philosophy and Opinions of Marcus Garvey,* published in two volumes (1923, 1925), *Garvey and Garveyism* (1963), and *Black Power in America* (1968) helped to stimulate a rebirth of interest in Garveyism. As a result, there has been a growth of historical scholarship focusing on the activities of Marcus Garvey and the UNIA. Amy Jacques Garvey was awarded a Musgrave Medal in 1971 in Jamaica for her distinguished contributions on the philosophy of Garveyism. On July 25, 1973, Amy Jacques Garvey died at University Hospital of the West Indies in Jamaica.

ULA TAYLOR

H

Hamer, Fannie Lou (1917–1977)

"I'm sick and tired of being sick and tired," the famous and radical words of Fannie Lou Hamer, summarized the essence of how many black Americans had come to feel by the 1960s. Her speeches and singing influenced everyone who heard and saw her. For many Americans, Fannie Lou Hamer symbolized the best of what the civil rights movement became.

Most people familiar with the civil rights movement of the 1960s know of Fannie Lou Hamer: sharecropper, determined voter registrant, fieldworker for the **Student Nonviolent Coordinating Committee** (SNCC), a founder (along with **Annie Devine,** Victoria Gray, Aaron Henry, and others) of the **Mississippi Freedom Democratic Party** (MFDP), orator, and political activist. In addition to these contributions, Fannie Lou Hamer abided by strong religious teachings and often expressed that religious zeal through a sacred hymn sung before each of her speeches. She opened many gatherings with "This Little Light of Mine," one of her favorite songs.

Fannie Lou Townsend was born to Jim and Ella Townsend on October 6, 1917, in rural Montgomery County, Mississippi. Ella and Jim Townsend moved to Sunflower County, Mississippi, when Fannie Lou was two years old, and the child received her early education there. At the age of six, Fannie Lou began working in the cotton fields and worked many long years

chopping and picking cotton until the plantation owner, W. D. Marlow, learned that she could read and write. In 1944, she became the time and record keeper for Marlow, and in 1945, she married Perry Hamer, a tractor driver on the Marlow plantation. For the next eighteen years, Hamer worked as sharecropper and timekeeper on the plantation, four miles east of Ruleville, Mississippi, the place where she and Perry made their home. All this changed in 1962 when she suffered economic reprisals after an unsuccessful attempt to vote in the county seat of Indianola. Familiar with the physical violence that would often follow economic reprisals, and having received threats, Hamer left her family to stay with friends. The move did not stay the violence, however, and Hamer and her friends miraculously escaped rounds of gunshots fired into the friends' home when a person or persons yet unknown discovered her presence there.

Despite the denial of the right to vote and the subsequent violence and economic intimidation, Hamer became an active member of SNCC in Ruleville. She took the literacy test several times in order to repeatedly demonstrate her right to vote. In 1963, she became a field secretary for SNCC and a registered voter; both put her life in jeopardy. From this point onward Hamer worked with voter registration drives and with programs designed to assist

For many Americans, sharecropper Fannie Lou Hamer, whose determination to vote led her to become a powerful political activist, symbolized the best of what the civil rights movement became. In 1967, she testified before the Senate's Subcommittee on Poverty. (SCHOMBURG CENTER)

economically deprived black families in Mississippi.

The youngest of twenty siblings whose parents seldom were able to provide adequate food and clothing, Hamer saw a link between the lack of access to the political process and the poor economic status of black Americans. She was instrumental in starting Delta Ministry, an extensive community development program, in 1963. The next year she took part in the founding of the **Mississippi Freedom Democratic Party** (MFDP), becoming vice chairperson and a member of its delegation to the Democratic National Convention in Atlantic City, New Jersey, in order to challenge the seating of the regular all-white Mississippi delegation. In this capacity she made a televised address to the convention. The 1964 challenge failed despite a compromise offered through Hubert Humphrey and

Walter Mondale that would have seated two nonvoting MFDP members selected by Humphrey. Instead, the MFDP's actions resulted in an unprecedented pledge from the national Democratic Party not to seat delegations that excluded black delegates at the convention in 1968. Hamer also unsuccessfully ran for Congress in 1964. Because the regular Democratic Party disallowed her name on the ballot, the MFDP distributed a "Freedom Ballot" that included all of the candidates' names, black and white. Hamer defeated her white opponent, Congressman Jamie Whitten on the alternative ballot, but the state refused to acknowledge the MFDP vote as valid. In 1965, Hamer, Victoria Gray, and Annie Devine appealed to the U.S. Congress, arguing that it was wrong to seat Mississippi's representatives (who were all white) when the state's population was 50 percent black. The three women watched as the House voted against the challenge, 228 to 143.

Hamer remained active in civic affairs in Mississippi for the remainder of her life and was a delegate to the Democratic National Convention in 1968 in Chicago. Her founding in 1969 of the Freedom Farms Corporation (FFC), a nonprofit venture designed to help needy families raise food and livestock, showed her concern for the economic plight of black Americans in Mississippi. The FFC also provided social services, minority business opportunity, scholarships, and grants for education. When the **National Council of Negro Women** started the Fannie Lou Hamer Day Care Center in 1970, Hamer became its board's chairperson. As late as 1976, even as she struggled with cancer, Hamer served as a member of the state executive committee of the United Democratic Party of Mississippi.

Fannie Lou Hamer in an interview in 1965 said: "I was determined to see that things were changed." Later in the same interview, and paraphrasing John F. Kennedy, she continued, "I am determined to give my part not for what the movement can do for me, but what I can do for the movement to bring about a change." On being tired, Hamer put it best when she said:

> I do remember, one time, a man came to me after the students began to work in Mississippi, and he said the white people were getting tired and they were getting tense and anything might happen. Well, I asked him, "How long he thinks we had been getting tired?" I have been tired for forty-six years, and my parents was tired before me, and their parents were tired; and I have always wanted to do something that would help some of the things I would see going on among Negroes that I didn't like and I don't like now.

Hamer consistently stated that she had always wanted to work to transform the South because she saw her parents work so hard to raise twenty children. Once her father bought two mules after much sacrifice, and simply because this meant he might experience semi-independence from the landowner, his mules were poisoned. Hamer said she never understood this kind of hatred, but fighting it gave her courage.

Fannie Lou Hamer's frankness, determination, courage, and leadership abilities made her a memorable figure in the 1960s civil rights struggle in general, particularly in the MFDP challenge to the Democratic Party in August 1964, and especially in its challenge to white Southern members of the party.

Fannie Lou Hamer received wide recognition for her part in bringing about a major political transformation in the Democratic Party and raising significant questions that addressed basic human needs. In 1963, the Fifth Avenue Baptist Church in Nashville, Tennessee, presented her with one of the first awards that she received, for "voter registration and Hamer's fight for freedom for mankind." Other awards include the National Association of Business and Professional Women's Clubs National Sojourner Truth Meritorious Service Award as a tribute to Hamer's strong defense of human dignity and fearless promotion of civil rights. **Delta Sigma Theta Sorority** awarded her a life membership. Many colleges and universities recognized her with honorary degrees, including Tougaloo College, in 1969.

Fannie Lou Hamer gave numerous speeches across the country into the 1970s. Suffering with cancer, she continued to accept invitations to speak about the issue most dear to her, basic human rights for all Americans. Indeed, she remained tired of being sick and tired until her life ended. She died of cancer on March 14, 1977, at Mound Bayou Community Hospital. A biography of Hamer by Kay Mills, *This Little Light of Mine: The Life of Fannie Lou Hamer,* was published in 1993.

LINDA REED

Harris, Louise (b. 1891)

Louise "Mamma" Harris was a rank-and-file leader of the Tobacco Stemmers and Laborers Union at Export Leaf Tobacco Company in Richmond, Virginia. Workers organized this independent union in 1937 with the help of activists from the Southern Negro Youth Congress to help win higher wages and improved working conditions.

Born in 1891, Louise Harris left school at the age of eight to begin caring for younger children and cooking in the homes of white people in Richmond. She entered the tobacco factories in her early forties and quickly appreciated the conditions that would lead to her involvement in the union. "It took me just one day to find out," she told *New Republic* writer Ted Poston, "that preachers don't know nothing about hell. They ain't worked in a tobacco factory."

Tired of wages that averaged between five and six dollars a week, Export workers struck the company in August 1938. The eighteen-day strike galvanized Richmond's Congress of Industrial Organizations unions, which donated money for strike relief and bodies for the picket lines. The sight of picketing white women from the International Ladies' Garment Workers Union horrified the police and the Richmond elite, but it was the presence of hundreds of tobacco workers, all "black and evil" according to Harris, that won the strike.

Although little is known about her life, Louise "Mamma" Harris exemplified the numerous black women workers who stepped forward in the South during the 1930s and 1940s to demand respect and an end to discrimination and exploitation. Black women dominated the tobacco factories, particularly those that processed the leaf for manufacture. For over a hundred years these plants had been their livelihood, and, despite the hardships, they developed a rich culture of mutuality and opposition.

Commenting on the power of women during the 1938 strike, Harris observed, "They [the police and bosses] 'fraid of the women. You can out talk the men. But us women don't take no tea for the fever."

ROBERT KORSTAD

Hernandez, Aileen Clarke (1926–)

"Some are suggesting," said Aileen C. Hernandez in the 1970s, "that it is time for black women to move to the back of the revolution. There is clear and present danger that if we do, the revolution will be aborted and black people—male and female—will have lost for the second time in 100 years the chance for real freedom. . . . No one can be free until all are free." These strong words reflect the dual concerns Hernandez—second president of the National Organization for Women (NOW)—has been advocating for decades. They are, unfortunately, as relevant today as they were then.

Born in Brooklyn, New York, Hernandez is the daughter of Charles Henry Clarke, Sr., and Ethel Louise Hall Clarke. She attended Brooklyn public schools, graduating from grammar school as valedictorian and high school as salutatorian. Winning a scholarship to **Howard University** in 1943, she pursued majors in political science and sociology. Active in the Howard University branch of the **National Association for the Advancement of Colored People** (NAACP), she picketed theaters and restaurants in the Washington area. She was editor of the campus newspaper during her junior and senior years and wrote a column on university affairs for the *Washington Tribune*. She graduated from Howard magna cum laude in 1947.

Hernandez stayed on briefly at Howard to work as a research assistant in the political science department. Later in 1947, she went to the University of Oslo with an international student exchange program in order to study comparative government. She studied public administration at New York University in 1950 and later attended the University of California at Los Angeles and the University of Southern California. She eventually received a master of arts degree in government with highest honors from Los Angeles State College in 1961.

Hernandez began working as a professional activist with the International Ladies Garment Workers Union (ILGWU). After serving an internship in 1951, she was assigned to the Los Angeles office, where she was a shop organizer and assistant educational director until 1959. At that time she was promoted to director of public relations and education, a post she retained until 1961. In 1960, she was sent to Latin America by the State Department in order to further understanding of the American political system and United States practices in unions with regard to the status of women and minorities.

In 1961, Hernandez went into politics more directly as campaign coordinator for Alan Cranston in his election for state comptroller. Cranston won the election and later became a long-serving senator from California. After Cranston's election, Hernandez was appointed assistant chief of the California Fair Employment Practice Commission. This period was the era when the government began to play an active part in the battle against widespread discrimination in public and private arenas. Hernandez held this post from 1961 to 1965.

In 1965, Hernandez was appointed one of the five members of President Johnson's Equal Employment Opportunity Commission (EEOC). Under the Civil Rights Act of 1964, the commission was intended to enforce federal laws against employment discrimination because of race, color, sex, religion, or national origin. Hernandez was the only female member of the commission. She was well aware of her symbolic value to the administration. "I think when people in politics make appointments to commissions," she commented, "they are always trying to balance out various parts of the community. They sort of hit the jackpot when they get someone who's black, who's a woman, who has a Mexican-American last name, who comes from California, and who's been in the labor movement." She resigned her position on the commission eighteen months later, because the commission lacked true enforcement powers.

In 1966, she returned to California and founded Hernandez and Associates, a public relations and management firm advising public and private organizations in their utilization of women and minorities. Her clients have included the city of Los Angeles, the University of California, and United Airlines. Thirty years later, her agency is still active and doing remarkable work.

Hernandez achieved national prominence in 1967 when she was appointed western vice-president of the National Organization of Women. In 1970, she became president of the national organization, taking over from Betty Friedan, NOW's first president. At this time, glaring inequalities between the sexes were not only common, but written into law. For instance, there were state laws that prohibited a married woman from controlling her own property. There were different penalties for men and women convicted of the same crime, with women getting the longer jail sentence. Labor laws that were intended to prohibit the exploitation of women were instead being used to bar women from high-paying jobs.

In the early seventies there was controversy over black women's participation in a women's rights organization. It became part of Hernandez's role to highlight the similarities in the goals of women and minorities, rather than allow the groups to be pitted against each other. As Hernandez once wrote, "Black women have to be supportive of both revolutions; we are 'twice cursed' by discrimination against blacks and discrimination against women. . . . But black men should be supportive of both revolutions, too—in equal partnership with black women." Hernandez was president of NOW until 1972.

In her years since NOW, Hernandez has been particularly active as vice-chair of the National Urban Coalition, an organization founded in response to the riots of the 1960s, to improve opportunity for urban people and further an urban agenda. She has been involved in work as varied as a study of South African apartheid and its links to American policy making, and serving on an advisory board for immigration issues for the Rand Corporation and the Urban Institute.

Hernandez has held many educational and advisory posts in addition to these. She was lecturer in political science at San Francisco State University from 1968 to 1969, and instructor on urban planning at the University of California at Berkeley in 1978 and 1979. She was a board member on the Ms. Foundation for Women, and

cofounder of Black Women for Action, an organization to endorse political candidates.

Hernandez's many honors include the distinguished service award from the National Urban Coalition and an honorary degree from Southern Vermont College. She was 1993 Regents Scholar in Residence at the University of California at Santa Barbara and, the same year, was also Tish Sommers Lecturer at the University of California at San Francisco, at the Institute for Health and Aging.

After decades of fighting for economic and civic justice for women and minorities, Hernandez is still a force for empowerment. As she pointed out many years before, it is not the hand that rocks the cradle that rules the world, it is the hand that controls the purse strings. Her tireless work for all disenfranchised people has taken her to China, Africa, and Latin America. As a policy maker, researcher, and activist, Aileen Hernandez has left her mark.

ANDRA MEDEA

Higgins, Bertha G. (1872–1944)

Suffragist and political activist Bertha G. Higgins worked tirelessly in Providence, Rhode Island, politics to benefit African Americans and women. Her activities spanned four decades, from the turn of the century until 1940. As a political activist, her goals included votes for women, political patronage for black men and women, antilynching legislation, and increased social services and jobs for the people of her community.

Bertha G. Dillard was born in Danville, Virginia, on November 18, 1872. A seamstress and clothing designer, she studied in London and Paris and for a time operated a clothing shop of her own after her marriage to physician William Harvey Higgins. The couple was married in Charlotte, North Carolina, in 1896, lived in Harlem for a time around 1899, and settled in Providence in 1906. They had one daughter, Prudence, who became a musician and a social worker.

Bertha Higgins began her political and community work shortly after moving to Providence by joining other black women in 1907 to petition the mayor and the school committee to hire a black teacher. She became involved in the Rhode Island black women's club movement, leading both cultural and political activities within a few years of her arrival in the city.

By 1914, Higgins was a suffragist, and with the support of her husband she led efforts to foster the work of the Woman Suffrage Party of Rhode Island. She wrote letters to federal and state elected officials and helped raise funds in support of the votes-for-women campaign. Several other black women worked in the Rhode Island woman suffrage movement during this period, including Mary E. Jackson, Susan E. Williams, and Maria Lawton. Of these women, however, Higgins was a prime mover. In 1916, for example, Higgins persuaded the Twentieth-Century Art and Literary Club, a group of black Providence women, to sponsor a minstrel show. Funds raised from this event benefited the Woman Suffrage Party, a racially integrated association.

Bertha Higgins was a founder and leader of several women's political organizations, including the Political League and, after the ratification of the Nineteenth Amendment,

the Julia Ward Howe Republican Women's Club. Higgins cooperated with nationally known Republican women such as **Mary Church Terrell,** who had significant roles not only in working for the passage of the amendment, but also in helping elect Warren G. Harding to the presidency in 1920. In appreciation of her work during the campaign, Harding invited the Higginses to his inauguration.

Through her various associations, Higgins fought for black women's political patronage in the Republican Party. However, in 1932, she became disillusioned with the failure of the party to recognize black political patronage and, as a result, led the women in her organization to the Democratic Party. Eventually, they changed the name of their organization to the Julia Ward Howe Democratic Women's Club.

Political activism was also a means for Higgins to push for legislation to improve black human rights. As president of her association, she pressured Congressman Clark Burdick and Senator Le Baron Colt to support the Dyer antilynching bill that went before Congress several times between 1918 and 1925. Burdick supported the bill, which managed to get through the House of Representatives a few times. Colt did not support the bill, which never passed the Senate.

During the 1930s and 1940s, Higgins worked diligently to gain meaningful employment for black people in her community. Numerous individuals sought her assistance in their efforts to gain state employment because they knew she would lobby on their behalf. As a result of her efforts, for example, in 1937, Higgins' daughter, Prudence, became the first black social worker at the Rhode Island Department of Public Welfare. Furthermore, in Bertha's efforts to end poverty among black people in Providence, she was instrumental in bringing the Urban League to the city during the 1930s.

By the end of the 1930s, Bertha Higgins had begun to slow down. In 1938, her husband passed away, and she withdrew to mourn for eighteen months. In 1942, at the age of seventy, she withdrew permanently from public life. She died December 30, 1944, at her home in Providence. This formidable woman never allowed barriers to hinder her battles to strengthen the rights of women and the people of her race.

ROSALYN TERBORG-PENN

Highlander Folk School

After attending a summer workshop on school desegregation at Highlander Folk School (HFS) in 1954, a black school-teacher from Columbia, South Carolina, reported to her community: "I always knew what I wanted to get done, but now I feel like I know how I'm going to get it done." Highlander provided both a gathering place and a philosophy of social change that engaged and supported the black freedom movement as it expanded in the aftermath of the 1954 *Brown* v. *Board of Education* decision. During the 1950s, interactions between Highlander and Southern black communities helped foster the development of indigenous local leaders. Women such as **Rosa Parks, Septima Clark,** and **Bernice Robinson** played pivotal roles in fusing Highlander's resources with the needs and aspirations of their communities in ways that helped to shape fundamentally the tactics and goals of the civil rights movement.

Cofounder Myles Horton described Highlander as a place "where people can share their experiences and learn from each other and learn to trust their own judgment" as they worked toward a more democratic and economically just society. HFS was established in Grundy County, Tennessee, in 1932, to serve industrial and rural workers in Southern Appalachia. Through its dynamic and flexible program of workshops and extension programs, Highlander quickly developed into a regional center for workers' education. Highlander became the primary training school for labor organizers who led the Congress of Industrial Organizations (CIO) drives to organize Southern industry. Although HFS was always open to all races, most unions were reluctant to sponsor interracial schools; black people did not begin to attend Highlander as students until 1944. The efforts of the 1930s and 1940s had demonstrated with increasing frequency, however, that racism was the main obstacle to achieving a democratic and economically just society in the South. By the late 1940s, Highlander's firm commitment to interracial unionism and its refusal to accommodate postwar anticommunism left it estranged from an increasingly conservative CIO, leading to a complete reassessment of HFS's program and goals.

Highlander was prepared to respond to the important developments in race relations that the 1950s would bring. In anticipation of the U.S. Supreme Court's ruling on *Brown* v. *Board of Education,* the HFS executive council resolved to focus its efforts on promoting the desegregation of public schools. Highlander initiated its new program in 1953 with a series of summer workshops to help prepare black and white

Rosa Parks (right) participated in a school desegregation workshop at Highlander Folk School in the summer of 1955. Several months later, back home in Montgomery, Alabama, Parks' refusal to give up her seat on a bus triggered the Montgomery bus boycott. Seated at the table (left to right) are Septima Clark; Dr. Parrish, University of Louisville; and Dr. Fred Patterson, president of Tuskegee Institute. Legend has it at Highlander that Parks remarked during the workshop "Nothing ever happens in Montgomery." (EMIL WILLIMETZ)

representatives of civic, labor, church, and interracial groups to lead in the transition to an integrated school system. In contrast to earlier days, at least half of the workshop participants were black. The workshops provided a valuable forum for individuals from throughout the South to share their experiences and frustrations, address common problems, and develop strategies and tools for achieving public school desegregation in their communities. For many, HFS workshops also created a unique experience of interracial community. Reflecting on her participation in a Highlander workshop during the summer of 1955, Rosa Parks recalled: "That was the first time I had lived in an atmosphere of complete equality with the members of the other race." Within months of her stay at Highlander, Rosa Parks' defiance of segregation would spark the legendary Montgomery bus boycott.

HFS's flexible program and workshop networks offered fertile ground for new ideas and new leadership to grow even as Southern states organized their resistance to the implementation of the *Brown* decision, along with a concerted assault on the **National Association for the Advancement of Colored People** (NAACP). When NAACP member and HFS workshop participant Septima Clark was fired from her job with the Charleston public schools in 1956, Myles Horton immediately hired Clark as full-time director of Highlander's workshop program. Septima Clark, along with Esau Jenkins and Bernice Robinson, two other workshop participants, gave substance to HFS's extension program to develop community leadership when they joined it to the concrete needs and aspirations of the people of the Sea Islands. Esau Jenkins, self-educated farmer and longtime community activist and leader on St. Johns Island, was convinced that the right to vote was the key to addressing other problems confronting the island's black community, and adult illiteracy was the primary barrier to meeting voting requirements. Jenkins' appeal to Highlander, first made during a 1954 summer workshop, resulted in the establishment of the first citizenship school on St. Johns Island in January 1957 as part of Highlander's extension program. Bernice Robinson, who served as the first teacher, and Septima Clark developed an adult literacy curriculum and program that provided the basis for citizenship schools throughout the South.

Bernice Robinson, a beautician and dressmaker, developed a curriculum around the life experiences and needs of her students. She and Septima Clark produced workbooks that included sample money order and mail order forms and voter registration applications, along with pertinent sections of the state's voting requirements, and short chapters on political parties, social security, taxes, the function of the county school board, and other topics. Robinson also rehearsed registration and voting procedures with the students. Jenkins, Robinson, and Clark organized mass meetings throughout the Sea Islands and in Charleston to build enthusiasm for the program and recruit teachers. Highlander ran workshops for more than 220 potential teachers, who represented a variety of occupational backgrounds and ages. By 1961, there had been thirty-seven citizenship schools in South Carolina alone, with 1,300 participants, which translated into a dramatic increase in the number of registered black voters. On St. Johns Island alone, black voter registration more than tripled between 1956 and 1960. Starting in 1959, Clark and Robinson produced materials for use in citizenship schools in Tennessee and Georgia, and they worked directly in helping to establish programs in Huntsville, Alabama, and Savannah, Georgia.

On April 1, 1960, Highlander's seventh annual student workshop hosted participants in the wave of sit-ins that swept the South earlier in the year. During the next year, Highlander sponsored several workshops for the new generation of activists and provided an important forum for addressing the role of white students in the movement. **Ella Baker, Dorothy Cotton, Ruby Doris Smith,** and **Diane Nash** were among the participants. In January 1961, fifty-two black beauticians from Tennessee and Alabama met at Highlander for a "new leadership responsibilities" workshop and explored how they and other women whose incomes were not dependent on white people could participate more effectively in the movement.

Highlander held its last workshop in May 1961. Years of harassment by state officials culminated in a Tennessee Supreme Court ruling revoking the school's charter and confiscating its property. Yet Highlander's contribution to the civil rights movement could not be so easily contained. The citizenship school program was transferred to the Southern Christian Leadership Conference (SCLC), where it continued to flourish under the leadership of Septima Clark. Bernice Robinson continued to work with the program from her position on the HFS staff, later joining the staff of the SCLC. Highlander reincorporated as the Highlander Research and Education Center and is currently located in New Market, Tennessee. Since the 1970s, it has worked primarily with the people of Appalachia, seeking to address labor, environmental, and health problems and concerns in the continuing struggle for social and economic justice.

PATRICIA SULLIVAN

Housewives' League of Detroit

The Great Depression of the 1930s was one of the most catastrophic periods in American history. All Americans suffered economic hardships, but especially African Americans. The thousands of black men and women who had left the South for Northern cities and Midwestern communities in search of a better future for themselves and their families as early as the mid-1920s found themselves embroiled in a fierce struggle for jobs, housing, education, and first-class citizenship. As their economic status worsened, African Americans in cities across the country encountered an increase in incidences of brutal violence, race riots, and blatant racial discrimination and segregation. During these dire times black women in Detroit created an ingenious organization based upon the principles of mutual aid, economic nationalism, and self-determination: the Housewives' League of Detroit.

The greatest weapon Detroit black women had at their disposal during the height of the Depression was the leadership and organizing skills they had cultivated during the previous four decades of involvement in club work. Black women's culture taught them how to identify issues needing to be addressed, how to mobilize their sisters, how to develop persuasive arguments, and how to fight for the survival and well-being of their families and communities. Grounded in a social welfare-oriented cultural tradition, they appreciated the necessity for collective action. As black women in Detroit experimented with new strategies to serve their people and to enhance their status as women, they seized upon the idea of harnessing their economic power.

On June 10, 1930, a group of fifty black women responded to a call issued by Fannie B. Peck, wife of Reverend William H. Peck, pastor of the 2,000–member Bethel

African Methodist Episcopal Church and president of the Booker T. Washington Trade Association. Out of this initial meeting emerged the Housewives' League of Detroit. Peck had conceived the idea of creating an organization of housewives after hearing a lecture by M. A. L. Holsey, secretary of the National Negro Business League. Holsey had described the successful efforts of black housewives of Harlem to consolidate and exert their considerable economic power. Peck became convinced that if such an organization worked in Harlem, it should work in Detroit. As an admirer later recalled, Peck "focused the attention of women on the most essential, yet most unfamiliar factor in the building of homes, communities, and nations, namely—'The Spending Power of Women.' "

The requirement for membership in the Housewives' League of Detroit was a commitment to support black businesses, buy black products, patronize black professionals, and keep black money in the black community. Founded in 1930, the league grew to a membership of 10,000 by 1934. Housewives' leagues exerted major influences in other large cities as well. (DETROIT PUBLIC LIBRARY)

The organization grew with phenomenal speed. From the original fifty members, its membership increased to 10,000 by 1934. Peck maintained that the growth was "due to the realization on the part of Negro women of the fact that she has been travelling through a blind alley, making sacrifices to educate her children with no thought as to their obtaining employment after leaving school."

Essentially, the Housewives' League combined economic nationalism and black women's self-determination to help black families and businesses survive the Depression. The only requirement for membership was a pledge to support black businesses, buy black products, and patronize black professionals, thereby keeping the money in the community. The leadership acknowledged that black women were the most strategically positioned group to preserve and expand the black internal economy. Members held the conviction that "it is our duty as women controlling 85 percent of the family budget to unlock through concentrated spending closed doors that Negro youth may have the opportunity to develop and establish businesses in the fields closest to them."

Each black neighborhood in Detroit had its own chapter of the Housewives' League. The community leaders attended monthly meetings of the executive board. Any woman who pledged to "help build bigger and better Negro businesses and to create and increase opportunities for employment" was welcomed to membership. "A belief in the future of Negro business and a desire to assist in every way by patronizing and encouraging the same is all that is necessary to become a member." The organization took pains to make sure that all interested women had the opportunity to join and participate in the league's work. This tactic lessened the development of class-based hierarchies within the organization.

Fulfilling the duties of membership in the league required considerable effort and commitment. Members of each chapter canvassed their neighborhood merchants, demanding that they sell black products and employ black children as clerks or stockpersons. In addition, chapter leaders organized campaigns to persuade their neighbors to patronize specific businesses owned by African Americans or white businesses with black employees. Across the city, league officers organized lectures, planned exhibits at state fairs, discussed picketing and boycotting strategies, and disseminated information concerning the economic self-help struggles of African Americans in other sections of the country. The Research Committee gathered data and made recommendations as to the types of businesses needed in various communities and neighborhoods and reported the results of "directed spending" tactics.

Black women's activism through the Housewives' League remained securely attached to concern for home, family, and community uplift. By the time of the modern civil rights movement, therefore, black women in Detroit perceived their advancement as being grounded upon the tripartite base of home, family, and community.

The league had an even more material impact however. During the Great Depression, historian Jacqueline Jones explains, the Housewives' Leagues "in Chicago, Baltimore, Washington, Detroit, Harlem, and Cleveland relied on boycotts" to secure "an estimated 75,000 new jobs for blacks."

Jones also notes that during the Depression these leagues "had an economic impact comparable to that of the CIO in its organizing efforts, and second only to government jobs as a new source of openings."

The league continued its work throughout the 1950s and into the 1960s. Ironically, however, just as the Black Power movement gathered momentum in the late 1960s, the Housewives' League of Detroit faded from view.

DARLENE CLARK HINE

Huggins, Ericka (1948–)

"I would like to see education given top priority for black and poor children, for all children." These were the words of Ericka Huggins, grass-roots activist, educator, and poet, after she won a seat in 1976 on the Alameda County Board of Education in Oakland, California. However, Huggins began her crusade to educate children long before 1976.

Ericka Huggins, born January 5, 1948, in Washington, D.C., was the oldest of three children. She began her undergraduate education at Cheyney State College in West Chester, Pennsylvania, with the intention of becoming a teacher of learning-impaired children and director of a school for them. In 1966, Huggins transferred to Lincoln University, in Oxford, Pennsylvania, where she worked toward a degree in special education. She completed her degree in 1979.

In the midst of her academic studies she became aware of the Oakland-based **Black Panther Party** (BPP) and, during her junior year in November 1967, left Lincoln University to actively involve herself in the struggle to improve conditions in black communities in America. Nevertheless, she did not lose sight of her dream to educate children, but rather began realizing her dream within the context of the BPP.

She married Jon Huggins in 1968, and they joined the Los Angeles chapter of the BPP in February 1968; in December 1968, she gave birth to a daughter, Mai. After her husband was murdered in January 1969, Huggins moved to his home in New Haven, Connecticut. She opened a BPP Liberation School for children where the children received meals in addition to an education. Huggins' BPP work was interrupted on May 22, 1969, however, when the New Haven police illegally arrested and incarcerated her. Huggins' case was dismissed May 25, 1971.

Ericka Huggins moved to Oakland, California, and resumed her grass-roots activism. Before her June 1972 election to the Berkeley Community Development Council Board of Directors, Huggins taught English and creative writing at the BPP-sponsored Oakland Community School, then called the Intercommunal Youth Institute. In 1973, she became editor of the *Black Panther Intercommunal News Service*.

From 1973 until 1981, she was director of the accredited Oakland Community School, the alternative school for Oakland youth established January 1971 by the BPP. As a consequence of the success of the model school, Huggins became a consultant for other alternative educational programs. In the midst of these activities, Huggins gave birth to a second child, a son, Rasa Mott, in August 1974. And in June 1976, Huggins became the first black person to serve on the Alameda County School Board. She was also a member of alternative school associations such as the Pacific Regional Association of Alternative Schools.

Between 1990 and 1992, Huggins taught part-time in the Women's Studies Department at San Francisco State University. And, until 1992, she also directed a program in underprivileged areas of San Francisco for individuals and families with HIV, through the Shanti Project. Similarly, during 1993, Huggins was the director of education for the AIDS project of Contra Costa.

Ericka Huggins continues to live in Oakland with her third child, also a son, Yadav Huyler, to whom Huggins gave birth July 1987. She also maintains her commitment to education and youth via consulting. Since 1994, she has been a trainer for the Mind Body Institute Education Initiative (based at Harvard University Medical School) to train educators in the south central Los Angeles, California, school district how to reduce their own and the students' daily stress levels and develop alternative healthy coping strategies. Huggins also performs similar consulting and training for other ages and organizations in the San Francisco Bay area.

ANGELA D. BROWN

Hurley, Ruby (c. 1913–1980)

In 1955, alone in Klan country, **National Association for the Advancement of Colored People** field representative Ruby Hurley went from plantation to plantation, asking questions about the death of Emmett Till. Her life was at risk, and she knew it; but she was just doing her job. That job began in 1939 when the Washington, D.C., native began organizing an NAACP youth council in her hometown. She was then about twenty-six years old. A few years later, in 1943, she became the national youth secretary of that organization. During the time she held that position, the number of youth councils and college chapters grew from 86 to 280.

In 1951, Hurley went into the Deep South. Racial tension and violence were intense as the white population struggled to maintain the most extreme state of oppression. When, in 1955, the Reverend George W. Lee encouraged thirty-one of his parishioners to register to vote and then to hold their ground against opposition, he was murdered. Hurley went to investigate. She saw Lee's body in the casket—reportedly the victim of a traffic accident—and wrote, "I saw his body in the casket—I will not be able to forget how the whole lower half of his face had been shot away. A man killed because he, as a minister, said that God's children had rights as God's children and as American citizens."

In the same year, young Emmett Till was lynched for supposedly whistling at a white woman. Hurley, along with Medgar Evers and Amzie Moore, found witnesses to the alleged crime in spite of the threat to themselves. Evers himself was murdered eight years later.

A few months after the Emmett Till investigation, Hurley stood next to Autherine Lucy as thousands of white racists tried to prevent that young woman from entering the University of Alabama. When Hurley went back to her home office in Birmingham, she was subjected to continual threats and harassment, from which she could expect no protection from the police department under the notorious commissioner "Bull" Conner. Eventually, she developed situational stress disorder, losing weight and suffering almost constant illness. She had to close the Birmingham office because of legal maneuvers against the organization.

In Atlanta, to which she moved, Hurley became involved in the struggles between the NAACP and the younger **Student Nonviolent Coordinating Committee** and Southern Christian Leadership Conference.

For the rest of her thirty-nine years in service to the NAACP, she found herself defending the older generation and trying to make the younger generation aware of civil rights activity before 1960. She retired from the NAACP on March 31, 1978. Hurley died in Atlanta on August 9, 1980, after an extended illness.

KATHLEEN THOMPSON

I

International Ladies Auxiliary, Brotherhood of Sleeping Car Porters

These black women trade unionists believed the American labor movement was not only for men but also for their wives and families. "Marching Together" (the title of the auxiliary's official anthem), the wives and female relatives of sleeping car porters, attendants, and maids helped the Brotherhood of Sleeping Car Porters (BSCP) American Federation of Labor become the first successful national black trade union. Membership figures varied, but in 1945, the auxiliary had more than 1,500 dues-paying members in the United States and Canada. Chicago, the largest local, claimed nearly 175 members, while smaller districts such as Portland, Norfolk, and St. Paul had core memberships of more than forty. Active between 1925 and 1957, the auxiliary also affiliated with the National Women's Trade Union League and American Federation of Women's Auxiliaries to Labor.

The Hesperus Club of Harlem became the first auxiliary in October 1925, with the encouragement of A. Philip Randolph, publisher of the *Messenger* and general organizer of the six-week-old BSCP. Other women's groups soon followed, along with Brotherhood locals in Philadelphia, Washington, D.C., Chicago, St. Louis, Omaha, Kansas City, Los Angeles, and elsewhere. For twelve years these auxiliaries, known formally as the Colored Women's Economic Councils, kept the faith during the "dark days" of the union's struggle for recognition.

Council activities varied with the Brotherhood's needs and differing locales. The new union always needed money. Often evicted, frequently without funds for heat and light, the struggle to keep the union going often fell to the councils. Using fundraising methods learned in church and other women's groups, they sponsored dances, bazaars, silver teas, chitterlings and chicken dinners, and apron and pajama sales to send Brotherhood officials on cross-country organizing tours. When Randolph and other organizers arrived in Washington, D.C., for example, Brotherhood women such as Rosina Corrothers-Tucker (1881–1987) housed and fed them. Lucy Bledsoe Gilmore, a porter's widow who sold insurance at the St. Louis Pullman yards and who was a popular speaker, had a knack for collecting large sums—even from Pullman Company spies—by passing the hat at mass meetings. In Los Angeles, Mrs. Tinie Upton, a Pullman maid fired for her labor activities, collected union dues and with her husband, a Pullman porter, preached the Brotherhood to the unconverted.

The Women's Economic Councils operated as local units until 1938, when President Randolph called women together in Chicago to found the International Ladies'

These two line drawings come from the sheet music of Rosina Corrothers-Tucker's "Marching Together." The chorus goes: "We are the Auxiliary, the ladies' Auxiliary of the B.S.C.P. Together we are marching proudly; Proudly marching as one pow'rful band; Singing our Union songs so loudly that they vibrate throughout the land. We are determined and won't turn away, But will steadfastly face the new day; And courage and unity shall lead us to victory."
(M. CHATEAUVERT)

Auxiliary Order to the Brotherhood of Sleeping Car Porters, "the first international labor organization of black women in the world" as Tucker wrote in her unpublished autobiography. Delegates from twenty-seven cities elected Halena Wilson as president, Rosina Corrothers-Tucker as secretary-treasurer, and recognized twelve other faithful wives with international offices. Brotherhood president Randolph became the international counselor to the auxiliary, maintaining his central advisory role in the women's organization.

Under the international structure, President Wilson, with Counselor Randolph's approval, developed a three-part program of organization, legislation, and cooperation designed to educate black women about the labor movement. The Ladies' Auxiliary believed labor solidarity meant family unity. The Brotherhood brought domestic security to porters' families through increased wages and better working conditions for husbands. The assumption was that women should take responsibility for the labor movement because women spent 85 percent of the family income; wives should spend their husbands' wages on union-label goods and services to guarantee organized labor's success. Members studied the consumers' cooperative movement; the Chicago and Denver auxiliaries founded cooperative buying clubs. One meeting each month focused on workers' education; each summer as many as a dozen members or their daughters received labor school scholarships to learn labor history, economics, union leadership, public speaking, and union homemaking.

Securing passage of federal and state legislation to advance labor and civil rights causes constituted the second part of the auxiliary's program. At each biennial convention, the Ladies' Auxiliary passed resolutions on poll taxes, lynching, lily-white primaries, the Fair Employment Practice Committee, desegregation of the armed forces, the Taft-Hartley Act, extending the Social Security Act to domestic and agricultural workers, and other current issues. As trade unionists, they voted against the Equal Rights Amendment and in favor of eight-hour-day labor laws for women. Through the auxiliary's page of the *Black Worker* the legislative committee kept members informed of recent congressional actions. President Wilson, a member of the executive board of the Chicago Women's Trade Union League, lobbied for legislation regularly in the state capital. Addie Booth of Seattle worked tirelessly for passage of a Washington State Fair Employment Practice Committee bill.

Armed with new consciousness, many porters' wives joined in labor and civil rights struggles. In Washington, D.C., they helped organize commercial laundry workers; in St. Louis and Oakland, they picketed discriminatory public utilities and defense plants; and in Little Rock, Arkansas, they often drove the black students who desegregated Central High School.

Auxiliary membership was open to wives and women relatives of any Brotherhood member, without regard to race, creed, or color. In Los Angeles, Mrs. T. B. Soares, wife of the local BSCP secretary-treasurer, and other Mexican-American and Filipino women joined; in Canada, several white women participated in the auxiliary. Pullman maids and other female members of the Brotherhood received complimentary auxiliary membership; Ada V. Dillon, a former Pullman maid on the Twentieth Century Limited, became president of the New York Ladies' Auxiliary in 1946. Husband-wife teams formed the leadership in several local auxiliaries and brotherhoods, but most union officials' spouses were rank-and-file members.

Before the Brotherhood gained recognition in 1937, porters earned less than $75 per month. Their wives often worked as domestics, laundresses, and seamstresses; Nora Fant, Auxiliary Executive Board member from Jersey City, New Jersey, also belonged to Local No. 25 of the International Ladies' Garment Workers Union. During World War II, many did defense work—jobs opened up as a result of Randolph's successful pressure on President Franklin D. Roosevelt to issue Executive Order 8802, banning race (but not sex) discrimination in defense industries. By 1949, porters' annual wages were in the top quarter of median black family incomes. The majority of auxiliary members were housewives, some held secretarial and factory operative jobs, and a very few held professional jobs or owned small businesses.

The Ladies' Auxiliary Constitution declared subordination to the Brotherhood, but men and women contested women's proper role in the union. Many men objected when Randolph announced he would encourage women to join the union's fight, believing that women's participation would complicate matters. In some locals, Brotherhood men appear to have deliberately sabotaged the women's efforts; in other locals, a few in the Ladies' Auxiliary insisted they had a right to attend the men's union meetings and to vote. Yet when the Chicago auxiliary debated the Brotherhood in 1951 on "Who Makes a Better Union Member, Man or Woman?" the women won by a majority vote.

M. MELINDA CHATEAUVERT

J

Johnson, Kathryn (1878–1955)

Lecturer, author, fieldworker for the **National Association for the Advancement of Colored People** (NAACP), and public school teacher, Kathryn Magnolia Johnson was born December 15, 1878, in the Drake County Colored Settlement near Greenville, Ohio. She attended public schools in New Paris, Ohio, and went on to study at Wilberforce University during 1897–98 and 1901–2. She studied at the University of North Dakota during the summer of 1908. Johnson began teaching in 1898, and worked in the Ohio and Indiana public school systems until 1901. She taught at the State Normal School in Elizabeth City, North Carolina, 1904–5, and then accepted a position as Dean of Women at Shorter College in Little Rock, Arkansas, 1906–7. From 1907 until 1910, Johnson instructed high school students who were attending summer school.

In 1910, Johnson, having moved to Kansas City, Kansas, shifted her career to "race work." Mary White Ovington, one of the white founders of the NAACP, credits Johnson as the first fieldworker of the NAACP. Johnson earned her living by making small commissions on branch memberships and *Crisis* (the official publication of the NAACP) subscriptions. Beginning in 1913, Johnson traveled extensively throughout the South and West, establishing branches, instigating educational campaigns to raise the consciousness of Southern blacks, and drumming up support for the national headquarters of the NAACP in New York City. In February of 1915, Johnson became a "reimbursed" field agent—she earned a small salary in addition to her commissions.

In January 1916, the NAACP publicly commended Johnson for her fruitful organization of all-black branches. Six months later, however, the NAACP dismissed her. Although no definitive explanation of this decision exists, some historians believe that Johnson's forceful personality, blunt conversational style, and emphatic beliefs that the NAACP leadership should be all-black hastened, if not caused, her dismissal.

Johnson and Addie Hunton were two of three black women who worked for the YMCA in France during World War I to guard the rights of the black American soldiers abroad. Hunton and Johnson co-authored *Two Colored Women with the American Expeditionary Forces* (1922) that detailed their observations and experiences.

After World War I, Johnson undertook a nationwide campaign to disseminate black literature. She traveled as a sales representative for Associated Publishers and the Association for the Study of Negro Life and History in Washington, D.C. She championed what she called her "two-foot shelf of Negro literature," which consisted of fifteen books published by the association.

Kathryn M. Johnson (along with Addie Hunton and Helen Curtis) worked in France for the YWCA during World War I, guarding the rights of black American soldiers in Europe. (NATIONAL ARCHIVES)

Johnson continued to teach, lecture, and agitate for social justice throughout her life. She was a member of the Independent Order of St. Luke, the African Methodist Episcopal Church, and the Republican Party.

THEA ARNOLD

Jones, Claudia (1915-1965)

Claudia Jones was among a tiny cadre of black women to rise within the ranks of the Communist Party of the United States. Born in Port of Spain, British West Indies (Trinidad), Jones was only nine years old when her family migrated to Harlem in 1924. As a teenager she earned a reputation as a promising journalist, but her education was cut short by the Depression—she was forced to drop out of school in order to work. Like many working-class Harlem residents, she was attracted to the Communist Party (C.P.) through the International Labor Defense's campaign to free the Scottsboro Nine, and at eighteen she joined the Young Communist League (YCL). Jones rose quickly within the ranks of the Harlem C.P., becoming editor of the YCL *Weekly Review* and the *Spotlight* and assuming the posts of chairperson of the national council of the YCL, YCL education officer for New York State, and eventually national director of the YCL.

As one of the preeminent young black Communists in Harlem during the popular front, Jones actively supported the National Negro Congress (NNC) from its inception, serving as a leader of the NNC youth council in Harlem. Although she had been associated with issues pertaining to African-American rights and was among the first to criticize Earl Browder's decision to abandon self-determination in the black belt, during World War II Jones developed a reputation as a relentless critic of male chauvinism and a leading party spokesperson for women's rights. After the war she was appointed to the women's commission, briefly serving as its secretary.

Following a series of arrests and attempted deportations beginning in 1948, she was eventually indicted in 1951 for violating the Smith Act and imprisoned in Alderson Federal Reformatory for Women. Although her case did not attract as much attention as **Angela Davis'** did two decades later, Jones became a symbol for a generation of radical black women who came of age on the eve of the civil rights upsurges of the 1960s, many of whom marched and petitioned on her behalf. Her incarceration is one of the clearest examples in history of an African-American woman serving time as a political prisoner in the United States.

Despite her deteriorating health, Jones was not released from prison until she had served her complete one-year sentence. In December 1955, she was deported to London, where she continued to work for radical black causes, including the Caribbean Labour Congress, the West-Indian Workers and Students Association, and the Communist Party. She served as editor of the left-wing *West Indian Gazette* during the late 1950s and in 1962 was guest editor of *Soviet Women*. Jones' life came to an end on Christmas Day, 1965; her death was caused in part by tuberculosis contracted as a teenager but aggravated by prison conditions in the United States.

ROBIN D. G. KELLEY

Jones, Rhodessa (1948–)

"I believe that my work is about changing people's realities," says Rhodessa Jones. "Art can be a parachute to save all our lives." Certainly that can be said of Rhodessa Jones and all those who are touched by her work and her art.

Born on December 9, 1948, in Bunnell, Florida, Jones is the daughter of Augustas and Estella Luci Eve Jones. She has three sisters and eight brothers. As a child, her family traveled the Eastern seaboard from Florida to New Jersey as migrant laborers.

In 1958, however, her parents decided that a more settled life was important for the family, and the Joneses moved to a truck farm in upstate New York.

At the age of seventeen, Rhodessa Jones gave birth to a daughter and at eighteen she graduated from Wayland Central High School. She attended the University of Rochester and San Francisco Community College. Though she never received a college degree, she has taught at colleges and universities around the country, including Smith and Yale.

The majority of the family migrated to the San Francisco area in the early 1970s, where they formed their own theater company, the Jones Company. Recalling her childhood, Jones has said that it might be the early years as migrants which led so many members of the family to the "gypsy life" of the arts. Brother Azel wrote plays for the Jones Company and another brother, Bill T., has become a world-renowned dancer and choreographer.

This tradition of the family working together has continued to this day. Rhodessa, Bill, and Rhodessa's longtime partner, Idris Ackamoor, collaborated on the production *Perfect Courage,* and Rhodessa performed in Bill's dance/opera *The Mother of Three Sons. Perfect Courage* won an Isadora Duncan Dance Award in 1991.

After the Jones Company closed, Jones worked with the Tumbleweed Dance Collective, and, in 1979, she created the performance monologue *The Legend of Lili Overstreet* with Ackamoor. In 1983, they became co-artistic directors of Cultural Odyssey, an interdisciplinary performance company where they have created such pieces as *Raining Down Stars* and *I Think It's Gonna Work Out Fine.*

In 1990, Jones created the one-woman show *Big Butt Girls, Hard-Headed Women* based on her experiences teaching aerobics to women in the San Francisco County Jail. She was inspired to create the show because in jail she "had entered another world, populated by wild, wounded, crazed, cracked, carefree, dangerous, devious, destructive, but colorful women . . . women who had met the devil and found him to be a very dull dude," she told the *Washington Afro-American* in 1994. "[The performance uses] theater, movement, and song to anchor the words born out of the silence that is so intrinsic to waiting . . . women waiting for bail, for mail, for the latest word concerning her child, money from her man, the next visit from her sister, her mother, and the word from her lawyer." In 1993, she won a "Bessie" (New York Dance and Performance Award) for the production.

Jail officials saw a performance of the show and asked Ms. Jones to create a workshop for women inmates. The Medea Project: Theater for Incarcerated Women was born. To date the Medea Project has developed three theater pieces, *A Taste of Somewhere Else: A Place at the Table* in 1994; *Food Taboos in the Land of the Dead* in 1993; and *Reality is Just Outside the Window* in 1992. *Reality is Just Outside the Window* won an Isadora Duncan Dance Award for Special Performance in 1993.

Her work in the prison system has led Jones to develop another solo piece, *The Blue Stories: Black Erotica About Letting Go,* which premiered at Sushi, Inc. in San Diego. Most recently, she led a two-month residency for Diverseworks in Houston, Texas, working with girls in a youth detention facility. The residency culminated in a public performance.

Jones won the 1994 "Fabulous Feminists Award" from the San Francisco National Organization of Women and the "Woman of the Year" Award from the Northern California *Women's Magazine.* She has performed and given talks all over the world and has been a California Artist-In-Residence and an Artist-In-Residence at New College of California, where she taught a graduate level performance seminar entitled "Creative Survival."

Rhodessa Jones' personal creativity has helped her survive. Now she is helping women all over the country learn that their own creativity can help them survive. As she has said, "If it hadn't been for theater, I would've been a memory or a bitch with a bad attitude."

HILARY MAC AUSTIN

K

Kennedy, Flo (1916–)

Florynce Rae Kennedy was born on February 11, 1916, in Kansas City, Missouri, the daughter of Wiley and Zella Kennedy. Her father was a Pullman porter who later owned a taxi business. Her mother worked outside the home only during the Great Depression. Her parents were fiercely proud and protective of their children. No one ever hit the Kennedy children, not their parents and not their teachers. They grew up feeling that they were precious and important and that authority and respect were earned, not granted. These teachings have stood her in good stead as she has demanded respect and gained authority through her civil rights, feminist, and gay rights activism.

Kennedy attended public schools in Missouri and in California during the two or three years her family lived in each place. After graduating at the top of her class from Lincoln High School in Kansas City, she worked at a variety of jobs, owned a little hat shop, sang on the radio, and generally had a good time. In 1942, after her mother's death, she moved to New York City. Two years later, she began taking prelaw courses at Columbia University. From there she went to Columbia Law School, turning a rejection into an acceptance by implying to the dean that a lawsuit based on racism was a possibility.

When she graduated in 1951, Kennedy worked first as a clerk in a law firm and then opened her own office. But progress was not easy—one Christmas she worked at Bloomingdale's to pay the rent on the office—and by the end of the decade the end of her time as a practicing lawyer was fast approaching. "Not only was I not earning a decent living," she wrote in her autobiography, "there began to be a serious question in my mind whether practicing law could ever be an effective means of changing society or even of simple resistance to oppression."

In the early 1960s, Kennedy began to get politically involved. In 1966, she created the Media Workshop, the purpose of which was to fight discrimination in and through the media. From the very beginning, Kennedy had the knack of knowing what would get people's attention, and she was not afraid to do whatever was needed. "When you want to get to the suites," she said repeatedly, "start in the streets."

In the suites, on the streets, in the courts, and wherever else she went, Kennedy soon learned that it does not pay to be polite. She developed a reputation for being rude, outrageous, foul-mouthed, and effective. "In 1967 I was up in Montreal at an antiwar convention," she explained in her autobiography, "and I got very mad because they wouldn't let Bobby Seale speak. He was more radical than the rest of the people there, and wanted to talk about racism, instead of limiting the discussion to the war. When they tried to stop him, I went berserk. I took the platform and started yelling and hollering. As a result, I was invited out to Washington to speak, for a fee of $250 plus expenses, and that was the beginning of my speaking career."

That career has continued to parallel Kennedy's political involvement. She has spoken, and acted, for black civil rights, feminism, and gay rights. She has been an advocate for prostitutes, ethnic minorities, and the poor. During the 1970s, she was a frequent speaking partner with Gloria Steinem. She formed the Feminist Party to support **Shirley Chisholm** as a presidential candidate. She also coauthored one of the first books on abortion, *Abortion Rap* (1976).

KATHLEEN THOMPSON

King, Coretta Scott (1927–)

The founding president of the Martin Luther King, Jr., Center for Nonviolent Social Change in Atlanta, Georgia, Coretta Scott King emerged as an African-American leader of national stature after the death in 1968 of her husband, Martin Luther King, Jr.

Born on April 27, 1927, in Marion, Alabama, Coretta Scott spent her childhood on a farm owned by her parents, Obie Leonard Scott and Bernice McMurry Scott. By the early 1940s, her father's truck-farming business had become increasingly successful, prompting harassment from white neighbors. The family suspected that resentful whites may have been responsible for a 1942 fire that destroyed the Scott family's home. Hoping for better opportunities for their offspring, Obie and Bernice Scott encouraged their three children to excel in school. Coretta Scott graduated

from Lincoln High School, a private black institution with an integrated faculty, and then followed her older sister, Edyth, to Antioch College in Ohio, where she received a B.A. in music and elementary education. An accomplished musician and singer, Scott made her concert debut in 1948 in Springfield, Ohio, performing as a soloist with the Second Baptist Church.

Enrolling in 1951 at Boston's New England Conservatory of Music with a grant from the Jessie Smith Noyes Foundation, Scott developed her singing talent and eventually earned a Mus.B. in voice. While there, she also began dating Martin Luther King, Jr., a doctoral candidate at Boston University's School of Theology. Despite the initial objections of King's parents, who wanted him to marry a woman from his hometown of Atlanta, the two were married at the Scott family home near Marion on June 18, 1953.

During the period of her husband's public career, Coretta King usually remained out of the spotlight, raising the couple's four children: Yolanda Denise (born November 17, 1955), Martin Luther III (October 23, 1957), Dexter Scott (January 30, 1961), and Bernice Albertine (March 28, 1963). While her primary focus was on raising children, in 1962, she served as a voice instructor in the music department of Morris Brown College in Atlanta, Georgia.

Coretta King also worked closely with her husband and was present at many of the major civil rights events of the 1950s and 1960s. In 1957, she accompanied her husband on a trip to Europe and to Ghana to mark that country's independence. In 1959, the Kings traveled to India, where Coretta King sang spirituals at events where her husband spoke. In 1960, after the family moved from Montgomery to Atlanta, she helped gain her husband's release from a Georgia prison by appealing to presidential candidate John F. Kennedy for his assistance. Kennedy's willingness to intervene to help the jailed civil rights leader contributed to the crucial support he received from African-American voters in the 1960 election. In 1962, Coretta King expressed her long-standing interest in disarmament efforts by serving as a Women's Strike for Peace delegate to the seventeen-nation Disarmament Conference held in Geneva, Switzerland. She also attended the 1964 ceremony in Oslo, Norway, awarding Dr. King the Nobel Peace Prize. In the mid-1960s, Coretta King's involvement in the civil rights movement increased as she participated in "freedom concerts," which consisted of poetry recitation, singing, and lectures demonstrating the history of the civil rights movement. The proceeds from the concerts were donated to the Southern Christian Leadership Conference. In February 1965, while Martin Luther King was jailed during voting rights protests in Alabama, she met with black nationalist leader Malcolm X shortly before his assassination. Prior to 1968, Coretta King also maintained speaking commitments that her husband could not fill.

After the assassination of Martin Luther King, Jr., in Memphis on April 4, 1968, Coretta King devoted her life to actively propagating her husband's philosophy of nonviolence. Just a few days after the assassination she led a march on behalf of sanitation workers in Memphis, substituting for her husband, and, later in the month, she kept his speaking engagement at an anti-Vietnam war rally in New York. In May she also helped launch the March on Washington of the Poor People's Campaign, and thereafter participated in numerous antipoverty efforts. In addition, during 1969, she published her autobiography, *My Life with Martin Luther King, Jr.*

In 1969, Coretta King began mobilizing support for the Martin Luther King, Jr., Center for Nonviolent Social Change. Her plans included an exhibition hall, a restoration of the King childhood home, an Institute for Afro-American Studies, a library containing King's papers, and a museum. As founding president of the center, she guided the construction of its permanent

Always a strong force in the civil rights movement, after her husband's death Coretta Scott King moved into the spotlight to help fulfill his dreams. (SCHOMBURG CENTER)

home, located on Auburn Avenue next to Ebenezer Baptist Church where Dr. King had served as copastor with his father. As of 1993, she retained her position as chief executive officer of the center.

By the 1980s, Coretta King had become one of the most visible and influential African-American leaders, often delivering speeches and writing nationally syndicated newspaper columns. In 1983, she led an effort that brought more than a half million demonstrators to Washington, D.C., to commemorate the twentieth anniversary of the 1963 march on Washington for jobs and freedom, where Martin Luther King had delivered his famous "I Have a Dream" speech.

Also during the 1980s, Coretta King reaffirmed her long-standing opposition to the apartheid system in South Africa. She participated in a series of sit-in protests in Washington that prompted nationwide demonstrations against South African racial policies. In 1986, she traveled to South Africa to investigate apartheid. Several black opposition leaders criticized her plans to meet with President P. W. Botha and with Chief Buthelezi, who was viewed by many as an accommodationist. Consequently, King canceled her meetings and, instead, met with African National Congress leader Winnie Mandela. After her return to the United States, she met with President Ronald Reagan to urge him to approve sanctions against South Africa.

Perhaps the most notable achievement of Coretta King's public life was her participation in the successful effort to establish a national holiday in honor of Martin Luther King, Jr. In 1984, she was elected chairperson of the Martin Luther King, Jr., Federal Holiday Commission, which was established by an act of Congress to formalize plans for the annual celebrations that began in 1986. Also notable are Coretta King's speeches at London's St. Paul's Cathedral in 1969 and at Harvard University's Class Day exercises. She was the first woman to speak at each of the events. King has also been involved in various women's organizations such as the National Organization for Women, the Women's International League for Peace and Freedom, and United Church Women.

CLAYBORNE CARSON/ANGELA D. BROWN

L

Lampkin, Daisy (c. 1884–1965)

When Daisy Elizabeth Adams Lampkin died at her Pittsburgh home on March 10, 1965, the whole nation took note. The Pittsburgh *Post-Gazette* carried an editorial stating: "Americans owe a debt to Mrs. Daisy Lampkin." The editors credited her with being "instrumental in advancing the cause of the **National Association for the Advancement of Colored People (NAACP),** and indirectly, the case which led to legally enforced desegregation of public schools." The *New York Times* characterized her as a "Negro leader," calling attention to her contributions to civil rights, to her thirty-six years as vice-president of the once-powerful *Pittsburgh Courier,* and to her work with the **National Council of Negro Women** (NCNW) and the **National Association of Colored Women** (NACW).

On August 9, 1983, the Pennsylvania Historical and Museum Commission dedicated a ten-foot-high, shining blue-and-gold official historical marker bearing the state insignia in front of her home at 2519 Webster Avenue, which was a mecca for national African-American activists for half a century. Lampkin was the first black woman to be so honored by the Commonwealth of Pennsylvania, which has erected more than 1,500 markers. Then Governor Dick Thornburgh (later U.S. attorney general) wrote in a statement issued for the ceremony, "Daisy Lampkin courageously sought full equality for blacks and women throughout the country. Today her work stands as an inspiration for countless citizens." Former Pennsylvania House Speaker K. Leroy Irvis recalled how Lampkin had guided young men like himself and Supreme Court Justice Thurgood Marshall in their public careers. Officials of city and county government, the Urban League, NCNW, **Delta Sigma Theta** sorority, **The Links,** and the Lucy Stone Civic League, as well as church and neighborhood groups, gave testimony of her numerous humanitarian achievements.

Daisy Elizabeth Adams was born in the District of Columbia in March 1884, according to the 1900 census for Reading, Berks County, Pennsylvania, which lists her as the stepdaughter of John Temple and his wife, Rosa. The record indicates that the couple had been married one year and that the sixteen-year-old girl was housekeeper for the adults who were employed as cooks. However, there have been several conflicting published reports, especially the data in *Who's Who in Colored America* (1950) stating that she was born in Reading, August 9, 1888, daughter of George and Rosa Anne (Proctor) Adams. She completed high school in Reading and is remembered as an active member of the Presbyterian Church. In 1909, Adams moved to Pittsburgh where she married William Lampkin, a native of Rome, Georgia, in 1912. That same year, the *Pittsburgh Courier* (December 20) ran an article commending

Best known for her work as national field secretary for the NAACP in the 1930s and 1940s, Daisy Lampkin was a tireless fundraiser and fighter for American civil rights organizations, as well as a longtime vice president of the Pittsburgh Courier. *She is shown here addressing the 1947 National Council of Negro Women convention.* (BETHUNE MUSEUM AND ARCHIVES)

her for promoting a successful woman's suffrage event. In 1913, Lampkin began her lifelong association with noted publisher and politician attorney Robert L. Vann. She won a cash award for selling the most new subscriptions to the *Courier* and traded it in for stock in the publishing company, continually augmenting her investment until she was named vice president of the corporation in 1929, a post she held for the rest of her life.

Lampkin was best known for her work as national field secretary for the NAACP, but she had established herself as a prominent national figure long before Walter White recruited her for the civil rights association. She had gained recognition for her leadership ability in Liberty Bond drives during World War I, when the black community of Allegheny County raised more than two million dollars. She started her political career as president of the Negro Women's Franchise League in 1915, affiliated early with the National Suffrage League, and held top positions in the women's division of the Republican Party. She was elected president of the National Negro Republican Convention in Atlantic City, New Jersey, in July 1924, when, according to the *New York Times*, the assembly passed a strong antilynching resolution. She was elected delegate-at-large to the Republican National Convention in Cleveland, Ohio, in 1928.

Before she joined the NAACP staff, Lampkin served as national organizer and chair of the executive board of the NACW. When James Weldon Johnson organized a group of African-American leaders to meet with President Calvin Coolidge at the White House in 1924 in an attempt to secure justice for the black soldiers accused in the 1917 Houston riot, he summoned Lampkin, the only woman among the twelve or more national leaders. Lampkin also was a delegate along with **Mary McLeod Bethune, Nannie Burroughs, Alice Dunbar-Nelson,** and Addie Dickerson, all noted clubwomen, when Sallie Stewart, NACW president, was elected a vice president of the National Council of Women of the United States, whose membership extended to the International Council of

Women. This November 1929 meeting marked the first formal recognition of African-American women as official participants in world affairs.

When the January 1930 edition of the *Crisis* announced the appointment of Lampkin as NAACP regional field secretary, the periodical noted, "The name of Daisy Lampkin will be known wherever colored women meet together. Her achievements have been so unusual that they have long been the subject of public knowledge and comment."

Significantly, Lampkin had been named vice president of the Pittsburgh Courier Publishing Company just a few months earlier and had been working closely with Walter White, then acting NAACP executive secretary, before she was hired by the board of directors.

She was able to use the connecting forces of the NAACP and the *Courier*—the two most effective civil rights institutions of the era—to assure success in numerous important campaigns. In fact, records show that Lampkin mediated numerous bitter fights among the men, which threatened the viability of a united African-American front in the battle against Jim Crow. Her devotion to the overarching cause of black progress earned Lampkin the respect of rivals and opponents throughout the community. Lampkin plunged into massive membership and fund-raising drives, using the NAACP's role in the defeat of U.S. Supreme Court nominee Judge John J. Parker of North Carolina as a rallying cry.

The NAACP announced that its staff and members would do everything possible to defeat senators who had voted for Judge Parker, whom they considered to be an archenemy of the black race, and in 1930,

Lampkin played a major role in the defeat of Senator Roscoe McCullough of Ohio. Even before she was hired, she had begun to reorganize the Ohio State NAACP Conference by working in twenty-three towns and cities, speaking two and three times a day, maximizing her superb oratorical skills. At the same time, Roy Wilkins, editor of the Kansas City *Call*, was out in front in the battle to bring down Senator Henry J. Allen of Kansas. His resounding victory in helping the NAACP make good its threat brought Wilkins into the NAACP fold as assistant secretary to White. Lampkin, Wilkins, and White formed a dynamic triumvirate whose relentless efforts laid the foundation for civil rights triumphs on battlefronts all over the nation.

Named national field secretary in 1935, Lampkin embarked on an astonishing fund-raising membership campaign schedule, often reporting more than forty meetings in one month. Almost as remarkable was her ability to garner nearly all of her expense money from the branches, thus keeping costs at the national office extremely low. Throughout her tenure as field secretary, Lampkin remained active with the NACW and NCNW, serving as a vice president of the former and on the board of directors and education foundation chair of the latter. She headed the drive to establish an NCNW headquarters in 1945 and turned over a check for $49,000 at the Washington, D.C., annual workshop. She also chaired the 1952 campaign to raise funds for Delta Sigma Theta's national home, sharing her triumph in a letter to her life-long friend, Nannie Burroughs.

Lampkin entered the Democratic Party camp along with Robert L. Vann and the *Courier* during the New Deal era of President Franklin Delano Roosevelt, skillfully skirting around NAACP nonpartisan directives to staff members. She asserted her right to speak for the women, telling White, "The public knows that I have many other interests in addition to the NAACP." However, in 1947 she used the NAACP nonpartisan stance to decline repeated efforts by Congressman William Dawson to recruit her for the committee to elect Harry Truman.

It is true that Lampkin's fund-raising ability was unmatched, but observers have grossly underestimated her worth to the civil rights movement by focusing only on this facet of her work. Due to extreme fatigue, she finally resigned her field position in 1947, despite fervent pleas from White, Wilkins, and Marshall that she hold on. To their great satisfaction she immediately accepted an assignment with the board of directors and continued to conduct membership drives in branches where leaders made it clear that they wanted no other person.

Lampkin began her job at $50 a week in 1930, and her salary never was higher than a meager $5,200 annually. During all those years she gave herself totally to what she always referred to as "the cause," the elevation of black people all over the world. Noted author C. L. R. James recognized her great influence when, in 1956, he wrote to her requesting that she make sure the Negrophobic pamphlet "Ordeal of the South" by Britain's Alistair Cooke was refuted. James described the articles as sneers and slanders, extremely harmful to international race relations. The NAACP's Henry Moon was joined by black journalists everywhere in voicing scathing rebuttals of Cooke's stories published by the *Manchester Guardian*.

Keeping her finger on the political pulse of the nation, Lampkin returned to the Republican Party in 1952 when the Democrats ran a segregationist, John J. Sparkman of Alabama, for vice president. Her switch was reported in the *New York Times* with a headline announcing, "Woman Newspaper Executive and Democrat Opposes Sparkman" (October 16).

Still campaigning for the NAACP in October 1964, Lampkin collapsed on the stage of a Camden, New Jersey, auditorium moments after delivering a stirring appeal. Lampkin was too feeble to attend the elaborate ceremony in New York's Waldorf-Astoria Hotel when the NCNW presented her its first Eleanor Roosevelt-Mary McLeod Bethune Award the following December 22. Lena Horne, who had formed a close friendship with Lampkin when the young singer lived in the same Pittsburgh neighborhood, accepted the tribute for her.

During the remaining few months of her life, Lampkin was cared for by her adopted family, Dr. and Mrs. Earl Childs, and their son, Earl Douglas Childs, who lived with her in the Daisy Lampkin apartment building, now a historic site.

EDNA CHAPPELL McKENZIE

Little Rock Nine

Few people know their names, but the nine black students who became known as the Little Rock Nine helped to bring widespread integration to public schools in the United States. In the fall of 1957, Americans who were impressed with their courage and curious about the confrontations

Three of the Little Rock Nine talk with National Guardsmen during the Little Rock Central High School crisis in 1957. From left to right they are Carlotta Walls, unidentified student, Gloria Ray, and Ernest Green. (BENITA RAMSEY)

they caused watched as these nine students braved repeated threats and other indignities from segregationists as they tried to attend classes at the all-white Little Rock Central High School. The determination of the Little Rock Nine in challenging Arkansas Governor Orval Faubus, who used armed troops to bar the nine students from entering the school, is legendary. Despite the obstacles they faced, the Little Rock Nine eventually entered the school and were able to attend classes, and as they did, their experiences continued to be documented and preserved as a testament to their characters.

In 1954, the U.S. Supreme Court ruled in *Brown* v. *Board of Education* that segregation in public schools was unconstitutional and that school systems should begin plans to desegregate. However, during the early years of his administration, President Dwight D. Eisenhower did not focus on education and, therefore, many states were slow to implement plans for or actively to pursue desegregation. Civil rights organizations like the **National Association for the Advancement of Colored People** (NAACP) continued to pressure state and federal officials about integration while implementing their own plans to facilitate the process. The Arkansas state president of the NAACP, **Daisy Bates** (who was elected in 1952), organized a youth council that included the first nine students to desegregate Little Rock Central High. Bates visited seventeen homes of black students selected by public school officials for their scholastic achievement and emotional stability to ask their parents whether they would allow their children to be assigned to Central High. The parents of nine of these students—Ernest Green, Elizabeth Eckford, Gloria Ray, Melba Patillo, Carlotta Walls, Terrance Roberts, Thelma Mothershed, Minnijean Brown, and Jefferson Thomas—agreed to enroll their children in Central High. The Little Rock Nine, as they became known, were to start school at Central High in September 1957.

Along with the worries of attending a new school, the Little Rock Nine also faced threats from Governor Faubus that he would take action to block integration of Arkansas schools and that he would use National Guard troops if necessary. On September 2, 1957, Faubus kept his promise and ordered units of the National Guard to bar the nine black students from entering Central High. Later that evening the school board issued a statement asking black students not to attempt to enroll at any of the white public schools. Faubus' action and others made by Arkansas officials (including an August 29 injunction against inte-

gration granted by Judge Murray Reed) were flagrant violations of the Supreme Court's decision, prompting a response from President Eisenhower. The Nine were now in the midst of a state/federal confrontation, with Faubus on one side claiming states rights and Eisenhower on the other side issuing a petition for "preliminary injunction against further interference with integration" and ordering Faubus to remove his troops.

Members of the black community in Little Rock also took action to counteract Faubus' actions. In response to Faubus' order to block the entrance with troops on September 2, Bates organized a group of ministers to escort the students from her house to Central the next day. She called the parents of all the students except Elizabeth Eckford to alert them of the change in plans. Too tired to drive to the Eckfords' (who had no phone), Bates retired for the evening. The next morning, Elizabeth went to Central High alone and was taunted and berated by hundreds of white students and citizens in front of cameras, reporters, and photographers from around the world.

National Guard troops were not the only hindrances to the Nine's entrance to Central High. On September 24, 1957, the day after Faubus withdrew the Guard in order to allow the students to enter Central, the Nine and their police escorts attempted unsuccessfully to enter the school. This time, they were forced to retreat by an angry mob consisting primarily of white students, their parents, and members of the local community. As the Nine approached the school's entrance, the mob became more violent and the situation more chaotic; both black and white newsmen were injured by mobsters trying to curtail the publicity the incident was receiving. Several white students protested by boycotting their classes. Virgil Blossom, the district's superintendent and the spearhead for the "Blossom Plan," which called for phased integration, expressed doubts that the Nine would attempt or even be able to attend classes the next day. Blossom underestimated the Nine's determination and persistence, and the next day (September 25), the Nine once again tried to enter the school. They succeeded with the assistance of National Guard troops, who had been federalized by President Eisenhower.

All but one of the Little Rock Nine stayed in school for the rest of the year, but they were continually harassed by groups of white students inside the school. Nevertheless, they had attempted to provide "a model of orderly transition for the thousands of other school districts across the South" who were "just beginning to face up to the reality of the mandate the United States Supreme Court had handed down." These "likeable, admirable young people," as they were called by Elizabeth Huckaby, a former teacher at Central High who taught the Nine, had changed the policy of a nation and triumphed over bigotry.

BENITA RAMSEY

Loving, Mildred (1942–)

Mildred Loving gained notoriety when the U.S. Supreme Court decided *Loving* v. *Virginia,* a case that declared antimiscegenation laws unconstitutional.

In October 1958, a Virginia grand jury indicted Mildred Loving and her white husband for violating the state's antimiscege-

nation laws. The Lovings pleaded guilty, and each received a one-year sentence. The trial judge suspended their sentences on the condition that the Lovings leave Virginia and not return to the state together for twenty-five years. The Lovings initially agreed to the conditions set by the trial judge and moved to the District of Columbia. However, they later became unhappy in Washington and moved back to Virginia, where they decided to fight to have the antimiscegenation statutes declared unconstitutional and have their convictions reversed. They were unsuccessful in the Virginia state court system, which upheld the constitutionality of the statutes. The Lovings appealed the Virginia court's decision to the U.S. Supreme Court, which, in a unanimous 1967 opinion, struck down the Virginia antimiscegenation laws and, by extension, similar laws that fifteen other states had in force at the time. Chief Justice Earl Warren wrote that the laws at issue were nothing more than "measures designed to maintain White Supremacy" and that restricting the freedom to marry along racial lines violated the equal protection clause of the Fourteenth Amendment. At the time of this decision, miscegenation was the last social institution still governed by de jure segregation laws. Loving's lawsuit put an end to such regulations.

Mildred Loving has led a quiet life since 1967. She and her husband had three children before he died in a car accident in 1975. In early 1992, her Central Point, Virginia, church awarded her a plaque to commemorate her struggle, and her minister compared her to **Rosa Parks.** Loving tends to downplay the role she played, suggesting that she really had no choice but to proceed as she did. Nonetheless, her efforts helped forge a world in which interracial relationships face one less barrier. Indeed, her daughter, Peggy Loving Fortune, married a man of mixed parentage.

PHILIP A. PRESBY

Luper, Clara (1923–)

In Oklahoma, the name Clara Luper is synonymous with civil rights sit-ins. As is true of many civil rights leaders of her generation, Luper is also closely associated with education and the black church. Perceived to be an agitator and vilified for leading the demonstrations on August 19, 1958, in Oklahoma City, which would continue off and on for more than ten years, Luper is now accorded the status of respected elder and is seen as a moderating voice in racial issues.

The daughter of Ezell and Isabell (Wilkerson) Shepard, she was born May 3, 1923, in rural Okfuskee County, Oklahoma. Clara Shepard grew up in the small community of Hoffman in Okmulgee County, Oklahoma. Her father was a laborer who did farmwork, drove buses, moved houses, chopped cotton on contract, and picked pecans, to name but a few of his jobs. Her mother took in laundry.

Luper went to a segregated school and wrote in her autobiography, *Behold the Walls* (1979), this account of those days: "The books . . . had been mainly discarded from the white elementary school. We were separate and we possessed through Education Calculated Manipulation an overabundance of *promises* for better books, equipment, and supplies that never came. We were Separate and Unequal."

In Oklahoma, Clara Luper's name is synonymous with civil rights sit-ins; she was jailed twenty-six times for her participation in nonviolent demonstrations to end segregation. Luper, left, received hugs and words of appreciation from her acquaintances and admirers after she spoke in April 1992 at a Watonga High School Heritage Club program commemorating the civil rights struggle in Oklahoma. (WATONGA REPUBLICAN)

She attended a segregated high school five miles away at Grayson. The microscope had no lenses, pages were missing from the handed-down history books, and the outdated encyclopedias and dictionaries were without some letters of the alphabet. After graduating with five other black seniors, she went on to Langston University, then a segregated institution in central Oklahoma. It also had inferior equipment, books, and supplies as compared to the white universities in the state. She earned her B.A. in mathematics with a minor in history in 1944. When she went to the University of Oklahoma, where she completed her master's degree in secondary education and history in 1951, Luper encountered separate restrooms and separate sections in the cafeteria. Classrooms had bars to segregate black and white students.

Luper's first marriage, to Bert Luper, an electrician, ended in divorce after thirteen years. In 1977, she married Charles P. (C. P.) Wilson, a truck driver. She has three children.

When she reviews her experiences, Luper tells about the twenty-six times she was jailed for her part in nonviolent demonstrations to end segregation. Her civil rights work began in earnest on August 19, 1958, when she and the local **National Association for the Advancement of Colored People** (NAACP) Youth Council carried out their first sit-in at the Katz Drug Store in Oklahoma City. When the group was refused service at the lunch counter and, in turn, refused to leave, police were called and the media came. Two days later, Katz announced that its thirty-eight outlets in Oklahoma, Missouri, Kansas, and Iowa would serve all people, regardless of race.

The sit-ins grew to involve hundreds of young black Americans and some white supporters. Participants would set out on foot from Calvary Baptist Church for various downtown establishments. Frequently, they would be jailed for trespassing, but they always kept coming back. Starting in August 1960, general boycotts were used as another tactic to force the end of segre-

gation. Luper helped spread the word and build support with her regular radio broadcast. Sit-in demonstrations continued off and on for almost six years until the Oklahoma City Council enacted a public accommodations ordinance on June 2, 1964, to resolve problems with hold-out establishments resisting integration.

Luper continued her efforts in other areas, working for a fair housing ordinance and establishing a Freedom Center for Youth Council activities—and rebuilding it after it was fire-bombed on September 10, 1968. At the insistence of the predominantly black sanitation workers, she led them in their strike in 1969 for better pay and working conditions. Though she had no lack of causes in Oklahoma, she joined the danger-filled civil rights march from Selma to Montgomery, Alabama, in 1965, among many other national activities. In 1972, she ran for the U.S. Senate from Oklahoma, but was not elected.

Throughout her many years of civil rights involvement, Luper taught in public schools and often drew criticism for her outside activities. For seventeen years she taught at Dunjee High School, a black school in Oklahoma City. She spent two years at Northwest Classen High School and then taught at John Marshall High School, both in Oklahoma City. In spring 1989, she was honored with a retirement dinner after forty-one years in education.

Clara Luper has received the NAACP Youth Council Advisor of the Year national award several times. Other honors include the Langston University Alumni Award, 1969; Zeta Phi Beta, Chi Zeta Chapter Woman of the Year, 1970; and Sigma Gamma Rho Service to Mankind Award, 1980.

In the thick of her sit-ins in June 1961, Luper wrote down her thoughts:

As I see it, blacks must become the active conscience of America, but conscience is a drowsy thing. It stirs, turns over, takes another nap and falls into a deep, dead sleep. "Leave me alone," conscience cries. "Let me sleep, let me sleep," conscience cries. "Let time take care of it—time, time is the answer. Maybe ten years or maybe another hundred years." Oh, no, America, your conscience, like old Pharaoh's of old, will not rest or sleep until we can eat here at John A. Brown's. We will arouse your conscience and will not let you rest until we can eat.

Clara Luper did not rest, and Oklahoma has been different for it ever since.

DARRELL RICE

M

Malone, Vivian (1942–)

She was the girl in front of the television cameras, walking behind a line of federal marshals and National Guard troops. It was 1963 at the University of Alabama. George Wallace, the diehard segregationist and governor of Alabama, blocked the doorway, refusing entrance to the all-white university. Soldiers marched up to him, Wallace stepped aside, and Vivian Malone walked in to register.

Malone was an undergraduate from Alabama Agricultural and Mechanical College in Huntsville when she decided to challenge the color barrier. The educational system in Alabama was divided along racial lines, with well-funded professional universities for whites and poorly funded technical and industrial schools for blacks. While desegregation had been mandated by federal courts nearly a decade earlier, Southern politicians continued to fight it tooth and nail. The confrontation at the University of Alabama was one of the most photogenic.

Desegregation had been an ugly business in the Deep South. In 1956, **Autherine Lucy [Foster]** had been the first black student at the University of Alabama, but rioting broke out, and she had to be spirited off campus, hidden on the floor of a squad car. She was ordered not to return by the university. Nine months before Malone registered, rioting had broken out at the University of Mississippi over desegregation. Malone was thinking about the Ole Miss riot as she walked behind the federal troops.

Malone was joined at registration by James Hood, another black undergraduate. He dropped out within a few months, citing illness and mental strain. Malone stayed on, for a while escorted to class by federal troops. Then the troops and the politicians went home, and Malone was left with the job of being the lone black student in a school that wasn't sure it wanted her.

Reactions from the white student body were mixed. Malone was prepared for the worst. She walked into a class only to have all of the rest of the students walk out. At one football game a bully dumped a cup of ice on her. But she also found a welcome among whites who agreed it was time for change. When Malone first went to her dorm, she found a group of white girls waiting for her in the lounge. They invited her to play bridge and watched television with her that evening. As Malone recalled, "Some girls even came by the room and said they were glad I could come there—that they thought they would profit by it personally." She learned to distinguish her true friends: "The lasting friends were those who, if I did something they didn't like, they'd tell me. The lasting friends were those I got in fusses with."

Malone graduated with a bachelor's degree in 1965, with better than a B average and a major in personnel management. Im-

Vivian Malone defied the governor of the state to enroll at the University of Alabama. In 1995, to commemorate the thirtieth anniversary of her graduation, the university endowed a scholarship in her name. The building where she confronted George Wallace now bears a plaque acknowledging her courage.

mediately she faced the job problems of being a woman. Having graduated from one of the best schools in Alabama, she went on interviews, only to be offered a job as a secretary. Instead she searched out better. Malone gained positions with the Justice Department and the Veterans Administration and later joined the Environmental Protection Agency as director of civil rights and urban affairs. In 1977, she became executive director of the Voter Education Project, based in Atlanta.

Married to Dr. Mack Jones, whom she met while he was enrolled at nearby Stillman College, Malone is now Vivian Malone Jones.

In 1995, to commemorate the thirtieth anniversary of her graduation, the University of Alabama endowed a scholarship in her name. She was honored outside Foster Auditorium, where George Wallace first tried to bar her entrance. The building now bears a plaque marking the 1963 confrontation.

ANDRA MEDEA

The Maryland Freedom Union (MFU) was born out of frustration by CORE staff in their failed attempts to assist black workers in attaining union rights and benefits. With encouragement from CORE field secretaries, some twenty employees of the Lincoln Nursing Home in Baltimore went on strike in February 1966 and became the nucleus for the new union. The MFU transcended the traditional limits of trade unions by organizing low-wage workplaces as an integral part of a movement to transform American society. (RAYA DUNAYEVSKAYA COLLECTION, WAYNE STATE UNIVERSITY)

Maryland Freedom Union

On February 9, 1966, some twenty black women, working as nurses' aides, housekeepers, and kitchen staff, walked off their jobs at Lincoln Nursing Home in Baltimore, Maryland. They called field secretaries from the Congress of Racial Equality (CORE) with whom they had met the previous week, and told them that Lincoln was "on strike," that the workers had named their union "Maryland Freedom Local No. 1," and that the CORE organizers had better come down to Lincoln Nursing Home immediately to show the workers how to "run a proper picket line."

The workers, who made as little as 25¢ an hour and worked up to seventy-two hours a week, became the nucleus of what they called a "new kind of union," the Maryland Freedom Union (MFU).

The concept of a "freedom union" of poverty-wage workers had been advanced by CORE staff frustrated with failed efforts to assist black workers in struggles for union rights and benefits. Convinced that the American Federation of Labor and Congress of Industrial Organizations (AFL-CIO) unions were not interested in organizing such workers, and exhilarated by the success of the **Student Nonviolent Coordi-**

nating Committee's (SNCC) 1965 Mississippi Freedom Labor Union project, CORE selected Baltimore as the site of its own freedom union experiment.

The Lincoln Nursing Home strikers were soon joined by black women workers at two other nursing homes. Meeting jointly, they elected Vivian Jones, a nurses' aide at Bolton Hill Nursing Home, as MFU president, and Ola Mae Johnson, an aide at Lincoln, as secretary. The union members, with no prior public speaking experience, spoke to church groups, student meetings, and outdoor rallies to explain the strike and appeal for funds.

Together with CORE members and supporters from local churches and schools, they picketed the suburban homes of nursing home owners and marched on city hall. By March 1966, they created a union study group on black and labor history, reading a history of black struggles, *American Civilization on Trial* (1963), and inviting its author, political philosopher Raya Dunayevskaya, to lecture at the MFU's Freedom House. Dunayevskaya's suggestion that the workers view themselves as "self-developing thinkers" made an impact.

After completing a covert study of retail stores along the mall shopping streets of the West and East Baltimore ghettos, the MFU opened an organizing drive among retail workers there. For the campaign, MFU President Vivian Jones designed a large button showing two black hands breaking a chain and the union slogan, "Breaking Free at Last." Thousands of the buttons, distributed in the black community, helped garner support for an MFU plan that any store they picketed was to be boycotted by black shoppers. The boycotts proved effective, and MFU strikers succeeded in winning union contracts at three of the largest retail chain stores in the ghettos by August 1966.

The campaigns aroused opposition from both merchants' associations and AFL-CIO unions. The unions accused the MFU of organizing in direct competition with them. Walter Reuther, then head of the AFL-CIO's Industrial Union Department, complained to Floyd McKissick, national director of CORE, about CORE becoming a union. McKissick, citing CORE's deep financial crisis, soon severed formal ties with the MFU.

Later MFU campaigns included food stores, hospitals, and a print shop, but its momentum slowed under the impact of tight finances and the ideological crises afflicting civil rights organizations in the late 1960s. The inner-city stores and nursing homes organized by the MFU closed in the early 1970s, victims of economic decline or neighborhood gentrification.

While it flourished, the MFU's membership, nearly all black and 90 percent women, and many of them recently arrived from the rural South, created a union quite different from the typical AFL-CIO affiliate. What drew so many of these workers to the MFU was not only the union's willingness to accept them as members—this organization called itself a *freedom* union and sought to organize low-wage workplaces as an integral part of a movement to transform the whole of American society. As a forerunner of both the black caucuses within established unions and black feminist critiques of civil rights organizations, the Maryland Freedom Union was a unique learning experience.

MICHAEL FLUG

McMillan, Enolia (1904–)

The first woman president of the **National Association for the Advancement of Colored People** (NAACP), Enolia Pettigen McMillan has had a long and distinguished career as an educator and administrator and is renowned for more than five decades of service to the cause of civil rights. Firmly believing in the need for increased educational and employment opportunities for black Americans, McMillan has worked through many different organizations to help bring an end to discrimination.

Enolia Pettigen was born on October 20, 1904, in Willow Grove, Pennsylvania, the daughter of Elizabeth (Fortune) Pettigen and John Pettigen, who had been born into slavery in Virginia. When Enolia was eight, her family moved to Baltimore, where they became active members of the Calvary Baptist Church. In 1922, after graduating from high school, and with much encouragement from her family and her high school principal, McMillan enrolled at **Howard University** in Washington, D.C., and graduated in 1926. Six years later she received her M.A. from Columbia University in New York City. In 1935, she married Betha D. McMillan, with whom she had one son, Betha D., Jr.

From 1926 to 1928, McMillan taught at Pomonkey High School. She was named principal of the school in 1928, a position she held until 1935. McMillan then taught junior high school students in Baltimore until 1956, when she was made vice principal of Clifton Park and Cherry Hill junior high schools, positions she held until 1969. In 1963, she also was made vice principal of Paul Laurence Dunbar Senior High School. Throughout her tenure as a teacher and administrator, McMillan worked hard to improve the status of black American schools. She was appointed as a lifelong principal by the Baltimore City School System in 1985.

McMillan's long service with the NAACP began in 1935 in the Baltimore chapter, and she became chapter president in 1969. McMillan's seventeen-year presidency was a busy and successful one as she strove to increase membership, especially of young people, and improve its fundraising potential. In 1985, McMillan became the first woman to be elected president of the national association. She was reelected to this unsalaried position each year until her retirement in December 1989. During her tenure as NAACP president, McMillan initiated moving the group's national headquarters to Baltimore, and she worked hard to raise funds for the building of its new headquarters, which opened in 1986.

In addition to her long-standing involvement with the NAACP, McMillan's community service includes being the only woman to be elected president of the Maryland State Colored Teachers Association, the first woman to chair the Morgan State College Trustee Board, and the first black person to serve as trustee to the executive committee of the Public School Teachers Association. She also has been a member of the Governor's Commission on the Structure and Governance of Education in Maryland and chairperson of the Joint Committee to Equalize Teachers Salaries in Maryland.

McMillan is the recipient of many awards and honors, including the NAACP Merit Medal in 1938 and the Distinguished Citizen Award from the Democratic Ladies

Guild in 1984. She was named one of the Top 100 Black Business and Professional Women of 1986. In 1984, McMillan received an honorary doctorate of humane letters from Sojourner-Douglass College and was inducted into the Douglass High School Hall of Fame in 1972. In honor of her dedication to education for black students, the Baltimore chapter of the NAACP created a scholarship fund in her name for students from low-income families.

Although her earliest ambition to become a doctor was never realized, Enolia Pettigen McMillan has dedicated much of her life to ensuring that the future ambitions of every young child, regardless of race or class, may be pursued to the fullest.

FENELLA MACFARLANE

Mississippi Freedom Democratic Party

Created in the spring of 1964, the Mississippi Freedom Democratic Party (MFDP) was a predominantly black independent political party set up alongside the state Mississippi Democratic Party at the height of the civil rights movement. At the time of the party's creation, black voters constituted 6.7 percent of the state's registered voters (the lowest figure for any state in the union), due largely to a variety of legal and extralegal voting restrictions ranging from literacy and poll tax requirements to economic intimidation and widespread indiscriminate violence. Thus, as the brainchild of many **Student Nonviolent Coordinating Committee** (SNCC) members and local activists throughout the state, the MFDP was formed in response to the

state's history of keeping black residents from registering as voters and participating in regular party activities such as precinct, district, and county meetings as well as primary and general elections. Contributing much to the MFDP's notable historical achievements were the activities of many well-known women civil rights leaders.

Arguably, the year of the MFDP's founding proved to be its most historically significant. With financial support from the Council of Federated Organizations, a coalition of various civil rights organizations set up to administer voter-registration drives throughout the Deep South, the grass-roots party ran a slate of candidates on a platform of statewide political inclusion and social justice. Black women candidates Victoria Gray and **Fannie Lou Hamer** were two of the four MFDP candidates running for office that spring of 1964, and black women constituted a sizable portion of the party's voter-registration workers during the campaign. Among the Freedom Party's local achievements that spring and early summer were the registration of more than 80,000 disenfranchised black voters in its Freedom Ballot campaign, a political demonstration that involved mock or protest elections, and voter registration signups with the MFDP.

In the late summer of 1964, the Freedom Party challenged the seating of the all-white Mississippi state delegation to the Democratic National Convention in Atlantic City, New Jersey. Among the MFDP's sixty-eight-member delegation and large, nationally based staff were such civil rights notables as **Ella Baker,** Fannie Lou Hamer, **Annie Devine,** and Victoria Gray. In its challenge, the MFDP argued that it best represented Mississippi's Democratic Party because it was open to all Mississippians of voting age, unlike the lily-white party that engaged in violence, intimidation, and other measures to keep black citizens from exercising their fundamental right. Thus, MFDP contenders argued that, even though the Freedom Party was not recog-

nized legally by its home state, only its delegates deserved seating and recognition because only they had faithfully adhered to the rules of the national party.

The highlight of the MFDP's summer challenge was the moving presentation of Hamer, who recounted one of the many instances of anti–civil rights violence, the

In 1964, the Mississippi Freedom Democratic Party challenged the seating of the all-white Mississippi state delegation at the Democratic National Convention in Atlantic City, New Jersey. The highlight of the summer challenge was Fannie Lou Hamer's moving account of a beating she and five other civil rights activists received in a Mississippi jail cell in 1963. Although the party wasn't seated, the Democrats did make some changes to ensure fairer representation of African Americans at future conventions. (SCHOMBURG CENTER)

horrible beating that she and five others received in a Winona, Mississippi, jail cell in 1963. By recounting the Winona incident in such vivid detail, Hamer tried to expose Mississippi's long and infamous history of political repression against black people and, by most accounts, was quite successful. Following her powerful presentation, hundreds of telegrams in support of the MFDP's challenge poured into the Freedom Party's temporary convention headquarters. In this regard, the MFDP attracted national attention and support for the civil rights movement.

Although the Democratic Party's credentials committee offered two at-large seats in response to the challenge, the Freedom Democrats rejected such an offer on the basis of its being a back-of-the-bus compromise that they could not accept and expect to return to their communities with their heads held high. Although the Freedom Democrats failed in their primary political crusade, they did influence the rules committee of the Democratic Party to make some changes by the 1968 and 1972 conventions. Beginning with the 1968 convention, the Democratic Party refused to seat any delegation that had been constituted through racially discriminatory means. Beginning with the 1972 convention, the party added to such a restriction a provision barring any delegation that failed to meet a gender quota for delegation membership.

After the 1964 challenge, the MFDP returned home and continued running candidates in local, county, and state elections. Before returning to full-time local organizing, however, the MFDP decided to issue yet another challenge in the national arena. In January 1965, Annie Devine, Victoria Gray, and Fannie Lou Hamer challenged the seating of the newly elected congressmen from their respective districts. Again, the charge was made that the three white men had won seats because black Mississippians had been effectively excluded from participating in the primary and general elections. Hamer, Devine, and Gray spent six months living in Washington, D.C., lobbying members of the U.S. House of Representatives to give fair consideration to their cause. Although this challenge also attracted a great deal of attention, it too ended in defeat, but not before the three women were given symbolic representation by being allowed seats on the floor of Congress during the debate, which made them the first black women in history to be given official recognition by the U.S. Congress. As with the previous challenge, however, Devine, Gray, and Hamer saw this as tokenism and dismissed its importance as they returned home to continue the struggle in their home districts.

During 1965–66, like many SNCC activists, many members of the MFDP returned to statewide civil rights activities with a more radical mind-set, particularly as it pertained to economic justice and international struggles against colonialism. In 1965, the Mississippi Freedom Labor Union (MFLU), a union of cotton and domestic workers, formed and received a great deal of organizational and moral support from the Freedom Party. This was particularly the case during the 1965 MFLU maid strike in Bolivar County, Mississippi, in which scores of women struck against several local hotels. By 1967, the MFDP added to its platform planks calling for a fair distribution of the nation's wealth and an end to U.S. involvement in the

Vietnam War. The MFDP also continued running candidates, many of whom were women, including local activist Emma Sanders, who participated in the landmark 1967 statewide elections where, among other historic achievements, twenty-two black Americans were elected to office in Mississippi, the most since Reconstruction.

By 1967–68, the MFDP was facing challenges from moderate black leaders and local white liberals within its own ranks. This eventually resulted in a faction of the party breaking off and forming the Loyal Democratic Party, a more moderate wing of the MFDP that had always desired a closer working relationship with the mainstream, national Democratic Party. Although momentarily left in disarray, the original MFDP rose again in true grassroots form not more than a year later when it resumed sponsoring candidates for election and participating in voter registration drives, labor activities, and poor peoples' cooperatives, all of which it continued to do through the mid-1970s.

CHANA KAI LEE

Moody, Anne E. (1940–)

Born on September 15, 1940, Anne Moody was the oldest child born to Fred and Elmira Moody of Wilkinson County, Mississippi. From the hardships of rural poverty, Moody would emerge as a vital civil rights activist and critically acclaimed writer.

As a child, Moody attended segregated schools and in 1964 received her bachelor of science degree from Tougaloo College. Upon graduating, Anne Moody was already a veteran of the struggle for civil rights; between 1961 and 1963 she served in the Congress of Racial Equality (CORE)

and afterward carried her activities north to Cornell University, where she served as civil rights project coordinator (1964–65). Moody's youth and her participation in the civil rights struggle are revealed in her autobiography *Coming of Age in Mississippi* (1968), an articulate and moving account of the often frustrating struggle of growing up black in the Deep South. She vividly recalls the succession of shacks in which her family lived, hunger, white prejudice, black apathy, and the birth of her racial consciousness.

Coming of Age in Mississippi, moreover, represents a confluence of the personal and historical and the reciprocal interaction between them. As part of a historical maelstrom, Moody's racial consciousness was raised by the lynching of Emmett Till. In her desire to combat race hatred, she became a vital force within the civil rights struggle. Unfortunately, Moody would later break with the movement; frustration with Northern whites and doubts about the direction of black liberation culminated in her departure.

In 1975, she published a book entitled *Mr. Death,* containing four short stories for children.

GINA BEAVERS

Moore, Audley (1898–)

In recalling the events of her life, "Queen Mother" Moore stated its theme: "There wasn't nothing to do but get into the struggle." A powerful street speaker and adept political organizer, Moore has been involved for almost a century in a host of crucial campaigns in support of Garveyism, the Harlem boycott and renters' rights movements, the Republican and Communist parties, the Scottsboro defense, Pan-Africanism, and the reparations movement.

Born in New Iberia, Louisiana, on July 27, 1898, Moore's experiences growing up in the South profoundly influenced her political vision. Her parents' lives had been shaped by white violence, and her own memories included lynchings, manhunts, and overt discrimination. Moore's father, St. Cyr Moore, born as a result of his mother's rape by a white man, ran a livery stable. Moore's mother, Ella Henry, was raised in a middle-class French Creole household after her father was lynched by whites and her mother driven from their property. Both parents died by the time Moore was in the fourth grade, ending her formal schooling. Moore trained in the Poro hairdressing system and at age fifteen became the primary supporter of herself and her two younger sisters, Eloise and Lorita.

Moore worked as a volunteer nurse during the 1918 influenza epidemic. She and Eloise lived in Alabama during World War I. They organized support services for black soldiers who were denied by the Red Cross. Moore joined the **Universal Negro Improvement Association** in New Orleans and embraced its tenets. She was attracted by Marcus Garvey's oratory and the beauty and self-fulfillment she found in his talk of the grandeur of ancient African civilization and pride in African culture and heritage. Moore often described an incident in New Orleans when she and other audience members defied white authorities by mounting benches and waving weapons while chanting for Garvey to speak. She remembered this as a victorious experience that contributed to the militancy of the grass-roots methods she used in later struggles.

Moore moved to Harlem in the 1920s. She organized domestic workers in the Bronx labor market and helped black tenants to defy evictions by white landlords. Arrested repeatedly for her activities, she used her jail sentences to organize fellow inmates. In the 1930s, she joined the International Labor Defense and the Communist Party, becoming one of the leading black Communist woman organizers in New York. An extraordinary and persuasive speaker, she agitated on such issues as the Scottsboro defense, the Italo-Ethiopian war, economic boycotts, black political representation, racial prejudice in film, and a myriad of other causes. She was a Communist Party candidate for the New York State Assembly in 1938 and for alderman in 1940, and she was campaign manager for Benjamin Davis' successful bid for the New York City Council in 1943.

Moore left the Communist Party in 1950. She and Eloise joined Mother Langley and Dara Collins in founding the Universal Association of Ethiopian Women, which worked on welfare rights, prisoners' rights, antilynching, and interracial rape issues. In the 1960s, she formed the Reparations Committee of Descendants of U.S. Slaves, Incorporated, demanding federal reparations to blacks as partial compensation for the gross exploitations of slavery and its aftermath.

In 1972, Moore traveled to Africa to attend Kwame Nkrumah's funeral. During the trip she was honored with the title of "Queen Mother" and spoke at the All-African Women's Conference in Dar es Salaam. Her tours of African farms and industries inspired her to found the Queen Mother Moore Research Institute and the Eloise Moore College of African Studies and Vocational and Industrial School in the Catskills (destroyed by fire in 1978).

Moore was a member of the **National Association of Colored Women** and a founding member of the **National Council of Negro Women.** Her view of the women's movement in the 1970s was negative, however, and she has described feminism as an "alien ideology emanating from the white woman," whereas the black woman's fight is "alongside of her man."

Moore's long career of political activism merged black nationalism, Pan-Africanism, and the left. Her simultaneous support of black women's organizations and alienation from the white feminist agenda speaks to the racial bifurcation of the women's movement.

BARBARA BAIR

N

Nash, Diane (1938–)

Civil rights activist Diane Nash was born on May 15, 1938, in Chicago and grew up on the city's South Side with her mother and stepfather, Dorothy and John Baker. Nash was raised Roman Catholic, attended parochial elementary school, and then Hyde Park High School. She attended **Howard University** for a year and then transferred to Fisk University in Nashville, Tennessee.

Moving to Nashville was a pivotal experience for Nash, who had never before experienced the horrors of Southern segregation. Feeling stifled, she began looking for a group that was fighting segregation and found James Lawson's workshops on nonviolence. At first, she was unconvinced by nonviolence as an approach to political and social change, but as the Nashville movement began to use it, Nash saw its power. Her own commitments had their roots and basis in Christianity, and Nash became an activist who saw nonviolence not only as a tactic but also as a lifestyle. She was elected chairperson of the Student Central Committee in Nashville, and they began organizing sit-ins at Woolworth, Walgreen, Kress, and two department stores. As a leader in the Nashville movement, Nash attended the first meeting of the **Student Nonviolent Coordinating Committee** (SNCC) in Raleigh, North Carolina, April 16–18, 1960, and was elected to the committee. Nash was not elected chair of the (temporary) committee only because she came late to the meeting, and Marion Barry, another Nashville student, had already been elected.

In February 1961, Nash was one of eleven students to be jailed in Rock Hill, South Carolina, the first group to go to jail, refusing to pay bail. The students spent one month in jail, a time of personal growth for the group. Nash, along with the Nashville group, also mobilized to keep the Freedom Rides going after the Congress of Racial Equality (CORE) pulled out. Nash was elected coordinator for the SNCC rides, which meant she had to stay out of jail and coordinate student efforts and act as liaison with the press and the U.S. Justice Department. In August 1961, SNCC, after a heated discussion, decided to develop two agendas: Diane Nash was to head direct action, and Charles Jones was to coordinate voter registration.

Also in 1961, Diane Nash married James Bevel, another civil rights activist, and they moved to Jackson, Mississippi, where they continued to organize. Expecting her first baby and facing a two-and-a-half-year jail sentence, Nash decided to turn herself in at the end of April 1962 and have her baby in jail in order to keep with the movement's idea of "jail-no-bail" and to dramatize the situation of black Americans in the South. The judge chose not to sentence her on that longer charge, but instead convicted her for refusing to move to the back of the

One of the original members of the Student Nonviolent Coordinating Committee, Diane Nash was in the first group of students to go to jail and refuse bail. Later, Nash joined the staff of the Southern Christian Leadership Conference. Her civil rights work eventually led her to the peace movement and later to the women's movement. (STATE HISTORICAL SOCIETY OF WISCONSIN)

courtroom. Her daughter, Sherrilynn, was born on August 5, 1962, in Albany, Georgia, where Bevel was working for the Southern Christian Leadership Conference (SCLC). Nash joined the staff of SCLC in 1962–63 and became a field staff organizer.

She and Bevel made an effective organizing team; their ideas were instrumental in initiating the 1963 March on Washington and the 1964–65 Selma campaign. For their work, Nash and Bevel together received SCLC's highest award in 1965, the Rosa Parks Award. Their second child, Douglass, was born on May 15, 1964.

Diane Nash's civil rights work led her to the peace movement, and at the end of 1966 she traveled with a group of women from the United States to North Vietnam. Her trip to Vietnam coincided with the rising feminist movement, and the combination profoundly affected Nash's growing feminism. She continued her political work through the 1970s, 1980s, and into the 1990s in Chicago, doing tenant organizing, welfare support, and housing advocacy. She has one granddaughter and one grandson.

JEANNE THEOHARIS

National Association for the Advancement of Colored People

Women played a large part in the early development of the National Association for the Advancement of Colored People (NAACP), founded in 1909. Among the more well-known black women activists were **Ida B. Wells-Barnett** of Chicago, Illinois, **Mary Church Terrell** and **Nannie Helen Burroughs** of Washington, D.C., and **Mary McLeod Bethune** of Daytona Beach, Florida. These women used existing social and community organizations established by black women to generate and sustain the NAACP's membership.

Until recently, few scholars have focused on the importance of women's roles in the

This dramatic photograph shows Myrlie Evers-Williams being sworn in as chairperson of the board of the NAACP in 1995. The men surrounding her are all federal judges. (DAVID SCULL/ NYT PICTURES)

association. Usually historical accounts of the NAACP focus on its male membership—most noticeably on the prominent scholar W. E. B. DuBois. However, there is a growing body of work documenting the crucial early contributions of women to this organization.

In 1905, a select group of concerned, prominent black and white American citizens were prompted by W. E. B. DuBois to begin a civil rights organization known as the Niagara Movement. Although the Niagara Movement had a predominantly black male membership, it also hosted a women's auxiliary whose members in- cluded **Maria Baldwin,** Carrie Clifford, and Mary White Ovington. Ovington was possibly the only participating white woman. Members of the Niagara Movement pushed for social equality and voting rights for black Americans. Within about four years of its founding, the organization faced bankruptcy and was forced to dissolve. Its members, however, remained dedicated to the cause of civil rights for black Americans, and they became some of the earliest members of the NAACP.

The NAACP began in response to a horrible race riot in Springfield, Illinois, in 1908. Socialist Southern journalist William

English Walling wrote an article about the riot in the *Independent* newspaper and challenged his readers to come forth and join forces to combat the rampant racism. Oswald Garrison Villard, the liberal activist grandson of famed abolitionist William Lloyd Garrison, was among the white supporters who responded to Walling's article. Villard was editor of the *New York Evening Post*. He issued what is referred to as "the call," inviting those who believed in justice for all in a true democracy to attend a national meeting. Sixty men and women signed the call. One-third were women, but only two were black women (Mary Church Terrell and Ida B. Wells-Barnett). Among those who responded to the call were several black activists and educators such as W. E. B. DuBois and Francis Grimké. Many white philanthropists and social activists, including Mary White Ovington, Jane Addams, William Walling, and William Dean Howells, signed the document as well. Although the majority of executive officeholders were white, this generally did not diminish the black members' commitment to the association.

One of the chief concerns of the newly founded organization was the issue of lynching. The early years of the twentieth century were plagued with reported and unreported lynchings of blacks. These heinous crimes not only were inflicted on usually innocent black men, but also on black women and children. Between 1909 and 1917, antilynching crusader Ida B. Wells-Barnett became increasingly disgusted with the NAACP's approach to this problem. Wells-Barnett thought the association was far too lenient concerning lynching. Moreover, Wells-Barnett disliked the dominance

of white leadership in the NAACP, in part because she thought they were insensitive to the impact of lynching on black Americans.

Kathryn Johnson, a black woman, served as the first field secretary for the NAACP from 1910 to 1916. Johnson's work was strictly voluntary until 1914.

Women played important roles in the NAACP, at all levels. Modjeska Simkins (right) was elected secretary of the South Carolina state organization in 1939, when James M. Hinton (left) was elected president. Under their leadership, the state organization launched several court cases to establish equality for black Americans, including Briggs v. Elliot, *which ultimately was combined with* Brown v. Board of Education. *Thurgood Marshall (center) was the NAACP's attorney for this case.* (BARBARA WOODS)

After a few disagreements with the national office, Kathryn Johnson resigned her position. It was not until 1920 that a black man, James Weldon Johnson, held a key position in the NAACP as national field secretary.

Several black women successfully pooled their talents to work with established women's club networks and the NAACP. For example, **Mary Talbert,** a key clubwoman from Buffalo, New York, served as president of the Empire State Federation of Colored Women and worked for a branch organization of the NAACP at the same time. Talbert was well trained in fundraising techniques and membership recruitment. Her skills contributed to the record growth in the number of branch organizations between 1909 and 1920.

During the early years of the NAACP, many black women served in various capacities to boost its membership, raise funds, increase its social and community service, and implement the association's commitment to woman's suffrage. Educators Mary McLeod Bethune and Nannie Helen Burroughs remained on the board of advisors for at least three decades. In 1920, Catherine Lealtad became the assistant director of branch organizations. Lealtad had previous experience working with the **Young Women's Christian Association** (YWCA). Once again, a black woman used her previous administrative and organizational talents to nurture the development of the NAACP.

The early women workers in the NAACP established a tradition of excellence that was maintained by women such as **Daisy Lampkin** of Pittsburgh, Pennsylvania, **Ella Baker** of New York, and, much later, **Daisy Bates** of Little Rock, Arkansas. The black women who worked with the NAACP were dedicated to the cause of securing civil rights for all—men and women. The NAACP was largely a grassroots organization that used its existing community, church, and professional networks to sell subscriptions to the association's official news publication, the *Crisis*. The *Crisis,* which began publication in 1910, was available at the subscription price of 10¢ a copy or $1 a year—affordable even for those with low or modest incomes.

In 1914, the NAACP instituted the renowned Spingarn Award, the brainchild of Joel E. Spingarn, who was then chairman of the NAACP board of directors. The award was established to honor African Americans who have excelled in their vocation. A modest number of women have been recipients of this medal; many of them were members or officers of the NAACP. Past female recipients include Mary B. Talbert (1922), Mary McLeod Bethune (1935), Daisy Bates and the **Little Rock Nine** (1958), and **Rosa L. Parks** (1979).

Black women remain a strong presence in the NAACP. Within the past decade and into the 1990s, women occupy a significant number of local and executive positions within the association. In February of 1995, **Myrlie Evers-Williams** was elected chairperson of the board of directors of the NAACP. She is determined to create a relevant, progressive agenda for the organization. "I do not intend to stay in this position for a lifetime, but I want to leave knowing that we have found a way to attract people who didn't go through the fire in the 1950s and 1960s to join the NAACP. I want to leave this organization healthy, knowing it can make a real difference in their lives."

LISA BETH HILL

National Domestic Workers Union

In early 1968, formal efforts to organize domestic workers began in Atlanta when eight women met at Perry Homes, a low-income housing project, to discuss the idea of an organization. This effort to organize was spearheaded by Dorothy Lee Bolden, who had worked as a maid for thirty-eight years. The women continued to hold meetings at the Butler Street Young Men's Christian Association, and as the group grew, they moved to the Wheat Street Baptist Church. Reverend William Holmes Borders, the church's pastor, was prominent in the African-American community and an encouraging force behind Bolden's organizing efforts. The group also received support and aid in the form of office space and telephone and secretarial help from John McGowan, executive director of the Georgia Human Relations Council. Although Bolden had in earlier years sought advice from organized labor representatives in Atlanta, the group decided not to affiliate with any existing labor organization, but to create their own group, the National Domestic Workers Union (NDWU).

By August 1968, the group had coalesced into a "mutual-benefit association," defined by social scientists and organizational theorists Peter M. Blau and W. Richard Scott as one "in which the membership is expected to be the prime beneficiary."

Thus, it was not a "union" in the true sense of the term. According to Bolden, she used the word "union" to "give the organization strength of its own. . . . The word 'union' gave it clout, and working-class members understood the word." Members were taught how to negotiate with and communicate their desires to their employers. The instruction proved successful, and most members got the wage increases and better working conditions they sought. Wages increased from $3.50–$5.00 per day to $13.50–$15.00 plus carfare.

The NDWU from its inception was characterized by volunteerism and an evangelical fervor. Members felt that by banding together, they could improve their lot. On September 19, 1968, Bolden was elected president, due to her charisma, self-confidence, competence, commitment to the mission of the group, and ability to articulate its ideological goals. She has served as president to the present.

The group agreed that its objective would be to "promote . . . organized and unionized Domestics, including all people." The group's charter, granted by the state of Georgia in 1968, states:

> This corporation is organized and chartered for the purpose of enhancing, protecting, and promoting the economic, social, and educational welfare of its members in Atlanta, Georgia, its environs and in the American Nation as a whole. The primary purpose of this organization shall be to benefit the community as measured by the increased wages, better working conditions, and more benefits to its members as reflected in improved living standards rather than monetary profits to its members.

To increase its membership, NDWU members agreed to promote the organization by contacting individuals, organizing meetings in various communities, distributing leaflets advertising the group at bus stops and other places frequented by domestic workers, and advertising on the radio. The group held spirited meetings, where community leaders were invited to speak. These tactics were extremely successful, and membership grew.

By the 1970s, the organization was considered a powerful political force in the community. Members participated in voter registration drives, protested against the Atlanta Mass Transit Authority (to get routes and fares that better accommodated domestic workers), and worked on local, state, and national political campaigns.

In an effort to pursue the goal of professionalizing the field of domestic work, the NDWU implemented several projects between 1971 and 1978 funded by government grants. Its homemakers' skills program was designed to train welfare recipients in consumer affairs, problem solving, resource use, and job hunting.

Another grant allowed the NDWU to develop a profile of Atlanta's domestic workers, which indicated that the group needed improved child care and training. As a result, the Office of Equal Opportunity and Economic Opportunity in Atlanta funded a career-training center, which operated for three years. Participants were paid a weekly stipend and received six months of training in reading, writing, mathematics, early childhood education, monetary budgeting, food preparation, first-aid, and general household duties.

In an attempt to create financial stability for the organization and honor women in domestic service, Bolden established a fund-raiser called Maids Honor Day in 1970. Employers nominated domestic workers for the Maid of the Year Award, and the winner and runners-up received cash and gifts. Former President Jimmy Carter's maid, Minnie Fitzpatrick, received the award in 1978. The fund-raiser was discontinued after 1978.

A major focus of the NDWU has been to provide a nonprofit employment placement and counseling service for its members. Between 1972 and 1980, over 13,000 members were served.

In 1979, Bolden was accused of misusing government funds. After a federal investigation, she was found innocent of the charge. However, her image was tarnished, and her credibility has continued to be questioned by some.

Between 1979 and 1984, the NDWU continued to provide counseling and placement services despite financial difficulties. During this period it was funded totally by donations from individuals and Bolden's personal funds. From 1984 to 1988, the NDWU received an annual grant of $12,000 from the Fulton County Board of Commissioners, to be used for job placement, training, and counseling. Since 1988, the NDWU has been dependent upon contributions and Bolden's personal funds.

By 1990, membership in the NDWU had declined considerably. In 1991, the NDWU placed and counseled approximately 300 members. During that time, members received domestic jobs paying from $50 to $80 per day. In spite of the organization's financial problems, Bolden continues to be committed to its goals.

DOROTHY COWSER YANCY

National Welfare Rights Organization

Throughout the 1960s and the early 1970s, a militant grass-roots movement of welfare recipients challenged the local, state, and national welfare bureaucracies. The National Welfare Rights Organization (NWRO) effectively coordinated the actions of numerous local welfare rights groups across the country between 1967 and 1975. This movement of poor, mostly African-American women and their supporters represented an important example of the active presence of the poor in the political process. It also brought attention to the ways in which race, sex, and class relations informed welfare policy decisions.

In 1966, a veteran civil rights activist and former associate director of the Congress of Racial Equality (CORE), George Wiley, created the Poverty Rights Action Center (PRAC) to establish a national communications network for the numerous welfare rights organizations that began emerging in the early 1960s. PRAC eventually became the headquarters for NWRO, established a year later in an effort to provide a tightly organized structure for the national efforts of local groups to challenge oppressive welfare policies. Several years before the national organization emerged, however, local organizations, like the one started by welfare recipient Johnnie Tillmon in Watts, began appearing around the country. Some of these organizations empowered welfare clients to plan their own job training programs—programs that stressed adequate opportunities for career advancement, education, and effective daycare facilities. Other organizations, like the Brooklyn Welfare Action Council (B-WAC)

gained the attention of local politicians who requested endorsements from welfare organizations and viewed welfare rights activists as viable political actors.

The NWRO emerged during the turbulent era of the 1960s when the nation's attention was directed at the stark contradiction of poverty existing in a country as affluent as the United States. President Lyndon Johnson spoke of the nation's ability to eliminate poverty and his newly developed national antipoverty programs were based upon the notion of "maximum feasible participation of the poor." Within this climate, the NWRO was able to utilize funds from middle-class liberal churches and government poverty programs for the operation of a national network.

In entering the highly contested welfare debate, welfare recipients added their voices to policy discussions that had historically excluded them. At its height in the late 1960s, NWRO-educated recipients and others eligible for benefits under existing laws pressured welfare agencies to provide such benefits in a dignified manner and articulated a unique and complex vision of welfare that guaranteed an adequate income for all families regardless of their composition. Welfare rights activists led sit-ins in welfare departments and utilized other direct action tactics to obtain immediate benefits for their members. Prior to the welfare activism of this era, many who were eligible for benefits were reluctant to apply for public assistance and many who did were denied relief. The assertive posture of the NWRO fueled an explosion in the welfare rolls as many more poor women applied for funds and became informed of their rights as recipients. As a result, many local welfare agencies were forced to change restrictive and demoralizing policies.

African-American welfare recipients/activists like Johnnie Tillmon, Beula Sanders, and Etta Horn gained national prominence as spokespersons and lobbyists for the national organization. The NWRO lobbied Congress for a guaranteed national income and fought against Social Security amendments that violated the constitutional rights of welfare recipients. As lobbyists, welfare women demanded that they be provided with the resources to manage their own lives. They criticized nonexistent or inadequate day-care facilities, ill-planned job training programs, degrading, low-wage employment, and welfare practices that scrutinized their personal lives before providing benefits they desperately needed. Furthermore, they exposed the problematic nature of white society's definitions of concepts like illegitimacy and matriarchy, and they affirmed the integrity and legitimacy of female-headed households. They criticized policies that purported to stabilize families by forcing mothers to accept low-wage work without guaranteeing adequate day-care facilities and transportation costs. Most important, these women asserted that their roles as mothers constituted valuable work for which they should be compensated. Their vision challenged existing assumptions about the proper composition of the family as well as notions about the meaning of work and welfare. The political participation of welfare women was met with fierce resistance from a powerful anti-welfare backlash in the early seventies. The organization was forced to file for bankruptcy in 1975 when financial support declined dramatically.

The NWRO represents a unique moment in the struggle for black liberation, because it brought together welfare rights and civil rights within a unified struggle. Welfare activists conceptualized the two as connected and stressed the impact of gender and race in the formulation of welfare policies. Women in the movement conceptualized welfare as a women's issue and undoubtedly influenced feminists who incorporated welfare into their agenda after the demise of the NWRO.

This empowering moment for women on welfare did not occur without many of the gender, race, and class hierarchies against which the movement defined itself. Black female organizers resisted the initiatives of professional organizers who were often sent by the national coordinating committee to direct the organization of local and state activities. Struggles of black women for autonomy within the NWRO were rooted in the organization's two-tiered leadership structure, which employed full-time organizers who were mostly male, white, and middle-class, while the elected leaders were all welfare recipients and mainly African-American women. Nonetheless, the strong challenge to the state represented in this movement exemplified the radical potential of organizations led by and for the poor.

AMY JORDAN

P

Parks, Rosa (1913–)

Rosa Louise McCauley Parks, held in high esteem because of her defiance of Southern law and tradition, frequently has been called the mother of the modern civil rights movement. Parks' act on December 1, 1955, of sitting down to stand up for equal chances at riding the bus in Montgomery, Alabama, took on enormous meaning. It became legendary, resulting in 42,000 black people's boycotting city buses. The Montgomery bus boycott lasted 381 days, and when it ended on December 21, 1956, the U.S. Supreme Court had ruled segregation on city buses unconstitutional, Martin Luther King, Jr., had become a national leader, and a mass movement of nonviolent resistance had begun that would continue into the 1960s.

When Leona McCauley gave birth to Rosa in Tuskegee, Alabama, on February 4, 1913, *Plessy* v. *Ferguson* and Jim Crow were in their second decade. McCauley reared her daughter in Montgomery, where Rosa attended the all-black Alabama State College. Rosa married Raymond Parks, a barber, in 1932, and they both became active in the local chapter of the **National Association for the Advancement of Colored People** (NAACP). Raymond Parks volunteered his time to help free the defendants in the Scottsboro cases of the 1930s. Rosa Parks served as youth advisor for the Montgomery NAACP, becoming its secretary in the 1950s. She first worked as a

clerk and an insurance saleswoman, and then she became a tailor's assistant at the Fair Department Store, making 75¢ an hour in 1955.

Sometime that year, E. D. Nixon, Pullman porter and president of the Montgomery NAACP, recommended Rosa Parks to white activist Virginia Durr, who sought a part-time seamstress. The Durrs on numerous occasions listened to Parks' complaints about segregation in the South, especially the situation involving Montgomery's public transit system. Parks deplored the custom of having to enter the front of the bus to pay the fare and then having to exit to reenter in the back of the bus. Frequently, white bus drivers pulled away before black riders could reboard at the back. Moreover, Parks kept the Durrs abreast of the efforts for a test case to end Montgomery segregated busing or at least improve the situation. Then, in March 1955, authorities arrested Claudette Colvin, a fifteen-year-old high school student, for refusing to give up her seat to a white passenger. At Parks' invitation, Virginia Durr attended an NAACP meeting concerning Colvin's case. An informal bus boycott had begun, but NAACP leaders decided not to initiate an organized resistance around this particular case. Upon learning that a scholarship was available for a 1955 summer workshop at the **Highlander Folk School** in Monteagle, Tennessee, the Durrs urged Rosa Parks to accept it. A reluctant Parks consented to go when friends of the Durrs offered to pay her travel expenses to and from Tennessee.

The Highlander Folk School was a training ground for labor organizers, and having been active in the NAACP in Montgomery, Parks knew of the struggle for justice and equality that that organization had maintained since 1910. Her mother, a schoolteacher, had benefited from the NAACP's efforts to secure equal salaries for black and white teachers in the 1940s. Parks believed that the historic *Brown* v. *Board*

Rosa Parks is a legend in the civil rights movement. She is shown here striking the Liberty Bell in Philadelphia. (SCHOMBURG CENTER)

of Education Supreme Court ruling in 1954 made most black Americans optimistic about their future in a newly desegregated America.

The Supreme Court decision marked a turning point in the long struggle against segregation, but the decision embraced only one aspect of racial equality, public education. Black Americans now had to overcome inequities in economic and political arenas. On the heels of *Brown*, black citizens made it evident in Montgomery that they would no longer tolerate racial injustice. This stand was sparked by Rosa Parks' refusal to give up her seat so that a white man could sit in the first row of a section of a transit bus reserved for non-whites. According to de facto custom, when the section reserved for white passengers was filled, black passengers were expected to give up their seats to those whites left standing. Parks was arrested for not complying and fined $14. Within four days of Parks' arrest and bond release, the black community of Montgomery rallied around the quiet, reserved, and hard-working woman as its symbol of courage.

Parks has said that she simply was too tired to move that day. The Durrs accompanied E. D. Nixon to get Parks out of jail. Indeed, the Durrs, Fred D. Gray (her black defense attorney), and E. D. Nixon (a principal organizer of the boycott) all played critical roles in organizing and sustaining the boycott. Though the gains from the Montgomery boycott were won by the many unsung participants who made it a success, Rosa Parks must be credited with providing the spark that made it all begin to happen.

For her actions in 1955, Parks lost her job, but history continues to reward her.

When she moved with her husband and mother to Detroit in 1957, she again worked as a seamstress, but Congressman John Conyers later hired her as a staff assistant. Detroit renamed its Twelfth Street in her honor in 1969. She received the Spingarn Medal from the NAACP in 1972. She continues to receive numerous awards and honorary degrees. *Ebony* readers chose her in 1980 as the living black woman who had done the most to advance the cause of black America, and the Martin Luther King, Jr., Center for Nonviolent Social Change awarded her the Martin Luther King, Jr., Nonviolent Peace Prize that same year. She fulfilled a personal dream in 1987 by founding the Rosa and Raymond Parks Institute of Self Development in Detroit. The institute addresses her lifelong commitment to career training for black youth, and affirms the Parkses' devotion and dedication to human rights struggles. Her autobiography (written with Jim Haskins) was published in 1992, *Rosa Parks: My Story.*

LINDA REED

Parsons, Lucy (1853–1942)

A veteran of the anarchist, socialist, and communist movements in Chicago during the late nineteenth and early twentieth centuries, Lucy Parsons was the first black woman to play a prominent role in the American left. A committed revolutionary, Parsons devoted sixty years of her life to improving the situation of the poor, the jobless, the homeless, women, children, and people of color.

Born in 1853 in Waco, Texas, of African, Indian, and Mexican ancestry, Lucy met and subsequently married Albert Parsons,

The first black woman to play a prominent role in the American left, legendary anarchist Lucy Parsons wrote powerfully on lynching and racial violence. (ARCHIVES OF LABOR AND URBAN AFFAIRS, WAYNE STATE UNIVERSITY)

a former Confederate army scout turned radical. Because of their mixed marriage, the couple was forced to flee Texas in 1873. They ultimately ended up in Chicago, where they both joined the socialist-oriented Workingmen's Party in 1876. Within three years, Lucy Parsons began contributing articles to the *Socialist* and became a primary speaker on behalf of the Working Women's Union. The Parsonses were eventually drawn to anarchism, which emphasized cooperative organization of production, the abolition of the state, and the free exchange of products without profit or market intervention. Along with her husband and several other white Chicago radicals, Lucy Parsons helped form the International Working People's Association (IWPA) in 1883. She continued to develop as a talented propagandist and radical intellectual, publishing a popular article in *Alarm* (a revolutionary socialist newspaper) in 1884 that called on the jobless to "learn to use explosives!"

Less known, however, are her early writings on lynchings and racist violence in the South, which were published several years before **Ida B. Wells'** famous pronouncements on the subject. She viewed racial oppression as primarily a class question and suggested that African-American working people adopt violent strategies of self-defense. Commenting on a multiple lynching that had occurred in Carrollton, Mississippi, in 1886, Parsons insisted that race had nothing to do with the brutal murders. "It is because [the black man] is *poor*. It is because he is dependent. Because he is poorer as a class than his white wage-slave brother of the North." Her tendency to focus on economic causes and de-emphasize the role of racism might be linked to her own denial of her black heritage. Her complexion and features not only enabled her to pass as Spanish, but her social world consisted almost entirely of white leftists. Because racism was not something she had to endure all of her life, it was difficult for her to see how it could have shaped the lives of African Americans.

Like so many other anarchists and radical labor leaders, Lucy Parsons helped organize the famous attempted general strike on May 1, 1886, demanding a general eight-hour workday. Three days into the strike, Albert Parsons and eight other IWPA members were arrested for allegedly throwing a bomb at police during a demonstration at Chicago's Haymarket Square. Lucy Parsons led a campaign to free her husband and the other seven political prisoners, but her efforts were to no avail: Albert Parsons and three other defendants were executed in 1887. (Just two years later she lost her youngest of two children, eight-year-old Lulu, to lymphadenoma.)

Despite these tragedies, Lucy Parsons continued her work on behalf of anarchist and socialist causes, addressing radical gatherings throughout the United States as well as in England. In 1891, she published and edited a short-lived newspaper, *Freedom: A Revolutionary Anarchist-Communist Monthly,* in which she began dealing with the woman question much more rigorously, publishing essays on rape, divorce, marriage, and the role of women's oppression as a function of capitalism. Like her views on racism, Parsons believed that sexism would automatically disappear with the construction of a socialist society.

By the turn of the century, Parsons had become somewhat of a legend of the left. She was one of two women in attendance at the founding convention of the Industrial Workers of the World (IWW) in 1905; she gained some notoriety for leading mass demonstrations of homeless and unemployed people in San Francisco (1914) and Chicago (1915); and she was a vocal opponent of World War I. In 1927, Parsons joined the International Labor Defense, a Communist-led organization devoted to defending "class war prisoners," notably incarcerated labor organizers like Tom Mooney and African Americans unjustly accused of crimes (e.g., the Scottsboro Nine and Angelo Herndon). After working closely with the Communists for more than a decade, the eighty-six-year-old Parsons joined the party in 1939. Three years later her life came to an end when a fire engulfed her home.

ROBIN D. G. KELLEY

Patterson, Louise (1901–)

An educator, cultural critic, early civil rights activist, and pioneering advocate of black women's rights in Harlem, Louise Thompson brought to the Communist Party an unusually sophisticated understanding of the complexities of race and gender oppression—a unique perspective for an organization that emphasized class exploitation above all else.

Born in Chicago, Illinois, on September 9, 1901, she was raised in several predominantly white, often racist communities in the West. Her family eventually settled in Oakland, California, in 1919. She earned a degree in economics from the University of California at Berkeley in 1923, but racism limited her career opportunities. She chose to go back to the Midwest and work toward a graduate degree at the University of Chicago, but she abandoned the idea soon thereafter. Giving up school, as well as a lucrative position at a black-owned Chicago firm, Thompson headed south to accept a teaching job in Pine Bluff, Arkansas, in 1925, and a year later accepted a faculty position at Hampton Institute in Virginia. Because of her open support of a student strike in 1927, the Hampton administration pressured Thompson to resign, after which she headed to New York City to accept an Urban League Fellowship to study at the New School for Social Research.

Unimpressed with social work paternalism as a means to improve the lives of the black poor, she discontinued her education in 1930 and turned to New York's Congregational Educational Society (CES), a liberal organization interested in the problems of race relations and labor. Simultaneously, she became a prominent figure in black cultural circles, serving as editorial secretary for Langston Hughes and Zora Neale Hurston, and offering her spacious apartment as a meeting place for black artists and intellectuals. Her involvement in social problems and cultural politics, compounded by the Great Depression, the Scottsboro case, and the growing strength of the Communist Party in Harlem, radicalized Thompson. She and artist Augusta Savage formed a left-wing social club called the Vanguard, out of which developed a branch of the Friends of the Soviet Union (FOSU). Soon thereafter, Thompson attended classes at the Workers' School, moving deeper into the party's inner circle.

As secretary of the Harlem chapter of FOSU, she became principal organizer of a group of black artists invited to the Soviet Union in 1932 to make a film about African-American life. Although the project was abandoned, she returned to New York with a deeper appreciation of socialism and a greater affinity for Communist politics. In 1933, she left CES and served as assistant national secretary of the National Committee for the Defense of Political Prisoners (NCDPP), through which she was officially asked to join the Communist Party. A year later she accepted a full-time position in the International Workers' Order (IWO) and continued to organize cultural and political events on behalf of the Communist Party in Harlem and elsewhere (including Alabama, where in 1934 she spent a night in a Birmingham jail). As black artists joined the Works Progress Administration (WPA) in the late 1930s, Thompson became an increasingly critical liaison linking black popular culture and Harlem's literati with Communist popular front politics. In 1938, for example, she and Langston Hughes organized the IWO-sponsored Harlem Suitcase Theatre that performed a number of works by black playwrights.

In 1940, Louise Thompson married longtime friend and veteran party leader William L. Patterson, who over a decade earlier had suggested she read Marx and look seriously at events in the Soviet Union. Soon afterward she joined "Patt" in Chicago and continued her work nationally and locally. Among other things, she served as national recording secretary of the IWO and helped establish a black community center on Chicago's South Side. Following World War II, she was among the founders and leading activists of the Civil Rights Congress (CRC), and in the 1950s she joined such luminaries as **Charlotta Bass,** Shirley Graham, and **Alice Childress** in forming the Sojourners for Truth and Justice, a black woman's auxiliary of the CRC.

ROBIN D. G. KELLEY

Porter, Carol Doe (1945–)

A "black conservative with a bleeding heart" and "card-carrying Republican" are what Carol Doe Porter calls herself. Others have dubbed her the "Mother Teresa of Houston," because out of her bungalow in the north sector of Houston, Texas, she and husband, Hurt Porter, Jr., have been feeding and in other ways caring for needy children in the city since 1985.

Their nonprofit organization, Kid-Care, Inc., accepts no government contributions as a matter of principle. A picture of former President George Bush—whose 1992 campaign for re-election advocated the "thousand points of light" philosophy of volunteerism—hangs on the Porters' wall.

Born in 1945, Carol married Hurt, Jr., in 1974 and the next year had a son, Hurt III, who now manages Kid-Care's transportation. A daughter, Jamilhah, was born in 1985, a year of great change in the couple's lives.

It was Carol's late mother, Lula Doe, who first inspired the Kid-Care idea. In 1984, Lula persuaded a supermarket not to throw blemished produce away but give it to the hungry. A year later, two events sparked definite action. A mother brought to Carol, then a registered nurse, a baby whom Carol had just a few months earlier helped deliver. But the baby had already died, of malnutrition. And after Carol witnessed children from a next-door apartment complex scavenging a McDonald's dumpster for food, the course of her life was decided.

The Porters' Kid-Care funds came from their paychecks, eventually from jobs as daycare inspectors and nutritionists for the U.S. Department of Agriculture. (Hurt, Jr., had been a musician and radio announcer.) Kid-Care started as a Saturday activity, when they loaded their car with blanket-covered pots of hot chicken, rice, and gravy and simply sought out hungry youngsters. But the more they provided, the more it was apparent to them how much was needed. They converted their garage into a pantry and their kitchen into both pantry and second kitchen. In time they acquired six refrigerators, four freezers, and two stoves. Soon they launched the nation's first meals-on-wheels program, carrying food directly to the hungry in their van. These included people with homes and those without.

By 1994, the Porters had a small paid staff and volunteers numbering fifty. They covered some 14,000 meals per month with a monthly donation-based budget of $30,000. Kid-Care gained a high visibility among corporations and counted among its sponsors Toys "R" Us, Quaker Oats, and Heartline Communications. By 1995, the annual budget grew to $500,000, and the number of meals served passed 20,000. Kid-Care's services expanded in the 1990s to include preschool, tuition, day care, medical, summer camp, and other programs.

The Porters were honored by groups as unalike as the Association of Black Social Workers and the Houston division of the FBI. At the White House they received the Presidential Volunteer Action Award.

Despite such honors and national media attention, there have been obstacles. In 1993, the Porter kitchen was cited as violating several Houston city codes, forcing the couple to replace hot meals with cold ones. As of 1995, Carol Porter intends to return to hot meals, once Kid-Care has transferred from her home to a 11,500-square-foot building equipped to produce 4,000 hot meals daily.

Carol Porter believes that welfare is "another form of slavery." Her critics cannot help but admire her services, even as they dispute her opinion that government has no business performing deeds similar to Kid-Care's. Their sharpest arguments may contain the highest praise, as in these words from Texas state senator Rodney Ellis, a black Democrat. "The harsh reality" he says, "is that there are too few Carol Porters in the world. If there were more, she'd be absolutely right in what she says."

GARY HOUSTON

R

Richardson, Gloria (1922–)

Violent conflict raged in the streets and in the hearts of black and white citizens when Gloria Richardson tried to lead the people of Cambridge, Maryland, to peace and freedom. "We live in a town where a man might be killed tomorrow," Richardson said in 1963, "where civil war might break out next week. It cannot get better while the white people fail to understand the mood of the Negro community and to realize that unless they grant the means of progress, their houses and ours may fly apart."

Gloria St. Clair Hayes Richardson came from a family of leaders. She was born on May 6, 1922, in Baltimore, the only child of John Edwards Hayes and Mabel Pauline St. Clair Hayes. When she was six years old, the Hayeses moved to Cambridge to be near other members of the prominent St. Clair family. Her grandfather, H. Maynadier St. Clair, was the second black American to be elected to the city council of Cambridge, serving from 1912 to 1946. He was not, however, considered to be a strong voice for his people, and when his son, Herbert, made a bid to replace him, Herbert was defeated.

In the meantime, Gloria St. Clair Hayes attended Frederick Douglass High School and **Howard University.** She married and had a daughter, Donna. She grew increasingly angry about the conditions of life in Cambridge. In 1962, she took up the leadership of the town's black community, but not by running for the city council. New methods were emerging in the struggle for justice, so Richardson assumed her leadership role as cochair of the Cambridge Nonviolent Action Committee (CNAC). She and others in Cambridge had been inspired to organize by a group of young freedom riders from New York and Baltimore. "There was something direct," she said, "something real about the way the kids waged nonviolent war. This was the first time I saw a vehicle I could work with." Richardson and other members of the St. Clair family became the nucleus of the new group, which was given support by the **Student Nonviolent Coordinating Committee** (SNCC).

On March 25, 1963, Richardson and her cochair, Inez Grubb, went before the city council with their demand—complete integration immediately. The alternative was public protest. Demonstrations began a few days later. There were sit-ins and picketing, demonstrations at the theater, the skating rink, the city hall, the county courthouse, and the jail. Eighty protesters were arrested in seven weeks, including Richardson. They were brought before the courts in May at the notoriously paternalistic "Penny Trials." Each defendant was given a suspended sentence and fined a penny. Judge W. Laird Henry lectured Richardson about disgracing her family name, and he trivialized the protesters' concerns.

Richardson went back out onto the streets. On May 14, 1963, three generations of women in her family were arrested. Donna Richardson was in a group of fourteen who were arrested for a sit-in in the lobby of the Dorset Theater. Gloria Richardson and her mother, Mabel St. Clair Booth, were arrested at the Dizzyland Restaurant. When protesters marched around the jail where they were being held, more were charged. That day, sixty-two black people fighting for their rights were put behind bars.

Four days later, Judge Henry, realizing that his judicial rap on the knuckles had not been effective, announced that he and other members of the white community were ready to take the demonstrators seriously. He would free those arrested and organize a committee to negotiate a settlement with the black community. The Committee on Interracial Understanding was set up, and the prisoners were released. The committee agreed that the basic demands of the demonstrators would be met. These included: complete desegregation of public places; complete desegregation of public schools; equal employment opportunities in industries and stores, with an initial quota of 10 percent; a public housing project and study of sewer and sidewalk needs; and an end to police brutality and appointment of a black deputy sheriff. There was, for a few days, peace.

Then arrests began again as peaceful demonstrations and an economic boycott continued. On May 31, Richardson asked Attorney General Robert F. Kennedy to investigate the violations of constitutional rights that were occurring in Cambridge. One fifteen-year-old girl, Dinez White, was being held without bond after having been arrested for praying outside a segregated bowling alley. Kennedy did not respond to Richardson's appeal. Dinez White was released on a writ of habeas corpus, but on June 10, she was sentenced to an indeterminate term in a correctional school, along with another juvenile protester. When violence broke out, Richardson again asked Kennedy for help.

Three days later, state troopers surrounded the black district. The governor of Maryland declared a state of martial law and sent in the National Guard. The guard remained in Cambridge until July 8. When it left, students again tried to enter the Dizzyland Restaurant, and again violence broke out. Just three days after they had left, the National Guard was back but could not stop the violence. On July 16, a commission of both black and white citizens was appointed to find a solution. A moratorium was called on demonstrations.

During this time, Gloria Richardson continued to search for peaceful solutions. She met with other civil rights leaders, black and white, to try to find a way to bring calm without compromise. On July 15, upon her return from a conference on racial problems in Annapolis that was chaired by Maryland's governor, she was arrested on the streets of Cambridge. On July 17, Robert Kennedy gave a speech in which he suggested that she was responsible for the violence there. She sent him a letter protesting the charge. Again, at a rally at a local church, she warned that the situation could no longer be controlled by guns and promises. Only justice would avert further violence.

On July 22, 1963, a conference was held in Washington, D.C. Gloria Richardson and other civil rights leaders met with Robert Kennedy, General George Gelston, who was in charge of the National Guard in Cambridge, and Maryland State Attorney General Thomas B. Finon, among others. A treaty was signed.

That might have marked the end of the open conflict and the beginning of progress toward justice. The treaty covered five points: (1) complete and immediate desegregation of the public schools and hospitals in the county; (2) construction of 200 units of low-rent public housing; (3) employment of a black advocate in the Cambridge office of the Maryland Department of Employment Security and in the Cambridge post office; (4) appointment of a human relations commission; and (5) adoption of the Charter Amendment providing for desegregation of public accommodations.

The fifth point contained a loophole. The Charter Amendment, by law, could be subjected to public referendum, so that treaty point was not firm. All present at the conference expressed the hope that no referendum would be called, but the hope proved baseless. Petitions were circulated, and more than enough signatures were obtained. When the referendum was placed on the ballot, Richardson took a highly controversial stand. She insisted that black Americans already had, by virtue of the U.S. Constitution, the rights outlined in the referendum and refused to ask black voters to support the referendum. When it failed, many people blamed Richardson.

In the years that followed the days of conflict and violence in Cambridge, black children began to enter white schools. The U.S. Civil Rights Commission issued a report vindicating the CNAC and criticizing Richardson's opponents. An on-the-job-training program was instituted in Cam-

bridge. In the same month that the National Guard finally withdrew from Cambridge, President Lyndon Johnson signed into law the 1964 Civil Rights Act. However, when Richardson participated in a demonstration on the night that George Wallace spoke in Cambridge, she was arrested.

Gloria Richardson left Cambridge in August 1964. She moved to New York and married her second husband, Frank Dandridge. Her commitment to the rights of others has led her to work with the Department of Aging in New York City.

KATHLEEN THOMPSON

Roberts, Lillian (1928–)

"Lillian Roberts Day" was proclaimed by Governor Hugh Carey of New York on January 9, 1981, in tribute to the labor leader's importance to the political and economic struggles of working people. As associate director of New York City's District Council 37, American Federation of State, County and Municipal Employees (AFSCME), Lillian Roberts had been at the forefront of labor battles for decades. Two months later Carey named her New York's State Industrial Commissioner; she was the first black woman appointed to this position. Such honors from the state stood in stark contrast to her stand against Governor Nelson Rockefeller in 1968 and her subsequent jailing, despite mass protests, for organizing a state hospital workers' strike in violation of a public employees no-strike law.

Lillian Davis was born on January 2, 1928, on Chicago's South Side to Lillian and Henry Davis, the second of five children. As part of the great migration of black people out of the South, her parents came to Chicago from Mississippi two years before her birth. Her mother's prayers and religiosity gave strength and emotional protection to the family while her leadership in community struggles for better education, humane welfare services, and housing provided young Lillian Davis with a model of committed womanhood. With her family's encouragement, she finished high school and was awarded a scholarship to the University of Illinois in 1945, but the scholarship did not cover her living expenses. After a year and a half, when the brother who was helping her was drafted and the welfare then supporting her family would not provide room and board, she was forced to quit her only formal higher education and return to Chicago to find work.

Lillian Davis was hired in 1946 as the first black nurses' aide in the nursery at Chicago's Lying-In Hospital when war-related positions were still pulling white women into better-paying jobs and black women's work in hospitals was primarily limited to the kitchens. The work fascinated her, and she took every opportunity to ask questions, to learn more, to become more skilled. As a so-called nonprofessional, she was never included in the shift report meetings of nurses, but she was often informally left in charge of the nursery and given teaching responsibilities with the new medical students. Davis married silkscreen operator William Roberts in 1948 and settled into a life of paid labor and homemaking.

After ten years, an overwork grievance pushed Roberts into work with the hospital workers' union, AFSCME. Her aggressiveness and sense of fair play quickly made her a shop steward and brought her into conflict with hospital management. The AFSCME organizer, Victor Gotbaum, recognized her skills and offered her a job with the union. It was the beginning of a lifelong labor alliance. Lillian Roberts quickly demonstrated her organizing skill, bringing both white and black workers together and into the union. Deeply committed to working-class empowerment, she fought against racism in all forms and for the union she saw as vital to democracy. Amid these struggles, tragedy struck her family. A brother was killed by the Chicago police, and her sister was murdered by her husband, leaving three young sons that Roberts and her husband began to raise.

By 1965, Victor Gotbaum had become executive director of District Council 37 of AFSCME in New York City, and he called Roberts to assist on a social service workers' strike. She subsequently directed a hard-fought campaign against the Teamsters Union that led to AFSCME's victory as the union for New York City's nonprofessional workers in nineteen municipal hospitals. Her organizing, three years later, of the state hospital workers led to violations of the state's no-strike law and her two-week jailing. At home, her mother assisted in the raising of her sister's sons while Roberts' marriage to William ended in divorce after twenty years.

Rising to director of the hospital division, then associate director of District Council 37 with its 600-person staff and 110,000 members, Roberts continued to fight for improved working conditions, better wages, and her own union project: a training program that made it possible for working union members to certify as licensed practical nurses. With Gotbaum, she built the union into a strong voice for labor in the maelstrom of New York City labor and municipal politics, and into the leader in worker education, with the creation of a District Council 37 campus at the College of New Rochelle. In recognition of her skills and renown, in 1981, Governor Carey named Roberts the state's Industrial Commissioner, a title she fittingly had changed to Labor Commissioner. She was reappointed to this position by Governor Mario Cuomo in 1982, as she was leading a fight against sweatshop conditions in the garment industry, promoting employment opportunities, organizing training programs, and working to see that surplus food was dispensed to the needy. She was awarded numerous honors, including an honorary doctorate from the College of New Rochelle, the **National Association for the Advancement of Colored People's** Roy Wilkins Award, and the Adam Clayton Powell Government Award.

Roberts was forced to resign in 1987 from the Labor Commissioner post after internal struggles with the governor. She became senior vice president of Total Health Systems, a health maintenance organization in New York, and directed their marketing to union, government, and commercial sectors. She is remembered for her dignity, her militancy, and her commitment to democracy and to the education of working-class people of all races.

SUSAN M. REVERBY

Robeson, Eslanda Goode (1896–1965)

Intellectual, writer, and activist Eslanda Goode Robeson was born on December 12, 1896, in Washington, D.C., where she grew up in a middle-class African-American family. Her maternal grandfather was Francis Lewis Cardozo, a noted black politician in South Carolina during Reconstruction. In the early 1900s, Eslanda's family moved to New York City, where she finished high school and studied chemistry at Columbia University, receiving a B.S. in 1923. She later attended the London School of Economics and then earned a doctorate in anthropology from Hartford Seminary.

In 1921, she married Paul Robeson, then one of the few African-American students attending Columbia University's Law School. In 1927, they had a child, Paul, Jr. Her husband eventually earned an international reputation as a singer, actor, and outspoken left-wing political activist.

Eslanda Robeson's main political activity, from the 1930s through the mid-1960s, focused on the colonized people of the world, primarily Africans. Along with her husband, she traveled all over the world and lived for extended periods of time in London and Moscow. In 1936, she visited Africa for the first time, accompanied by her young son, and later published a book, *African Journey,* which was the diary of her trip. In 1938, she traveled to Spain to support anti-Fascist troops fighting in the Spanish Civil War against Franco. These experiences fueled an international perspective and a commitment to decolonization and independence for all nations.

She was a pioneer advocate for African self-determination. In 1941, Robeson cofounded the Council on African Affairs, a group of African Americans who lobbied aggressively against colonialism in Africa. The group hoped that in the wake of World War II the reordering of the world political map would include decolonization. Robeson represented the council as a delegate observer to the founding convention of the United Nations in 1945. In 1951, she was one of three protesters who disrupted the United Nations postwar conference on genocide to argue, unsuccessfully, that ending vigilante violence against African Americans should be a part of the agenda. In 1958, she attended the All-African Peoples Conference in the newly independent African nation of Ghana as a representative of the Council on African Affairs and one of the few women delegates.

In addition to her staunch opposition to colonialism, Eslanda Robeson was also a strong supporter of socialist countries like the Soviet Union and China after its 1949 revolution, and although neither she nor her husband was ever an open member of the Communist Party, many of their friends were, and the couple made no apologies for these associations or their left-wing sympathies. Her dissident political views led to her being called before the House Un-American Activities Committee (HUAC) in 1953 to defend her past political affiliations. Robeson refused to cooperate with what she deemed the anti-Communist hysteria that was the impetus for the committee's investigations. She was reprimanded by the HUAC and Senator Joseph McCarthy for her actions. In the late 1940s and early 1950s, Paul Robeson was denied work because of his political views, and both he and Eslanda were labeled Communist subversives. In 1958, the couple moved to the Soviet Union to escape the political persecution and racial discrimination they faced in the United States. They lived there for five years. When they returned to the United

Often overshadowed by her brilliant husband, Eslanda Goode Robeson had a distinguished career as an opponent of racism, colonialism, and all forms of oppression. In 1951 she was one of three protesters who disrupted the United Nations' postwar conference on genocide to argue, unsuccessfully, that ending vigilante violence against African Americans should be a part of the group's agenda. (SCHOMBURG CENTER)

States in 1963, the Vietnam War was under way. Eslanda did not hesitate to immediately speak out against the war and in support of the growing peace movement. It was one of her last acts of political defiance. Two years later, in 1965, she died of cancer.

BARBARA RANSBY

Robinson, Bernice (1914–1994)

Bernice Robinson was an educator and activist during the civil rights movement in the American South. She served as the first teacher in the citizenship school program developed in the South Carolina Sea Islands in the late 1950s. This program eventually spread across the South and was responsible for encouraging thousands of black Americans to register to vote in the early 1960s, changing the political face of the South.

Robinson was born in Charleston, South Carolina, on February 7, 1914. Her father, James Christopher Robinson, a bricklayer, was a union organizer, although his daughter did not know this until she became an activist herself many years later. Her mother, Martha Elizabeth Anderson Robinson, was a seamstress and homemaker. Both parents taught their children to be self-reliant and, in particular, to avoid relying on the white community. This would be an important factor for Robinson when she became politically active.

Finishing high school in the segregated system in Charleston, Robinson hoped to pursue studies in music. She decided to live with her sister in New York City and work in order to earn tuition for a music conservatory in Boston. Over the next ten years she held a variety of jobs in New York City in the garment industry, as a beautician, and in civil service. In 1947, when her parents became ill, she postponed her hope of entering the conservatory and returned to Charleston. By this time she had married and divorced and was raising a daughter, Jacquelyn, on her own.

Her time in New York heightened her awareness of racial discrimination and injustice, and when she returned to South Carolina, she became active in the NAACP and the YWCA, working on the issues of job discrimination and political disenfranchisement. In 1954, an aunt, **Septima Clark,** invited Robinson to attend a workshop at the **Highlander Folk School** in Tennessee.

The workshop experience was a pivotal one. There she worked with another South Carolina low country leader, Esau Jenkins, who spoke of the need for an adult education class to help rural black residents learn basic literacy skills in order to pass the voter registration test. The Highlander Folk School and Jenkins joined forces to begin the citizenship education program in the Sea Islands. Septima Clark became director of the program, and Robinson was asked to be the first teacher.

Reluctant at first, she eventually agreed, acknowledging that as an independent person (a beautician who did not rely on white customers) and as someone not wedded to formal ideas about teaching, she could play an important role in this unusual school. She told the students, "I'm really not going to be your teacher. We're going to work together and teach each other." Robinson and Clark built the curriculum for the adult classes around the specific needs and interests of the students. The schools were so popular they spread quickly throughout the Sea Islands. As word of them spread, requests came in from across the South for literacy classes aimed at political empowerment and for the training of teachers like themselves. The citizenship school program became the prototype for the Southern voter education program that was eventually taken over by the Southern Christian Leadership Conference (SCLC).

Robinson spent the 1960s and 1970s as a civil rights activist and teacher. She worked first at Highlander, and later for SCLC. She traveled the South, providing workshops on political empowerment. When she returned to live in Charleston, she was urged to run for the state legislature in 1972. Though unsuccessful, she remained active in local politics and community affairs. She served on Highlander's board of directors for many years. She was honored with a distinguished service award from the NAACP and from the Black Caucus of the South Carolina State Legislature.

Bernice Robinson died in September of 1994 in Charleston, South Carolina.

CANDIE CARAWAN

As a professor of English at Alabama State College and as president of the Women's Political Council of Montgomery, civil rights activist Jo Ann Robinson was an influential and leading figure in the Montgomery Bus Boycott of 1955–56.

Robinson, Jo Ann Gibson (1912–)

As president in the early 1950s of the **Women's Political Council (WPC) of Montgomery, Alabama,** Jo Ann Gibson Robinson was one of several crucial initiators of the Montgomery Bus Boycott of 1955–56. Robinson was an influential and leading figure both during the two years of black civic activism leading up to the boycott and as a major player in the significant events that transformed the arrest of **Rosa Parks** into a communitywide protest movement.

Jo Ann Gibson was born near Culloden, Georgia, on April 17, 1912, the youngest of twelve children. Educated in the segregated public schools of Macon and then at Fort Valley State College, she became a public school teacher in Macon, where she was briefly married to Wilbur Robinson. After their one child died in infancy, Robinson left Macon after five years of teaching and went to Atlanta, where she earned an M.A. in English at Atlanta University. In the fall of 1949, after teaching one year at Mary Allen College in Crockett, Texas, Robinson accepted a position at Alabama State College. She was a professor of English at Alabama State throughout the boycott.

In Montgomery she joined both the Dexter Avenue Baptist Church and the WPC, which had been founded three years earlier by another Alabama State English professor, **Mary Fair Burks.** At Christmastime in 1949, Robinson endured a deeply humiliating experience at the hands of an abusive and racist Montgomery City Lines bus driver, and she resolved then and there that the WPC would target racial seating practices on Montgomery buses. Many other black citizens had had similar experiences, and for the next several years the WPC repeatedly asked city authorities to improve racial seating practices and address the conduct of abusive bus drivers. In May 1954, more than eighteen months before the arrest of Rosa Parks, but just several days after news of the U.S. Supreme Court's *Brown* v. *Board of Education* decision began to sweep the country, Robinson wrote to Montgomery's mayor as WPC president, gently threatening a black boycott of city buses if abuses were not curtailed.

Following Rosa Parks' arrest in December 1955, Robinson played a central role in beginning the protest by immediately producing the leaflets that spread word of the hoped-for boycott among the black citizens of Montgomery. She became one of the most active board members of the Montgomery Improvement Association, the new black community group created to lead the boycott, but she remained out of the limelight in order to protect her teaching position at Alabama State as well as those of her colleagues. In 1960, Robinson left Alabama State (and Montgomery), as did other activist faculty members.

After teaching one year at Grambling College in Grambling, Louisiana, Robinson moved to Los Angeles, where she taught English in the public schools until her retirement in 1976 and where she was active in a number of women's community groups. Robinson's health suffered a serious decline just as her memoir, *The Montgomery Bus Boycott and the Women Who Started It,* was published in 1987. She was honored by a 1989 publication prize given by the Southern Association for Women Historians, but was unable to accept the award in person.

DAVID J. GARROW

S

Shabazz, Betty (1936–)

Betty Shabazz, the widow of Malcolm X (El Hajj Malik El Shabazz, the Black Muslim civil rights leader assassinated in 1965), has definite goals for carrying on the work for which her husband lived and died. Shabazz devotes her time to black community affairs in the areas of health, child care, and education.

Born May 28, 1936, in Detroit, Michigan, she attended Tuskegee Institute, Brooklyn State Hospital School of Nursing (R.N.), and Jersey City State College (Certified School Nurse and B.A. Public Health Education). She has certification in early childhood education and completed a thesis on sickle-cell anemia for her master's degree in public health administration, and then completed a Ph.D. in education administration at the University of Massachusetts at Amherst. She is the mother of six children.

Shabazz shows a strong interest in education and children and devotes her time to improving conditions for the disadvantaged. She is a volunteer in early childhood education and on the Sickle-Cell Telethon Advisory Board, and performs local PTA work in a high school for pregnant students. Shabazz has served as director of the African-American Foundation, the Women's Service League, and the Day Care Council of Westchester County, and she is a trustee of the National Housewives League. She is a member of the board of education of the Union Free School (District 13) and is cochair of the advisory board of the *Amsterdam News* in New York City.

She has worked as a university instructor, community activist, and registered nurse. She has served as chair of the forty-first **National Council of Negro Women** Convention in New York City. At Mount Holyoke College in South Hadley, Massachusetts, a cultural center has been named in her honor. She remains active in **Delta Sigma Theta** sorority.

She is currently director of communications and public relations at Medgar Evers College of the City University of New York.

LAVONNE ROBERTS-JACKSON

Simkins, Modjeska (1899–1992)

"I cannot be bought and I will not be sold!" These words of Mary Modjeska Monteith Simkins characterize the bold, outspoken, and defiant stance that the human rights activist claimed for herself. Born in Columbia, South Carolina, on December 5, 1899, Modjeska Simkins, as she was popularly known, lived for ninety-two years, during which she became legendary in her hometown, native state, and beyond for the role she played in furthering the cause of justice and equality among all peoples.

Henry Clarence Monteith and Rachel Evelyn Hull Monteith were a prosperous married couple who decided to make a secure home for the large family they planned; much to their joy, their first child was a daughter, whom they named both for Rachel's younger sister, Mary Ellen, and for a favorite Polish actress, Helena Modjeska. To provide the best family life possible, the couple purchased a farm on

Named for Polish actress Helena Modjeska, Modjeska Simkins was prepared by her upbringing, with its emphasis on education, racial pride, and activism, for a public career. An activist for more than six decades, she worked with over fifty progressive reform organizations to advance the struggle for human and civil rights in the United States. (BARBARA WOODS)

the outskirts of Columbia so that Modjeska and their other seven children could grow and develop into women and men with few distractions from outside influences.

Modjeska's mother, a public school teacher, exposed her daughter to culture and erudition to the greatest possible extent. The young girl was taken to church and given a leadership role; she was taught the rudiments of reading, writing, and mathematics before she entered grade school; and she was exposed to music, to cultural affairs and education, to drama and the social graces, to all that a nineteenth-century mother thought would refine a little girl into a Southern lady, replete with the charms and eloquence that would make her the choice of a fine Southern gentleman when it came time for her to marry.

The Monteith home was filled with various reading materials, both on classical subjects and on worldly affairs. This inspired the children to read and explore the world outside their home, to open their minds to problems that lay outside of Columbia, South Carolina, and even America. Her younger siblings looked to Modjeska for guidance and for an example in academic pursuits. She was placed into the second grade upon enrollment at Benedict College, for she had been so well trained that she was head and shoulders above the other young children her age who were entering the school. (Benedict College, like many private black institutions of higher education in this period, offered quality primary and secondary curriculums in addition to college courses in order to provide the education denied black Americans in segregated public schools.) Modjeska excelled in mathematics and decided to become a mathematics teacher after she graduated from the college course.

A few months after she received an A.B. degree in 1921, Monteith started teaching in the teacher-training department of Benedict; the next year she found employment in the elementary division of Booker T. Washington School in Columbia. Two years later she was assigned to teach mathematics at the school. She maintained this position until December 1929, when she married Andrew Whitfield Simkins, and had to resign because married women were not allowed to teach in the city's schools. By 1931, she had found employment at the South Carolina Tuberculosis Association as the agency's first Director of Negro Work. This position lasted until 1942, when she was released because of her involvement in civil rights activities. Before she retired, she worked at Victory Savings Bank in Columbia, where she held various positions, including heading a bank branch and serving on the board of directors.

The historical and familial circumstances into which Modjeska was born and reared—including an emphasis on education, racial uplift, and activism—prepared her for a public career. Columbia was the state's capital and the seat of two private black colleges, Benedict College and Allen University. Within forty miles, there were three other black colleges, Morris College in Sumter, and Clafin College and South Carolina State College in Orangeburg. Living in the center of black higher education in the state prompted her to complete graduate studies. She attended Columbia University in New York, the University of Michigan at Ann Arbor, and Michigan State Normal School (now Eastern Michigan University). This commitment to education was in harmony with the Monteiths' family heritage of participation in racial uplift projects, and she continued the tradition. Moreover, older relatives, particularly her mother and two maternal aunts, Rebecca Walton and Mayme Dunmore, were active in the Columbia branch of the **National Association for the Advancement of Colored People** (NAACP), and they brought Modjeska into the organization.

In the 1930s, Modjeska Simkins was active with the Civil Welfare League, a local organization that sought improved municipal conditions for black residents in Columbia, including securing better housing, ending police brutality, and regaining the franchise. Also, she worked diligently with the Columbia branch of the NAACP as publicity director, and she took part in the founding meeting of the South Carolina Conference of Branches of NAACP in 1939.

Perhaps her greatest public work during the 1940s and 1950s was with the South Carolina NAACP. From the outset, she worked as corresponding secretary; in 1941, she was elected as head of the publicity committee and a member of the speakers' bureau. In 1942, she was elected state secretary, a position she held until 1957. During the period in which she held elective office, the South Carolina NAACP launched several court cases to establish equality for black Americans, and Simkins was at the heart of these proceedings. They won their first lawsuits, for equalization of teachers' salaries, in Charleston in 1944 and in Columbia in 1945. The NAACP set up a Teachers Defense Fund, and Simkins

"I cannot be bought and I will not be sold!" These words of Modjeska Simkins characterize the bold, defiant, and outspoken nature of this longtime activist, a major figure in South Carolina history. (BARBARA WOODS)

was secretary of this project. Then, with *Elmore* v. *Rice* in 1947 and *Brown* v. *Baskins* in 1948, the South Carolina NAACP dismantled the all-white primary. The most significant lawsuit in which Simkins played a major role was the NAACP lawsuit to end segregation in South Carolina's public schools and, ultimately, the nation's public schools. *Briggs* v. *Elliott* was filed in federal district court in May 1950, the initial hearing before a three-judge court was held in May 1951, and it later became the first of five cases to be decided by the U.S. Supreme Court as *Brown* v. *Board of Education* in May 1954.

Simkins was active in many organizations that fought racism and injustice on local, regional, and national levels in voter registration, education, and health care. In the mid-1940s, she worked with the Columbia Women's Council and with the Richland County Citizens Committee; both were political action groups. She participated in regional organizations such as the Commission on Interracial Cooperation, the Southern Regional Council, the Southern Conference for Human Welfare, the Southern Organizing Committee for Economic and Social Justice, and the Southern Negro Youth Congress. At the national level, she was a member of the Civil Rights Congress, the National Negro Congress, and the United Negro and Allied Veterans of America.

Her work with political parties spanned more than half a century. Her activities in the early years were tied to the national Republican Party; in 1948 she was named to the National Convention Committee on Permanent Organization from South Carolina. She became disenchanted with the Republicans during this period because many politicians who had disapproved of President Harry Truman and Democrats' support of civil rights moved into the Republican Party, and later, she changed party affiliation. Simkins never was a strict one-party person even so. In 1948, she supported Henry Wallace's candidacy for the U.S. presidency. In South Carolina, she also supported two predominantly black third-party platforms, the Progressive Democratic Party in the 1940s and the United Citizens Party in the 1970s. Her involvement in politics led her to run for public office four times, but she was never elected.

Because of her work with more than fifty progressive reform organizations over a period of six decades, Modjeska Simkins is a major figure in South Carolina history and a major figure in women's history. She was a steadfast, persistent, and courageous activist in the struggle for human rights in the United States.

She received many honors in her lifetime, including being awarded the highest commendation given by her home state, the Order of the Palmetto. The Columbia branch of the NAACP named a scholarship for her—the Modjeska Simkins Scholarship Award. In 1980, the Modjeska Simkins

Endowment Fund was established "to make small grants to non-profit organizations whose grass-roots activities in South Carolina exemplify Mrs. Simkins's spirit and work on behalf of human rights, social dignity, and economic justice." The American Civil Liberties Union of South Carolina Foundation is a trustee of this fund. At Benedict College, the research archives have been named in her honor to keep her memory alive.

She died on May 15, 1992. After her death the Columbia branch of the NAACP established the Modjeska Simkins Scholarship Award.

BARBARA WOODS

Simmons, Althea T. L.   (1924–1990)

Civil rights activist Althea Simmons was born in Shreveport, Louisiana, on April 17, 1924, to Lillian Littleton Simmons and M. M. Simmons. She attended Southern University in New Orleans, from which she received a B.S. with honors. From there she went to the University of Illinois at Urbana, earning a master's degree in marketing, and then to **Howard University**, where she received a law degree.

After graduation from law school, Simmons went to work for the W. J. Durman law office in Dallas, Texas. She soon became active in the **National Association for the Advancement of Colored People (NAACP)**, first serving as a volunteer and later as a paid staff person. She was executive secretary of the Texas State Conference of NAACP branches and chairperson of the executive committee of the Dallas branch. She then moved to Los Angeles as a field secretary. From 1964 to 1974, she was secretary for training for the entire country, developing handbooks and setting up training sessions, coordinating the entire massive educational program of the NAACP at that time.

When the 1964 Civil Rights Act passed, Simmons was director of the NAACP's National Voter Registration Drive. She also went to Mississippi to help teach black citizens how to use the new law.

In 1979, Simmons became chief lobbyist for the NAACP in Washington, D.C. Her position was an enormously important one, as she worked to persuade legislators to pass laws that would give black Americans justice and opportunity. Her predecessor in the job, Clarence Mitchell, was legendary. "I recall quite vividly when Mr. [Benjamin] Hooks took me to the White House to introduce me to President Carter," she said in an interview for *I Dream a World*. "The president said, 'Miss Simmons, you've got some very big shoes to fill.' And I said respectfully, 'Mr. President, nobody can fill Clarence Mitchell's shoes. I'll have to walk in my own footsteps.' "

Simmons' own footsteps turned out to be legendary as well. She became one of the most effective lobbyists in Washington, playing a crucial part in the 1982 extension of the Voting Rights Act, sanctions against South Africa, and the naming of a national holiday to honor Dr. Martin Luther King, Jr.

Althea T. L. Simmons died in September 1990 in Washington, D.C.

KATHLEEN THOMPSON

Sister Souljah (1964–)

Taken in context, the line was not that dramatic. Talking about the hard-pressed people who took part in the Los Angeles riots after the Rodney King trial, Sister Souljah (also known as Lisa Williams) said, "I mean, if black people kill black people every day, why not have a week and kill white people?" That remark, quoted by Bill Clinton during his presidential campaign, sparked a nationwide uproar. Whites were upset about the implied violence of the statement. Blacks were upset because once again, whites failed to hear the essential point that was being made. Sister Souljah seized the opportunity before the national press to say a lot more.

Souljah was born in the Bronx in 1964, the second of four children. Her father was a truckdriver who lost his job after being diagnosed with epilepsy. Her mother was a housewife at the time. Her father began having emotional problems after losing his position, and her mother left him while Souljah was a child. The family had to go on welfare and move into a housing project.

The family attempted to stay united and spiritually connected, even while living in a dangerous situation. Souljah's great-grandmother was the pastor of the church they attended. Her mother found work, and the family eventually got out of the project, but Souljah never forgot her experiences there.

Souljah was a gifted and competitive student. She attended Cornell University's advanced summer placement program and went to Spain with a project from the University of Salamanca. After high school graduation she attended Rutgers University, where she was active in demonstrations and developed her skill at public speaking. While at Rutgers, she majored in

African studies and American history, but she left school just one semester before graduating.

While still in college, Souljah founded the African Youth Survival Camp, a program for homeless children, located in Enfield, North Carolina. This program was run in cooperation with the United Church of Christ. When the church organization relocated to Cleveland, Souljah was invited to move with them. Instead, she decided to stay in New York and take a job as vice president with a small, independent, black-owned record label.

Souljah had learned music production skills by producing benefits for political causes. With her new job at the recording company she began to match production skills with marketing and creative skills. She saw music as a way to educate and reach young black people, the way that political speeches or rallies could reach older people. She combined her interests when she brought out a rap album of her own, titled *360 Degrees of Power*. It was released in 1990.

The album was not a critical or commercial success, but Souljah became known as a spokesperson for the new generation. Rap music as a whole was receiving heavy criticism at the time. While Souljah was not as confrontational as other rap artists, the public was not used to hearing radical political rap from a woman. Souljah was comfortable on television and radio talk shows as well. She was quick in debate and did not pull her punches. The quote that caused the controversy appeared in the *Washington Post*.

The statement came out during an election year. Some speculated that Clinton seized on the remark because he needed to distance himself from black militants during his presidential campaign. He chose to criticize Souljah while speaking at a convention of Jesse Jackson's Rainbow Coalition. The Coalition had asked Souljah to speak at the same convention, and Clinton criticized them for giving her time at the podium.

This was not an entirely fair criticism of the Rainbow Coalition, Souljah, or her statements. It was true that she was both radical and outspoken. She was not fond of white people, but little in her experience

Sister Souljah says "I see my role as a person who places pressure on white America. There are a lot of African people throughout the world who would love to, but they have no idea how to go about doing that. I'll do that, and by doing that, it may make it easier for somebody else."

had given her reason to like them. At times Souljah said things that were not well thought out. On the other hand, she was a young voice who could criticize the establishment and even bring her black elders to task. The Rainbow Coalition wanted to reach out to young people and wanted to reach out to women. It was willing to brave her criticism in the interests of hearing what the younger generation had to say.

The subsequent publicity was particularly good for Souljah the activist. She welcomed the public debate. She said, "I see my role as a challenger. I see my role as a person who places pressure on white America. There are a lot of African people throughout the world who would love to, but they have no idea how to go about doing that. I'll do that, and by doing that, it may make it easier for somebody else."

Souljah followed up this controversy by putting out an even more controversial music video titled "Slavery's Back in Effect." The video showed black people being enslaved once again in the United States. Again, this was no mild statement, but writers had written novels postulating the possibility that different groups—including women—might be enslaved after a conservative backlash in the United States. These other writers became part of a serious debate in the press. Souljah just drew criticism.

In 1994, Souljah's first book, *No Disrespect,* was published by Random House. It was an autobiography and took the reader on an emotional roller-coaster concerning her upbringing and search for relationships. In many ways she spoke for the chaos and confusion of a young girl under pressure. While a novelist might have gathered praise for a tough rendition of a young, black life with its assets and errors, *No Disrespect* did not win praise as an autobiography. Nevertheless, a lot of young people could probably relate to exactly these situations.

It may be unfair to hold Souljah to account as a fully matured, well-rounded, political thinker. She is young, intelligent, and fiery. These are her gifts. She can also reject wise counsel, get into situations that she does not know how to manage, and substitute politics for common sense. These are her flaws. One hopes that her political insights will continue to grow and mature, since she clearly has something important to contribute to her people, her country, and the world.

ANDRA MEDEA

Sloan, Edith Barksdale (1940–)

Edith Barksdale Sloan was a champion of the rights of domestic workers and consumers.

Sloan was born on November 29, 1940, and grew up in the Bronx, the daughter of Odell Barksdale and Elizabeth Watts Barksdale. Her father was a postal worker and electrician, and her mother was a buyer and homemaker. She was one of six children.

Sloan's parents were not prosperous, but they made sure their children were exposed to the cultural advantages of New York. The Barksdales brought up their children with cultured tastes and took them to lectures by the great black leaders of the day. As a child, Sloan met such famous figures as **Mary McLeod Bethune** and Eleanor Roosevelt.

Sloan completed high school at the age of sixteen. Many of her high school teachers were openly racist, and black students were often subjected to mistreatment. She went on to Hunter College, where treatment was more fair. At Hunter she thrived. She went to Europe while still in college, which opened her eyes to the joys of travel. When she graduated in 1959 at the age of 19, she was ready to play an active role in the world.

Sloan applied both to the Peace Corps and to the World Council Mission for assignments overseas. She had to turn down a Peace Corps assignment to Ghana because she had just accepted an offer from the World Council Mission to join a work camp program in Lebanon. Lebanon was fascinating in itself, but a side trip to Egypt put her in touch with her roots. Experiencing Egypt, she realized she belonged to a race of world leaders.

Sloan briefly returned to New York before accepting a Peace Corps assignment in the Philippines. She was reluctant at first, thinking the Philippines were too Americanized. Once she arrived in the Philippines, she realized that American influence was found merely on the surface, and the true, rich culture survived. Among the people, Sloan taught school and worked to help disfigured children.

In 1963, while living in Western Leyte, she received two pieces of news that changed her life. President Kennedy had been killed, and four little black girls had been killed in a church bombing in the South. Sloan decided then to go back to the United States and fight for what was right in her own country.

Back in New York, Sloan spent a year as a human rights intern at the Eleanor Roosevelt Memorial Foundation. She was assigned to the New York Urban League, where she worked on housing code violations and assisted in voter registration for the 1964 general election.

In 1965, Sloan moved to Washington D.C., where she took a government post as public information specialist for the U.S. Commission on Civil Rights, helping private groups plan programs to further civil rights. In 1967, she served as assistant manager of the National Conference on Race, a position that included preparing White House statements on civil rights.

In 1971, Sloan became Executive Director of the National Committee on Household Employment. Domestic workers were still underpaid, underinsured, and underrespected. The going rate for domestic workers in large parts of the South was as little as fifty cents an hour. There was no union, no job security, and no respect. Domestic workers were reluctant to organize, but they were tired of being treated with widespread disrespect. For the first time they began to organize and demand what they deserved. As Sloan exhorted them, "The next time somebody calls you Sally or John, tell them your name is Miss Sally or Mr. John. And if somebody calls you Auntie, ask them, 'Which of my sister's children are you?' "

In the summer of 1971, the first conference of the National Household Workers was held. It received national television coverage and made the Sunday front page of the *New York Times*. Still, legal protection for domestic workers was not easily gained. The first bill to ensure fair wages and hours for domestic workers was vetoed by President Nixon in 1973. Then Sloan lobbied George Meany, the union leader, to back their cause. The balance was tipped in 1973, when Meany insisted that unless household workers were included in the minimum wage act, there would be no minimum wage act for that year.

With this victory won, the momentum of the movement started to ebb. In 1976, Sloan turned her attention to consumer rights when she became the director of the District of Columbia's Office of Consumer Protection. She held this post for two years. In 1978, she was asked by President Carter to be a commissioner for the Consumer Product Safety Commission. This was a five-year appointment that carried her into the Reagan administration. When her commission ended in 1983, Sloan decided to leave politics.

Sloan became a lawyer with the firm of Fortas, Porkop and Hardman. She then left law to enter the Wesley Theological Seminary, where she was a divinity student from 1989 to 1993.

Smith-Robinson, Ruby Doris
(1942–1967)

Ruby Doris Smith-Robinson worked with the **Student Nonviolent Coordinating Committee** (SNCC) from its earliest days in 1960 until her death in October 1967. She served the organization as an activist in the field and as an administrator in the Atlanta central office. She eventually succeeded Jim Forman as SNCC's executive secretary; Ruby Smith-Robinson was the only woman ever to serve in this capacity. Her SNCC colleagues realized how important she was. SNCC freedom singer Matthew Jones recalled, "You could feel her power in SNCC on a daily basis." Smith-Robinson demanded hard work and dedication from everyone around her. Jack

Minnis, a member of SNCC's research staff, insisted that people could not fool her. Minnis was convinced that she had a "100 percent effective shit detector."

This hard-nosed administrator and legendary activist was born in Atlanta, Georgia, on April 25, 1942, and she spent her childhood in Atlanta's black Summerhill neighborhood. She was the second oldest of seven children born to Alice and J. T. Smith. The Smith children lived a comfortable existence in their separate black world. They had strong adult support, and they had their own churches, schools, and social activities. No matter how insulated they were, however, the reality of American racism and segregation intruded from time to time. Smith-Robinson recalled her feelings about segregation in those early years. "I was conscious of my blackness. Every young Negro growing up in the South has thoughts about the racial situation." She also remembered her reaction to the white people she came in contact with when she was a youngster. "I didn't recognize their existence, and they didn't recognize mine. . . . My only involvement was in throwing rocks at them."

In this atmosphere young Ruby, like many young black Americans of her generation, became convinced that change was possible. A few years later, when Ruby Smith entered **Spelman College**, she quickly became involved in the Atlanta student movement. She regularly picketed and protested with her colleagues who were trying to integrate Atlanta, and she soon moved from the local scene to the national arena. As early as February 1961, she became involved in activities sponsored by the fledgling SNCC. She was a bold and daring colleague, the creator of SNCC's "jail no bail" policy and one of the original Freedom Riders.

Because of her attitude and her actions, Ruby Doris Smith-Robinson soon became a legend. Most early SNCC members could recount at least one Ruby Smith-Robinson story. For example, Julian Bond remembered that when a delegation of SNCC staff was preparing to board a plane for Africa in the fall of 1964, an airline representative told them the plane was overbooked and asked if they would wait and take a later flight. This angered Ruby Smith-Robinson so much that without consulting the rest of the group she went and sat down in the jetway and refused to move. They were given seats on that flight. The innovative and determined spirit displayed in her activism was also part of her administrative demeanor. By 1963, she had become a full-time member of the central office staff. Then, in 1966, she was elected to the post of executive secretary. Throughout this period Ruby Smith-Robinson devoted an enormous amount of attention to SNCC, but there was another part to her life as well. She married Clifford Robinson in 1964, and they had a son, Kenneth Toure Robinson, in 1965. In the meantime, she managed to graduate from Spelman with a bachelor's degree in physical education.

Because of her talent and commitment, Ruby Smith-Robinson was able to juggle all of these demanding roles—for a time. By January 1967, however, her health began to decline precipitously. At that time she was admitted to a hospital. In April of that year she was diagnosed with terminal cancer. She died on October 9, 1967.

CYNTHIA GRIGGS FLEMING

Somerville, Vada Watson (1885–1972)

As a civil rights activist and health care professional, Vada Watson Somerville was a leader in the African-American community in Los Angeles, California, for nearly fifty years. As a member of a new generation of professional elites—whose leadership supplanted that of the pioneering black families—she crafted myriad organizations and strategies that shaped black Los Angeles' response to racial discrimination.

The child of migrants from Arkansas, Somerville was born in Pomona, California, on November 1, 1885. After attending public schools, Somerville won an academic scholarship from the *Los Angeles Times* in 1903 that allowed her to enroll at the University of Southern California. After leaving the university prior to graduating, from 1906 until 1912 Somerville worked as a telephone operator and bookkeeper. In 1912, she married dentist John Somerville, who encouraged her interest in dentistry. She went back to college, and in 1918, Somerville received a D.D.S. degree from the University of Southern California, practicing until 1930 when she "retired to devote her time to social welfare and civic work." In 1927, Vada and John Somerville built the Hotel Somerville, an elegant, all-black hostelry that symbolized both the possibilities of racial advancement and the realities of racial segregation.

The Somerville home was at the center of much of the reform and political activities of black Los Angeles. Vada Somerville was one of the founders of the Los Angeles branch of the **National Association for the Advancement of Colored People** (NAACP) in 1913, the Los Angeles chapter of the **National Council of Negro Women** in 1938, and the Los Angeles County Human Relations Committee in 1948. Her commitment to better health care for African-American women led Somerville to establish the Pilgrim House Community Center, to service the health needs of black families who migrated to Los Angeles during World War II, and to support the creation of black women's service organizations like **The Links** and the **Alpha Kappa Alpha** Sorority. To foster interracial cooperation, Somerville created the Stevens House of the University of California at Los Angeles, a multiracial dormitory that she hoped would prove that a new order of race relations was possible. Vada Somerville died in Los Angeles on October 28, 1972.

LONNIE BUNCH

Student Nonviolent Coordinating Committee

African-American women activists played a major role in the founding and development of the Student Nonviolent Coordinating Committee (SNCC). **Ella Baker** (1903–86), director of the Atlanta headquarters of the Southern Christian Leadership Conference (SCLC), organized the April 1960 conference in Raleigh, North Carolina, that resulted in the formation of SNCC. A strong advocate of group-centered rather than leader-centered organizations, Baker encouraged student protesters attending the conference to form their own organization rather than become the student arm of SCLC or other existing civil rights groups. During its first months of existence, SNCC's operations were conducted in a

corner of SCLC headquarters, and the fledgling organization made use of Baker's extensive contacts with black activists throughout the South. Baker remained an advisor to SNCC through the mid-1960s, consistently arguing for organizing strategies that emphasized the nurturing of grass-roots leaders in areas where SNCC established projects.

Women who were active in the lunch counter sit-in movement of 1960 led in the transformation of SNCC from a coordinating office into a cadre of militant activists dedicated to expanding the civil rights movement throughout the South. In February 1961, **Diane Nash** (1938–   ) and **Ruby Doris Smith** (1942–67) were among four SNCC members who joined the Rock Hill, South Carolina, desegregation protests, which featured the jail-no-bail tactic—demonstrators serving their jail sentences rather than accepting bail. In May 1961, Nash led a group of student activists to Alabama in order to sustain the Freedom Rides after the initial group of protesters organized by the Congress of Racial Equality (CORE) encountered mob violence in Birmingham. During May and June, Nash, Smith, and other student freedom riders traveled on buses from Montgomery to Jackson, Mississippi, where they were swiftly arrested and imprisoned. In August, when veterans of the sit-ins and the Freedom Rides met to discuss SNCC's future, Baker helped to avoid a damaging split by suggesting separate direct-action and voter-registration wings. Nash became the leader of the direct-action wing of SNCC.

During the period from 1961 to 1964, as SNCC established a staff of full-time office workers and field secretaries, women continued to play a central role in the organization. While Nash's activity in SNCC declined after her marriage to SCLC organizer James Bevel and the birth of their first child, Smith's role in the organization increased. In 1962, Smith (later Smith-Robinson) left her position as executive secretary of the Atlanta student movement to become the full-time Southern campus coordinator for SNCC. The following year, she became SNCC's administrative secretary and then its executive secretary. She remained one of SNCC's most forceful administrators until her death in 1967 from a rare form of cancer. Other African-American women served on SNCC's office staff or in its support network, including Roberta Yancy, Smith's successor as Southern campus coordinator, Norma Collins, Judy Richardson, Jean Wheeler Smith, Lenora Tate, and Carol Merritt.

SNCC's community organizing projects involved many African-American women. In Georgia, Albany Movement participants **Bernice Johnson Reagon** (1942–), Ruth Harris, and Bertha Gober became members of SNCC's Freedom Singers. In August 1962, Prathia Hall (1940–) left Temple University to join SNCC's southwest Georgia project. Boston native Peggy Dammond also worked in southwest Georgia. **Gloria Richardson** (Dandridge) sustained a protest movement in Cambridge, Maryland. Hall, Martha Norman, Annie Pearl Avery, Colia LaFayette, Ruth Howard, and Fay Bellamy (1938–) played important roles in SNCC's voting rights campaign in Alabama.

Many African-American women were active in SNCC's voting rights campaign in Mississippi. These included Victoria Jackson Gray (1937–) of Hattiesburg, who ran in the 1964 Democratic primary to represent Mississippi in the U.S. Senate and later ran for Congress on the **Mississippi Freedom Democratic Party** (MFDP) ticket. Muriel Tillinghast, a former **Howard University** student, served as SNCC's project director in Greenville and later worked under Ruby Smith-Robinson in Atlanta. Another Howard student, Cynthia Washington, also served as a project director in Mississippi. Dorrie and **Joyce Ladner** first became active in their hometown of Hattiesburg. Other SNCC activists and organizers in Mississippi included Brenda Travis, Mary Lane, Dona Richards, Janet Jemmott (Moses), Amanda Purdew, **Eleanor Holmes (Norton)**, Freddye Greene, Gloria House, Doris Derby, Helen O'Neal, June Johnson, Ruth Howard (Chambers), and Emma Bell.

The best known of the local leaders who were drawn into the struggle by SNCC's organizing efforts was **Fannie Lou Hamer** (1917–77), a native of Ruleville, Mississippi. In 1962, after attending a SNCC meeting, Hamer attempted to register to vote and was promptly evicted from the plantation where she worked. After enduring a beating in jail, Hamer became a SNCC field secretary and, in 1964, ran for Congress as a candidate of the MFDP. Hamer received national attention in August 1964, when she testified about her beating before the credentials committee of the Democratic National Convention as part of an effort to unseat the regular Mississippi delegation to the convention. Hamer and other MFDP delegates rejected a compromise that would have given them two at-large seats.

After the convention, SNCC grew increasingly concerned with issues beyond civil rights reform. Reflecting a long-term interest among SNCC workers in Pan-Africanism, a SNCC delegation, including Hamer, Hall, Smith-Robinson, and Richards, toured Africa during fall 1964. Most African-American women in SNCC were initially reluctant to affiliate with the white-dominated women's liberation movement of the late 1960s. Nevertheless, at the November 1964 staff meeting in Waveland, Mississippi, two white SNCC workers, Casey Hayden and Mary King, wrote a controversial paper on the position of women in the group that has since been described as a pioneering statement of the modern women's liberation movement.

During SNCC's Black Power period in the late 1960s, African-American women remained active in the organization's ideological discussions. Ethel Minor edited SNCC's newspaper and worked closely with SNCC chair Stokely Carmichael. The shift in SNCC activities away from sustained community organizing toward Black Power propagandizing was accompanied by increasing male dominance. The Black Women's Liberation Committee, founded by Frances Beal, was one of SNCC's few significant initiatives of the post-1966 period. Beal later was founder of the Third World Women's Alliance. By the early 1970s, external repression and internal ideological conflicts had destroyed the organization's effectiveness.

CLAYBORNE CARSON/HEIDI HESS

T

Terrell, Mary Church (1863–1954)

"A White Woman has only one handicap to overcome—a great one, true, her sex; a colored woman faces two—her sex and her race. A colored man has only one—that of race." This provocative statement was made in 1890 at the National Woman Suffrage Association convention in Washington, D.C., by Mary Eliza Church Terrell, one of the leading twentieth-century black women activists. For more than sixty-six years, she was the ardent champion of racial and gender equality.

Born into the black elite of Memphis, Tennessee, on September 23, 1863, as the Civil War was coming to a close, she was the oldest child of Robert Reed Church and Louisa Ayers. Her early years were spent in Memphis, a city convulsed by violent and bitter racism. Although she was sheltered as much as possible by her parents, who attempted to obliterate any trace of their own slave beginnings, she could not avoid encountering racism when, after her parents' divorce, her mother sent her to school in Ohio. In response to her growing awareness of discrimination, she resolved to excel academically to prove the abilities of African Americans and especially black women. After graduating from **Oberlin College** in 1884, and living with her father for one year, she took a teaching position at Wilberforce University in Ohio and, a year later, at M Street Colored High School in Washington, D.C. It was at the high

school that she met her future husband, Robert H. Terrell.

Between 1888 and 1896, Terrell was faced with two major decisions. First, as an intellectual, she had to decide whether to remain in the United States, where she would not be judged by her abilities but by her race and gender, or to seek a world free of prejudice. Second, as a woman, she had to decide whether to accept the Victorian ideal that a woman's place is in the home. She decided to go to Europe. After two years, she returned to the United States as an advocate of racial elevation.

In 1896, Terrell became the founder and first president of the **National Association of Colored Women** (NACW). Symbolizing unity among black women, this self-help organization offered sisterly support for its members and created programs that addressed racial problems through the elevation of black women. Terrell believed that the amelioration of discrimination was contingent upon "the elevation of black womanhood, thus both struggles are the same."

Aware of the preponderance of black married women in the workforce, Terrell led the NACW in establishing socially progressive institutions such as kindergartens, day nurseries, and Mother Clubs. Mother Clubs functioned as depositories and disseminators of information on rearing children and conducting the home. Terrell's objective was to improve the moral standards of the "less favored and more igno-

Mary Church Terrell is shown here in her wedding gown in 1891. Because her husband also taught at M Street Colored High School, she was required to resign her teaching position there when she was married.

rant sisters," because the world "will always judge the womanhood of the race through the masses of our women."

Because of the contact between Mother Clubs and the masses of women, and the rapid loss of jobs held by black women, Terrell broadened the functions of Mother Clubs to include social as well as economic concerns. She advised directors of Mother Clubs to study the effects of the lack of employment for black men as well as women. In addition, she launched a fundraising campaign to establish schools of domestic science. The NACW also established homes for girls, the aged, and the infirm. It emerged as a leading women's organization, enhancing the lives of the masses and providing a vehicle for the emergence of middle-class women.

From 1896 to 1901, Terrell defined and developed her role as a "New Woman," which resulted in the development of purpose, independence, and vitality in her life. By 1901, Terrell was prepared to function as a leader outside the confines of women's organizations. She began to move from an approach of black self-help to one of interracial understanding, advocating education as the way to this understanding. She hoped that unbiased research and intelligent dissemination of information to both white and black peoples would spark better cooperation.

Terrell's advocacy of advancing the race through improving the lives of black women led to opportunities to comment on broader issues facing her race. She gave numerous speeches highlighting the improved living conditions of black people and their progress in spite of discrimination. In a stirring address delivered in 1904 at the International Congress of Women in Berlin, she vividly described the numerous contributions of the black race. She delivered the speech in German (she spoke three languages fluently), receiving accolades for her depictions of black life and her intellectual abilities. Through her speeches, she became a booster of black morale, as she exhorted her people to improve themselves.

Terrell also wrote articles and short stories on lynching, chain gangs, the peonage system, defection of mulattoes, and the disfranchisement of African Americans. In her writings, she sought to further interracial understanding by educating white people about the realities of black life.

Terrell's actions were undertaken with the same conviction of racial equality that she demonstrated in her writings and speeches. Uncompromising and unequivocal, she never hesitated to criticize Southern white liberals, Northerners, or even members of her own race if she felt that their positions were not in the best interest of humanity. When Republican President Theodore Roosevelt disbanded several companies of black soldiers, she vehemently attacked his decision, despite the fact that her husband owed his federal judgeship to the Republican Party. In an article, "Disbanding of the Colored Soldiers," she asked African Americans to "regard the terrible catastrophe which has filled the whole race with grief as an evil out of which good will eventually come."

The last two decades of her life marked a transition in her position on race relations and politics. Frustrated by the economic hardships of African Americans during the Great Depression and the New Deal era, dismayed by the irony that African Americans were fighting for democracy abroad during World War II but were denied it at home, and grieved by the death of her husband, Terrell became a militant activist, working assiduously to bring a definitive end to discrimination in the United States, particularly in the nation's capital.

Terrell's later life is most noted for leading a three-year struggle to reinstate 1872 and 1873 laws in Washington, D.C., that "required all eating-place proprietors to serve any respectable well-behaved person regardless of color, or face a $1,000 fine and forfeiture of their license," which had disappeared in the 1890s when the District code was written. On February 28, 1950, Terrell, accompanied by two black and one

By the last two decades of her life, Mary Church Terrell had become a militant activist. The most notable achievement of her later life was leading the successful three-year struggle that ended segregation in public eating places in Washington, D.C. (AFRO AMERICAN NEWSPAPER ARCHIVES AND RESEARCH CENTER)

white collaborator, entered Thompson Restaurant, one of several segregated public eating establishments. Thompson refused to serve the black members of the interracial party. Immediately Terrell and her cohorts filed affidavits. The case of *District of Columbia* v. *John Thompson* became a national symbol against segregation in the United States.

Throughout the three-year court struggle, Terrell targeted other segregated facilities. Confronted with the intransigence of proprietors of restaurants, she realized that the earlier weapons of moral suasion and interracial dialogue were incapable of abolishing segregated public facilities. She armed herself with such direct-action tactics as picketing, boycotting, and sit-ins. Finally, on June 8, 1953, the court ruled that segregated eating facilities in Washington, D.C., were unconstitutional.

This ardent fighter for civil rights lived to see the U.S. Supreme Court mandate the desegregation of public schools in *Brown* v. *Board of Education*. Two months later, on July 24, 1954, she died.

BEVERLY JONES

U

Universal African Black Cross Nurses

The Universal African Black Cross Nurses, organized in May 1920, was a female auxiliary of the **Universal Negro Improvement Association** (UNIA). The UNIA, a black nationalist organization, was founded in Jamaica by Marcus Mosiah Garvey in 1914. Black Cross nurses, active members of the UNIA, were trained in their local divisions throughout the United States and internationally by a head nurse or registered nurse. Their aim was to provide services to their local communities and ultimately to prepare for liberation wars in Africa.

Like the Red Cross nurses, these women were primed in first aid and relief measures in case of calamities. They were encouraged to raise funds by giving public lectures and instruction in first aid. They disseminated professional knowledge on safety devices, nutrition, and geriatric care by utilizing pamphlets and a column on the women's page in the *Negro World,* the UNIA's weekly newspaper published in New York. In addition, Black Cross nurses assisted at local hospitals and supported social service agencies.

Though there are photos of children in Black Cross nurse uniforms, only black women between the ages of sixteen and forty-five took a solemn oath to administer medical care and educate their public on health and home care. One of many UNIA auxiliaries, the Black Cross nurses followed protocol and each division elected a president, head nurse, secretary, and treasurer. Often featured in UNIA parades wearing long white robes with an emblem of a black Latin cross on their caps, these women represented the epitome of activists committed to the welfare of their black communities.

ULA TAYLOR

Universal Negro Improvement Association

Marcus Garvey's Universal Negro Improvement Association (UNIA), the grassroots Pan-Africanist organization that began in Jamaica in 1914 and was reconstituted in the United States in 1917–18, is characteristically seen as one manifestation of the post–World War I New Negro movement—a movement in which patterns of racial accommodation were exchanged for resistance, pride, and the proclamation of black manhood. It is less commonly recognized that the UNIA also challenged dominant definitions of black womanhood. Women were an important part of the UNIA, making up at least half of its membership and serving in leadership positions on the local, national, and international levels. Garvey acknowledged that women made up the backbone of the grass-roots movement, but his idealized and patriarchal vision of women dominated the formal affairs of the UNIA. Nevertheless, the thousands of women who participated in the movement effectively broadened the internal debate over what women should do and be.

Garvey's view of women was consistent with his larger nationalist philosophy of racial unity, self-help, and identification with Africa. His poems, notably "The Black Woman" and "The Black Mother," idealized the African woman as a virginal goddess-queen or as the mother who is a source of unconditional support for the son. Garvey used such visions of black womanhood to reverse white-defined standards of beauty and lift black women above white stereotypes of immorality.

Similarly, the UNIA worshiped a black Christ and canonized the Virgin Mary as a black Madonna, countering white images of the Holy Family. While the issue of birth control was debated within the UNIA (with some seeing it as a boon to women and others as genocide), Garvey, a Catholic, denounced it as interference with divine will. At the same time, he criticized single motherhood and exalted the nuclear, patriarchal family, with women in companionate, supportive roles. He credited the UNIA with lifting black women out of domestic service in white homes and into dignified clerical work in UNIA offices and businesses. As with his poetry and religious instruction, his views on women, work, and family addressed the historical separation of black families and workforce exploitation of black women. His ideal of manhood was that black men should protect black womanhood, and chivalry was a prevalent theme in UNIA rhetoric. While he saw the ideal woman's role as that of

wife, Garvey also praised women as leaders in the UNIA and referred to successful women entrepreneurs (**Maggie Lena Walker, Madam C. J. Walker, Annie Malone**) as role models to emulate in building a black economy. He admired **Sojourner Truth** and other black heroines of history. Africa was often given female form in his speeches as a woman in need of rescue and redemption, and as the Motherland.

The UNIA's Declaration of Rights and Constitution defined men's and women's official roles. On the local level, each UNIA division had a general president (male) who oversaw the activities of the division as a whole. Each division also had a woman president, who had authority over the women members and female auxiliaries. Children were divided into separate courses by gender, with girls instructed by women. Female auxiliaries in the UNIA included the Black Cross Nurses, the Motor Corps, and the elite Ladies of the Royal Court of Ethiopia.

Women also played a role in UNIA enterprises, serving on the boards of the Black Star Line and the *Negro World*, and having primary roles as workers and consumers in UNIA restaurant, laundry, hat-making, and dress-making businesses. Women were delegates to the famous UNIA conventions, which also featured women's days and exhibits of women's industrial arts and crafts. Women participated in important organizational rituals, marching in UNIA parades, appearing in pageants and concerts, and singing at UNIA mass meetings. They were frequent contributors to UNIA fundraising projects and owned Black Star Line stock. The *Negro World* newspaper featured columns, letters, articles, poetry, and short stories by women as well as men. Women participated in Garvey's African School of Philosophy, an officer-training course he developed in the 1930s, and held key positions as regional organizers.

Several women were instrumental to Garvey's success as a race leader. **Amy Ashwood,** who later became Garvey's first wife, helped found the UNIA in Jamaica and drew women into the movement as members and benefactors in its early years. Madam C. J. Walker gave money to help Garvey begin the *Negro World* and purchase Liberty Hall, and **Ida B. Wells-Barnett** was a guest speaker for the fledgling organization. **Henrietta Vinton Davis** also lent her fame to the movement in its beginnings, and as International Organizer, traveled on many national and international tours to found or reorganize hundreds of local divisions and to win support for the UNIA's business enterprises. Ashwood was supplanted as UNIA headquarters manager and Garvey's personal assistant by **Amy Jacques,** who became Garvey's second wife. Jacques emerged as a forceful speaker, writer, and administrator and carried out UNIA business according to Garvey's instructions during the years of his imprisonment. She became the movement's premier propagandist, publishing the two-volume *Philosophy and Opinions of Marcus Garvey* (1923, 1925). After Garvey's death, she devoted herself to preserving his name and reputation. M. L. T. De Mena, another great UNIA organizer, followed Davis as the leading female officer in the late 1920s. Daisy Whyte, one of a series of personal secretaries who handled Garvey's affairs, cared for the UNIA leader in his final illness in London in 1940. Ethel Collins emerged

as a local leader in New York and, as UNIA Secretary General, orchestrated the reorganization of the movement after Garvey's death.

Despite women's participation in the UNIA and Garvey's praise of their abilities, their authority in policy and leadership positions remained largely token. Amy Jacques Garvey, for example, never held official office in the organization. Davis was for many years the only woman in any international office; she was also the only woman to participate in UNIA diplomatic delegations. There were no women staff members of the *Negro World* until 1924. Men far outnumbered women as business executives, diplomats, and editors and were generally granted greater status as UNIA employees, officers, and delegates. While all UNIA officials suffered from the organization's lack of financial solvency, women were more likely to be seen as fulfilling a calling or support service and thus less in need of remuneration, promotion, or personal recognition than men. Some women protested this state of affairs: women delegates rose at conventions to demand greater equality, a voice in policy, freedom from male restriction, and access to positions reserved for men. Davis, De Mena, and Jacques all made militant appeals for the recognition of and equal opportunity for women. De Mena wrote in the *Negro World* (1926), "We are sounding the call to all the women in the UNIA to line up for women's rights."

Jacques's "Our Women and What They Think" page, the women's section of the *Negro World,* details the ways in which UNIA women redefined the prevailing standard of womanhood set by Garvey. The women's page offers a full range of opinion, including antifeminism, domestic feminism, and liberal feminism as well as coverage of women in political movements around the world and in racial and party politics, accounts of outstanding black women achievers, articles about women who succeeded in traditionally male professions and businesses, and debates about women's traditional roles as mother, wife, laborer, and homemaker.

BARBARA BAIR

W

Wells-Barnett, Ida B. (1862–1931)

Ida Bell Wells-Barnett was an ardent advocate of African Americans' civil rights, women's rights, and economic rights. Throughout her life, she maintained a fearless devotion to justice, which often placed her in physical danger or social isolation. As a journalist and an activist, Ida B. Wells-Barnett made an indelible mark on the history of the United States and offered a critique of racial, sexual, and economic exploitation that still rings true.

Born on July 16, 1862, in Holly Springs, Mississippi, Ida Bell Wells was the eldest of the eight children of Jim Wells and Lizzie Warrenton. Jim Wells was born in Tippah County, Mississippi, the son of his master and a slave woman, Peggy. He was trained as a carpenter and apprenticed to a white contractor in Holly Springs. Lizzie Warrenton was one of ten children born into slavery in Virginia. Separated from her family and auctioned as a slave for several years, she began working as a cook on the plantation where Jim Wells was employed. They were married not long after and once emancipated, the couple remained in Holly Springs.

Like many black Americans in the post-bellum South, the Wellses ardently believed in education and sent their children to school as early as possible. In 1866, the Freedman's Aid Society established Shaw University in Holly Springs, later renamed Rust College, for freed black students. As an interested father and community activist, Jim Wells became a trustee at Shaw. Lizzie Wells, having no formal education, often accompanied her children to classes so she could learn to read and write.

A yellow fever epidemic swept through Holly Springs in 1878. Jim and Lizzie Wells and their nine-month-old son, Stanley, were among the victims. Another son, Eddie, had died several years before of spinal meningitis. Sixteen-year-old Ida Wells assumed the responsibility of caring for the other five children. Her training at Shaw enabled her to pass the teacher's exam for the county schools and gain employment at a school six miles from her home at a monthly salary of $25. A year later, on the invitation of her mother's sister in Memphis, Tennessee, Wells left Holly Springs. Her paralyzed sister, Eugenia, and two brothers remained behind with relatives. She took the two younger girls with her to Memphis and secured a teaching job in the Shelby County school district at a higher salary than she had earned in Mississippi.

In May 1884, Wells boarded a train owned by Chesapeake and Ohio Railroad and sat down in the ladies' coach. The conductor informed her that he could not take her ticket where she sat and requested that she move to the segregated car. She refused to move. After scuffling with the conductor, she was forcefully removed from the train. In retaliation, she hired a black lawyer and sued the railroad. Disap-

Outrage at the lynching of three friends propelled Ida B. Wells-Barnett into a lifelong battle against racism. In her clearminded, relentless pursuit of justice and equality, she achieved true greatness. (SCHOMBURG CENTER)

pointed with his lack of attention to her case, she hesitantly turned to a white lawyer. She was awarded $500. Victory was bittersweet, however, because the state supreme court reversed the ruling of the lower court.

A prolific reader and debater, she became a member of a lyceum of public school teachers that met on Friday afternoons. After each Friday afternoon pro-

gram, the lyceum closed the meeting with a reading of a weekly newspaper, the *Evening Star.* It reached hundreds and was one of the few sources of communication in the black community. So, when the editor of the paper returned to his position in Washington, D.C., Wells took the editorship. Not long afterward, she also accepted the editorship of the weekly newspaper *Living Way.* Under the pen name "Iola," her weekly column reached mostly rural, uneducated people. She committed the column to writing "in a plain, common-sense way on the things which concerned our people." Her popularity grew, and over the years she contributed articles to local and national publications such as the Memphis *Watchman,* the *New York Age,* the *Indianapolis World,* and the Chicago *Conservator.*

In 1889, she bought one-third interest in the Memphis *Free Speech and Headlight* and later became editor. At first, she spent much of her time writing about the poor conditions of local schools for black children. Wells argued that inadequate buildings and improperly trained teachers contributed to the mediocre education of black children. Conservative black leaders dismissed her argument, and the white school board did not renew her contract for the following year. To financially support herself, Wells began to promote subscriptions for the *Free Speech.* She successfully canvassed and secured subscriptions throughout the Delta region in Mississippi, Arkansas, and Tennessee.

In March 1892, three black male colleagues were lynched. Thomas Moss, Calvin McDowell, and Henry Steward were successful managers of a grocery business in a heavily populated black section just outside Memphis. The owner of a competing white grocery store in the area charged them with conspiracy. News of the indictment spread throughout the black community. The three men and several other black supporters held a meeting and voiced threats against whites. They were arrested and incarcerated. Chaos erupted in the black community. After four days of shooting, Moss, McDowell, and Steward were indicted for inciting a riot and thrown in jail. Later they were removed from the county jail, taken about a mile from the jail, shot, and hanged.

The deaths of Moss, McDowell, and Steward forced Wells to question not only the rationale of lynchers, but also to rethink her own ideas about the reasons for lynching. She, like most Americans, black and white, believed that lynching happened to accused rapists; that is, black men raping white women. Yet the men brutally murdered in Memphis had not been accused of rape. Instead, they were outstanding community citizens whose only crime was economic prosperity. Wells began to investigate cases in which lynch victims were accused of rape. She concluded that lynching was a racist device for eliminating financially independent black Americans.

Wells expressed indignation and outrage that "the city of Memphis has demonstrated that neither character nor standing avails the Negro if he dares to protect himself against the white man or become his rival." Therefore, she urged the black citizens of Memphis to "save our money and leave a town which will neither protect our lives and property, nor give us a fair trial in the courts, when accused by white persons." In addition, she wrote a scathing editorial attacking white female purity and suggested that it was possible for white

Ida B. Wells-Barnett believed that the vote for all African Americans was key to equality. In 1913, she formed the Alpha Suffrage Club, the first black female suffrage club in Illinois. As a delegate to the National American Woman Suffrage Association's suffrage parade in Washington, D.C., that year, Wells-Barnett refused to march with the black delegates, at the back of the procession, and instead joined her white colleagues in the Illinois delegation, thereby integrating the U.S. suffrage movement. (THE JOSEPH REGENSTEIN LIBRARY, THE UNIVERSITY OF CHICAGO)

women to be attracted to black men. The suggestion infuriated the white Memphis community.

When the editorial appeared, Wells was en route to Philadelphia to attend the African Methodist Episcopal Church's general conference. The Free Speech office was destroyed, and threats were made that Wells' life would be in danger should she dare return to Memphis. So Wells went to New York, joined the staff of the New York Age, and continued her exposé on lynching. In October 1892, her thorough investigative research culminated in a feature story, "Southern Horrors: Lynch Law in All Its Phases." The publications and speaking tours on lynching and the plight of African Americans that followed gained her a national audience.

Still, it was international pressure on the United States, she argued, that offered the best means of change for African Americans. She toured England and Scotland, using her investigations as proof of atrocities toward black Americans. Her efforts spawned the growth of several organizations pledged to fight segregation and lynching.

Wells' second tour of England in 1894 became highly controversial when she harshly criticized and denounced the activities of prominent white leaders considered to be supporters of black American causes. Wells argued that these leaders did not take a strong enough stance on lynching and that their silence on the issue sanctioned mob violence. In addition, she maintained that white leaders who addressed racially segregated audiences in effect condoned segregation and discrimination. These people, she concluded, were not friends of black Americans.

The president of the Missouri Press Association, in an effort to discredit Wells, published a letter that denounced the activities of Wells and characterized black women "as having no sense of virtue and altogether without character." It was in part in response to this blatant attack that black women nationwide banded together and formed the **National Association of Colored Women** in 1896.

Wells was also an energetic and strong voice at the Chicago World's Fair in 1893.

She solicited funds and published 20,000 copies of a protest pamphlet, *The Reason Why the Colored American Is Not in the Columbian Exposition,* to publicize the inherent racism of the fair's administration. She remained in Chicago and helped spawn the growth of numerous black female and reform organizations. The Ida B. Wells Club and the Negro Fellowship League were two such associations. She served as president of the Ida B. Wells Club for five years and led the club in the establishment of the first black orchestra in Chicago and in the opening of the first kindergarten for black children.

Wells married Ferdinand Barnett, owner of the *Chicago Conservator,* in 1895. Barnett, a widower with two children, was a strong advocate for black equality. He contributed to her pamphlet *The Reason Why the Colored American Is Not in the Columbian Exposition,* was her strongest supporter, and encouraged her to continue her antilynching and political activities. The couple had four other children, Charles Aked, Herman Kohlsaat, Ida B. Wells, Jr., and Alfreda M. Often traveling with one or more children, she was persistent in speaking to groups about opposition to lynching and other reform activities.

In 1910, Wells opened the Negro Fellowship League to provide lodging, recreation facilities, a reading room, and employment for black migrant males. By the end of the first year, the league boasted of finding employment for 115 black men. Depleting funds, waning public support, and competition, however, limited the continued success of the league. Philanthropic support dwindled, the Young Men's Christian Association for black men opened in 1913, and the Urban League opened its doors in 1916. By the end of the decade, the Negro Fellowship League disbanded altogether.

Her antilynching activities were instrumental in making her one of two black women to sign the call for the formation of the **National Association for the Advancement of Colored People** (NAACP) in 1909. She later broke with the association because of its predominantly white board and because it was timid when confronting racial issues.

She had a strong belief that the vote for all African Americans was the key to reform and economic, social, and political equality. In her 1910 article "How Enfranchisement Stops Lynching," she asserted that if "the constitutional safeguards to the ballot" are swept aside, then "it is the smallest of small matter . . . to sweep aside . . . safeguards to human life." Because she believed that economic and political empowerment for black citizens required the cooperative effort of black men and women, she organized the Alpha Suffrage Club. Formed in 1913, the club was the first black female suffrage club in Illinois. The club sent Wells-Barnett as an Illinois delegate to the National American Woman Suffrage Association's suffrage parade on March 3, 1913, in Washington, D.C. White Illinois delegates pleaded with her to march with the black delegates at the back of the procession. She refused and argued that "the southern women have tried to evade the question time and again by giving some excuse or other every time it has been brought up. If the Illinois women do not take a stand now in this great democratic parade then the colored women are lost." Moreover, she continued,

"I shall not march at all unless I can march under the Illinois banner." Despite support from white allies, Wells-Barnett's motion to march with the state contingent fell on deaf ears.

Afterward, Wells-Barnett disappeared from the parade site. Illinois delegates assumed she had admitted defeat and decided to march with the black contingent; but as the delegates began marching down Pennsylvania Avenue, she quietly stepped out from the crowd of spectators and joined her state colleagues. By her bold action, she successfully integrated the suffrage movement in the United States.

In 1915, she played a pivotal role in steering the Suffrage Club to endorse the election of Oscar DePriest, an election he won, to become the first black alderman of Chicago. The club's loyalty to the Republican machine also sustained the reign of white Republicans in Chicago politics. Throughout the twenties, Wells-Barnett maintained her interest in the political arena, and in 1930, she ran unsuccessfully for the Illinois senate as an independent candidate.

Her anti–Booker T. Washington stance and alliances with Timothy Thomas Fortune and Marcus Garvey often placed Wells-Barnett at odds with her peers and with the federal government. She believed agitation, activism, and protest were the only means of change in the United States, and she saw Washington's philosophy as accommodationist. Wells-Barnett supported the editor of the *Age*, Timothy Thomas Fortune, in his efforts to resuscitate the National Afro-American League because the organization expressed some of her own grievances—disfranchisement, lynching, inequitable distribution of education funding, the convict lease system, and Jim Crow laws. She spoke at **Universal Negro Improvement Association** meetings and hailed Garvey as the person who had "made an impression on this country as no Negro before him had ever done. He has been able to solidify the masses of our people and endow them with racial consciousness and racial solidarity." As a result, the U.S. Secret Service branded her a dangerous radical.

Wells-Barnett continued writing and reporting despite the controversies surrounding her. She wrote exposés on several riots, including the riot in East St. Louis in July 1917, and she pointed out that similar conditions existed in Chicago. "With one Negro dead as the result of a race riot last week, another one very badly injured in the county hospital; with a half dozen attacks upon Negro children, and one on the Thirty-fifth Street car Tuesday, in which four white men beat one colored man, . . . the bombing of Negro homes and the indifference of the public to these outrages. It is just such a situation as this which led up to the East St. Louis riot." Then, for fourteen days in July and August 1919, black and white Chicagoans battled. In the end, thirty-eight died and 537 were injured.

After a thirty-year exile from the South, Ida Wells-Barnett returned in 1922 to investigate the case of the Arkansas black farmers who were indicted for murder in what was known as the (Elaine) Arkansas race riot, and she published the pamphlet *The Arkansas Race Riot.*

Wells-Barnett was a reformer and one of the first black leaders to link the oppression and exploitation of African Americans to white economic opportunity. She believed that black citizens had to organize themselves and take the lead in fighting for their own independence from white oppression. Through her campaigns, speeches, reports, books, and agitation, she raised crucial questions about the future of black Americans.

Wells-Barnett died in Chicago of uremia in 1931. Her autobiography *Crusade for Justice: The Autobiography of Ida B. Wells,* edited by her daughter, Alfreda Duster, was published posthumously in 1970. A diary she kept from 1885 to 1887 was published in 1995 under the title *The Memphis Diary of Ida B. Wells.* It was edited by Miriam DeCosta-Willis.

WANDA HENDRICKS

Wilson, Margaret Bush (1919–)

"There is no progress without struggle," is a quote widely attributed to black nationalist Marcus Garvey, but Margaret Bush Wilson embraced this philosophy as her own. Wilson's life has been characterized by fights against unfair laws and practices, segregation, housing discrimination, and poverty. Her first victory came when, as a young lawyer, she assisted her father, James T. Bush, president of the local real estate brokers association, in what became the framework for *Shelley v. Kraemer,* the case that led to the 1948 U.S. Supreme Court decision declaring restrictive housing covenants unenforceable under the law.

Not all of Wilson's battles have been with the establishment, however. She stands for her beliefs, even in the face of opposition. For example, Wilson endorsed the nomination of Clarence Thomas as associate justice of the Supreme Court in 1991, despite his denunciation by many women's and civil rights groups, including the **National Association for the Advancement of Colored People** (NAACP), to which she has given her life's work.

Wilson's courage and single-mindedness typify her determined personality and deep convictions. In 1983, after years of troubled administration at the NAACP, where she had served as chairperson of the national board since 1975, Wilson tried to correct the association's continuing management problems. However, instead of a productive meeting of minds, old feuds and bitter feelings between Wilson and NAACP Executive Director Benjamin Hooks distorted the issues. Wilson suspended Hooks but was pressured to reinstate him a week later. Wilson has characterized this struggle as the "moment of truth," when she came face to face with what she calls "sexism in the most ironic place." Although ridiculed, Wilson stayed the course and fought even harder for the ideals of the organization to which she had committed herself for more than sixty years.

Born Margaret Berenice Bush on January 30, 1919, she recalls, "I was literally born and raised in the NAACP, and the issues that it faces have been a part of my earliest experiences." Activism in the NAACP was indeed a family tradition. Both her parents were active members of the St. Louis branch. Her mother, Berenice Casey Bush, served on the executive committee. Her brother, James, Jr., and sister, Ermine, also were members. Ermine regularly modeled for the NAACP's national journal, *The Crisis*.

In addition to being exposed to the inequities of life through the work of the NAACP, growing up in St. Louis during the Great Depression made Wilson sensitive to the plight of poor people. She realized very early on that the only way to help oneself and others was through education. After graduating from Sumner High School in 1935, she enrolled in Talladega College, Talladega, Alabama, where she obtained her bachelor of arts degree in economics cum laude. Her desire to better people's lives inspired her to pursue a career in law, and in 1943, she received her law degree from Lincoln University School of Law. At Lincoln she met Robert E. Wilson, whom she later married; they have one son, Robert Edmund Wilson III.

Wilson returned to St. Louis to practice law as U.S. attorney at the Department of Agriculture and later as assistant attorney general. She also deepened her commitment to the NAACP, assuming leadership positions on the local executive board. In 1958, she was elected president of the St. Louis branch and, in 1962, president of the Missouri state branch.

In the 1960s, Wilson's commitment reached the national level. In 1963, her excellent leadership and organization of the NAACP's first statewide conference in Missouri earned her a seat on the national executive board. President Lyndon B. Johnson appointed her to the Anti-Poverty and Civil Rights Act of 1964 task force. The Johnson administration introduced the Model Cities program, a federal initiative to increase aid to severely distressed urban areas. Having worked for the Missouri Office of Urban Affairs and as founder of the Model Housing Corporation, which was designed to secure federal grants for housing, Wilson was a highly qualified candidate to fill a vacancy in the position of deputy director of the St. Louis Model Cities Agency in 1968.

Her other professional positions include administrator for Community Services and Continuing Education, legal specialist for the state Technical Assistance Office, professor for the Council on Legal Education Opportunity at Lincoln University School of Law, assistant director of the St. Louis Lawyers for Housing, chair of the Land Reutilization Authority of St. Louis, and senior partner in the firm of Wilson, Smith, Wunderluch, and Smith.

Wilson is a member of many community, professional, and service organizations, including **Alpha Kappa Alpha** Sorority; the Missouri Council on Criminal Justice; the St. Louis Lawyers Association; and the Mound City, Missouri, the American, and the National Bar associations. She has served on the board of the Monsanto Company and of the Police Foundation and as a trustee of Washington University and Saint Augustine's College.

Although she is the recipient of many awards, one of her most treasured is the Democracy in Action Award, given to her in 1978 by the American Jewish Conference, an organization committed to human rights.

FRANCELLO PHILLIPS-CALHOUN

Women's Political Council, Montgomery, Alabama

The Women's Political Council (WPC) of Montgomery, Alabama, was a grass-roots organization of black professional women formed to address the city's racial problems. The group led efforts in the early 1950s to secure better treatment for black bus passengers, and in December 1955, it initiated the thirteen-month bus boycott that culminated in a U.S. Supreme Court decision ordering desegregation of the city bus system.

The WPC was founded in 1949 by **Mary Fair Burks,** head of the Alabama State College English Department in Montgomery, after a personal encounter with racist treatment by the police. A majority of the council's middle-class membership were teachers at the college or in local public schools; many were congregants at Dexter Avenue Baptist Church (where Martin Luther King, Jr., became pastor in 1954). The group's initial purposes were to foster women's involvement in civic affairs, to promote voter registration through citizenship education, and to aid women who were victims of rape or assault. One of its most successful programs was an annual event called Youth City, which taught black high school students about politics and government and "what democracy could and should mean." During election campaigns the WPC worked with the white-only League of Women Voters to inform black citizens about political candidates.

In 1949, Jo Ann Robinson, a newly hired English professor at Alabama State College, joined the council. Her firsthand experiences with segregated seating on buses prompted Robinson to succeed Burks as WPC president in 1950 and to shift the council's primary focus to challenging the seating policy. Under her leadership the council grew to over 200 members and expanded to three chapters in different areas of the city. It built a reputation as the city's most dynamic and effective black civic organization, in part because it directly challenged racial injustice. During the early 1950s, WPC leaders met regularly with Mayor W. A. Gayle and the city commission to lobby for bus reforms and other civic improvements. Although they succeeded in pressuring the city to hire its first black police officers and to increase funding for the black community's parks and playgrounds, they made no progress in their effort to ameliorate bus segregation. (Publicly, at least, they did not seek to end segregated seating but to make it more equitable.) Robinson expressed the group's frustration in a May 1954 letter to Mayor Gayle, four days after the Supreme Court's *Brown* v. *Board of Education* school desegregation ruling, in which she warned him of a possible bus boycott if conditions did not improve.

The WPC first considered organizing a boycott in March 1955 after Claudette Colvin, a fifteen-year-old high school junior, was arrested for refusing to give up her seat in the unreserved middle section of a city bus to a white passenger. Robinson and WPC colleagues helped arrange two meetings that black representatives held with city and bus company officials and took the lead in demanding reform, but to no avail. Colvin's arrest and conviction angered and unified the black community. In a spontaneous protest, large numbers refused to use the buses for several days.

When **Rosa Parks** was arrested on December 1, 1955, for the same offense as Colvin, WPC leaders were ready to implement the boycott that they had been discussing since the earlier incident. Parks, a longtime NAACP activist who was deeply respected in black Montgomery, seemed the ideal community symbol around which to mobilize a mass protest. Robinson pre-

pared a flyer calling upon black citizens to refuse to ride the buses the following Monday, the day of Parks' trial. She spent Thursday night mimeographing the 50,000 flyers that she and two students distributed all over town the next day. The resulting one-day boycott was so successful that several thousand participants voted at a mass meeting to continue the protest until they won decent treatment.

Although Martin Luther King, Jr., and other male leaders, particularly ministers, took over the visible leadership of the boycott after it began, several WPC activists—including Robinson, Burks, Irene West, and Euretta Adair—played crucial roles in organizing and sustaining it. They served on all major committees, shared in planning and strategy, helped to manage the car pool system, and handled many of the boycott's day-to-day details. Robinson negotiated skillfully with white officials concerning the bus demands and edited the monthly newsletter. In addition, dozens of active council members assisted the boycott in various ways.

Ironically the council's indispensable role in ending city bus segregation contributed to its organizational decline. Partly because its central goal was achieved, and partly because the WPC was overshadowed by the Montgomery Improvement Association (MIA) that was created to direct the boycott, the council subsequently found itself with a diminished leadership role in the black community. After the boycott the MIA took on some of the major issues that had animated the WPC, such as voter registration and public parks. Still, the women's organization coexisted and cooperated with the MIA for a number of years.

Younger women reinvigorated the council, guided by older members serving as role models. "Members felt that young, concerned women, with their futures ahead, would benefit by the WPC," Robinson recalled, "and that we would help them to organize and select goals and directions for their future."

Robinson and Burks left Montgomery in 1960, after several Alabama State College professors were fired for civil rights activities, to take teaching positions in California and Maryland, respectively. Information is not available on the extent to which the younger women became involved in the later civil rights movement in Montgomery and elsewhere.

STEWART BURNS

Chronology

1619

The first African women arrive in North America, at Jamestown, Virginia.

1663

In Glouchester, Virginia, African slaves and white indentured servants plan a revolt. They are betrayed and the rebels are executed.

1681

An unnamed black woman is executed for burning down a barn in Roxbury, Massachusetts.

1688

The first known document protesting slavery in the British colonies, the "Germantown Mennonite Resolution Against Slavery," is drafted.

1708

In Long Island, New York, a slave rebellion results in the deaths of seven whites. Four slaves are executed.

1711

A group of fugitive slaves leads an attack on a settlement in South Carolina.

1712

Slaves in New York City revolt. After the revolt twenty-one are captured and executed.

1720

Slaves thought to be involved in a revolt near Charleston, South Carolina, are executed or banished.

1727

In Glouchester and Middlesex, Virginia, a rebellion involving blacks and Native Americans is uncovered before it can be carried out.

1729

Slaves, with either the help or the influence of the Chickasaw tribe, attempt to revolt and establish their own community near New Orleans, Louisiana. Their plan is discovered.

1730

At least 200 slaves in Virginia plot a rebellion, believing that whites are not following an alleged decree by King George of England to free all slaves who are Christian. The plan is revealed before it can be carried out.

1739

In Stono, South Carolina, slaves rebel and try to escape to Florida. Armed, they kill any white who stands in their way. Most are captured, but twelve succeed in their flight.

1741
Slaves are found to be planning to burn down Charleston, Massachusetts.

1765
Jenny Slew sues for her freedom in a Massachusetts court and wins.

1775 to 1783
South Carolina loses more than a fifth of its slave population to escape.

1777
Vermont is the first state to abolish slavery.

Jenny, a slave woman to John Lewis, is condemned and executed for conspiracy.

1778
Rachel, a slave of Lockey Collier, is executed for murder.

1780
Elizabeth Freeman, also known as Mum Bett, goes to court, in Massachusetts, in search of freedom and wins.

1782
Passing as a man for more than a year, **Deborah Gannet** fights as a member of the revolutionary forces, and her bravery is noted. According to some accounts, she is an African-American.

A guerrilla war by a group of ex-slaves called the King of England's Soldiers, is carried out in Georgia and South Carolina.

1787
The Free African Society is established in Philadelphia. It is the first organization formed specifically to improve the condition of black Americans.

The African Union Society, the first official organization to foster blacks' return to Africa, is founded in Newport, Rhode Island.

1791
In Louisiana, a slave rebellion is crushed. Twenty-three slaves are executed and three whites are banished.

1793
The Fugitive Slave Act is passed, making it criminal to harbor a fugitive slave or to attempt to prevent his or her arrest.

1803
Black protesters burn portions of New York City.

1804
In New Haven, Connecticut, the African Friendly Society and the Female Benevolent Society are founded.

1807
African slaves arriving in Charleston, South Carolina, die by starving themselves rather than submit to enslavement.

1808
The African Association for Mutual Relief is established in New York City.

1811
Slaves rebel outside New Orleans. Government troops are called in and the rebellion is put down. One hundred slaves are killed.

1815
The Underground Railroad is begun by Levi Coffin, a Quaker.

1820

Members of the American Colonization Society in New York City send the first expedition of African Americans to Africa, where they create the Republic of Liberia.

1822

A revolt in Charleston, South Carolina, spearheaded by Denmark Vesey, a free black, is revealed by another slave resulting in the arrest of 139 blacks and forty-seven executions, including Vesey's.

1826

Nashoba, a colony for free blacks, is founded near Memphis, Tennessee, by black woman Frances Wright. It exists for only four years and the surviving inhabitants emigrate to Haiti.

1827

The first black newspaper, *Freedom's Journal,* is founded. It actively campaigns against slavery. The Female Literary Society of New York is a main source of financial support.

1831 to 1861

75,000 slaves escape from the South using the Underground Railroad.

In Virginia, Nat Turner's rebellion begins with five other slaves and soon grows to at least sixty. Fifty-seven whites are killed during the revolt. Turner is eventually captured and executed.

In Philadelphia, the Colored Female Society is established.

The first Annual Convention of the People of Color is held in Philadelphia. They officially stand in opposition to the Ameri-

can Colonization Society's attempts to send African Americans to Africa.

1832

Maria Stewart, the first American-born woman to give a series of public lectures, calls for self-determination for all African-American men and women.

The Afric-American Female Intelligence Society is founded in Boston, Massachusetts. It is both a literary and self-help group.

1833

The **Philadelphia Female Anti-Slavery Society** is founded.

1834

Colored Female Anti-Slavery Societies are founded in both Middletown, Connecticut, and Newark, New Jersey.

1835

Held in Philadelphia, the Fifth Convention for the Improvement of Free People of Color proposes that the term African not be used in the names of black institutions and that blacks cease to use the term colored to describe themselves.

Groups of African Americans and Native Americans lead two separate revolts in Florida.

The first "vigilance committee" is formed in New York City. These committees are established to help fugitive slaves and protect them from kidnapping.

1836

In Boston, a group of black women forces its way into a courtroom and rescues two fugitive slave women before they can be returned to the South.

1837

Held in New York City, the Anti-Slavery Convention of American Women holds its first meeting. One-tenth of the participants are black.

1838

Free blacks protest segregation in transportation in Boston and, in Philadelphia, protest the Pennsylvania Reform Convention, which bans them from voting.

1839

When a faction loyal to William Lloyd Garrison comes to power in the American Anti-Slavery Society, women gain higher roles of responsibility in the organization.

Sojourner Truth begins her career as an abolitionist.

1848

Ellen Craft and her husband, William, escape from Georgia by impersonating a female slaveowner and her servant.

1849

Mary Ann Shadd [Cary] adds her voice to the call for black self-reliance with a pamphlet entitled "Hints to the Colored People of North America."

Harriet Tubman escapes from slavery and begins her career as "Moses," one of the bravest and most successful conductors of the Underground Railroad.

To help raise money for Frederick Douglass' newspaper, *North Star*, The Women's Association of Philadelphia is formed.

In Ohio, a group of women demands inclusion in a discussion on black suffrage. The women are allowed to participate.

1850

A revised Fugitive Slave Law is enacted, which not only allows Southern slave owners to pursue escaped slaves into the North, but states that the federal government must capture and return any slave who escapes into the free states.

Mary Ann Shadd [Cary] moves to Canada after the passage of the revised Fugitive Slave Law.

1851

At a woman's right convention in Akron, Ohio, **Sojourner Truth** delivers her famous "Ain't I A Woman?" speech.

1852

Mary Ann Shadd [Cary] publishes another pamphlet, strongly encouraging blacks in the United States to go to Canada.

1853

In Rochester, New York, the National Council of Colored People is founded.

1854

Women are one-third of the delegates at the National Emigration Convention, and Mary E. Bibb is elected second vice president.

1855

Ann Wood is among a group of slaves who succeed in escaping from Virginia to Philadelphia.

Mary Ann Shadd Cary is made a corresponding member of the National Convention of Colored People.

1856

Slave rebellions are recorded in almost every Southern state.

Margaret Garner, caught while attempting to escape with her family, kills three of her four children rather than have them return to slavery.

1858

John Brown holds his antislavery convention in Chatham, Canada. Thirty-four blacks and twelve whites attend.

1859

John Brown leads his raid against the Federal arsenal in Harpers Ferry, West Virginia.

1860

Harriet Tubman begins speaking publicly for women's rights and abolition.

1861

The Civil War begins at Fort Sumter, South Carolina.

Five black women join Clara Barton in nursing wounded soldiers in Baltimore, Maryland.

Freedmen's aid and relief organizations form in major cities all over the North to assist newly freed slaves.

Harriet Tubman leads guerrilla raids during the Civil War, as well as scouting and spying for the Union Army.

1863

In California, **Mary Ellen Pleasant** succeeds in pushing through a law that gives African Americans the right to testify in court.

Functioning as a servant in the Confederate White House, **Mary Elizabeth Bowser** is a successful spy for the Union forces.

The Emancipation Proclamation is signed.

1869

The American Equal Rights Association splits over the question of black male suffrage versus woman suffrage. As a result of the split, the National Woman Suffrage Association, headed by Susan B. Anthony, and the American Woman Suffrage Association, headed by Henry Ward Beecher, are formed.

1871

Mary Ann Shadd Cary addresses the U.S. House of Representatives on the issue of woman suffrage.

1875

The Civil Rights Act is passed in the U.S. Congress. This act states that there can be no discrimination in public places or on means of transportation within the United States.

Carrying clubs, black women in South Carolina ensure that, on election day, black men have access to polling places all over the state. They do the same the following year.

1876

The National Woman Suffrage Association elects Harriet Purvis as vice president. She is the first black woman to serve in that position.

The Colored Women's Progressive Franchise Association is founded by Mary Ann Shadd Cary.

1877

Union troops are withdrawn from the South.

1881

More than 3,000 black women are involved in a strike by the Washerwomen's Association of Atlanta.

The first of the Jim Crow laws is passed in Tennessee.

Black women are excluded when the American Federation of Labor (AFL) is founded.

1885

Suffragist and activist **Gertrude Mossell** publishes her column "Our Woman's Day" in the first issue of the New York City newspaper *Freeman.*

1890

Locust Street Settlement House is started by **Janie Porter Barrett** in Hampton, Virginia.

1892

Fannie Barrier Williams, wife of a prominent black attorney, is appointed a clerk in charge of exhibit installations at the Columbian Exposition in Chicago. A New York black women's club puts together an exhibit that is accepted for display.

Three black store owners are lynched in Memphis, Tennessee. One of them is the close friend of Ida B. Wells, prompting her to begin her antilynching crusade.

Southern Horrors, Ida B. Wells' first book, is published. The money to finance it comes from a fund-raising event in New York that is called "the greatest demonstra-tion ever attempted by race women for one of their own number."

1895

The First National Conference of Colored Women of America meets in Boston. There are 104 delegates, representing fourteen states and the District of Columbia. Out of this conference comes the National Federation of Afro-American Women.

1896

The National League of Colored Women, headquartered in Washington, D.C., and the National Federation of Afro-American Women merge to form the **National Association of Colored Women** (NACW). **Mary Church Terrell** is its first president.

In the *Plessy* v. *Ferguson* case, the Supreme Court declares that separate but equal facilities in interstate railroad transportation are legal. This sets a precedent that will be used in court cases concerning everything from public washrooms to public schools.

1897

The **White Rose Mission** is founded in New York City by **Victoria Earle Matthews** to aid black women moving from the South.

1899–1903

At least four black women are lynched.

1900

London, England, is the sight for the first Pan-African Conference. **Anna Julia Cooper** and Anna H. Jones are the only black women to address the Conference.

1903

Georgia Anderson and other working-class women from Savannah submit a petition to the Georgia legislature requesting $2,000 to emigrate to Africa.

1904 to 1908

At least six black women are lynched.

1905

The Niagara Movement is founded.

The constitution of the Industrial Workers of the World (IWW) allows for membership in the union regardless of sex, creed, or color.

Black women in New York City found the National League for the Protection of Colored Women.

1906

The second Niagara Movement meeting is held. One hundred black men and women attend.

1908

After a devastating race riot in Springfield, Illinois, socialist journalist William English Walling issues a challenge to fight racism. The result is a call to meet and act signed by sixty people, including **Ida B. Wells-Barnett** (now married to Ferdinand Barnett) and Mary Church Terrell.

Josephine Allensworth and her husband found an all-black town near Bakersfield, California.

The **Atlanta Neighborhood Union** is founded, under the leadership of **Lugenia Burns Hope**.

1909

The **National Association for the Advancement of Colored People** (NAACP) is estab-lished by a group of black and white activists.

1909 to 1913

At least six black women are lynched.

1910

Kathryn Magnolia Johnson becomes the first field worker for the NAACP.

The Negro Fellowship League votes Ida B. Wells-Barnett its first president.

1911

The Committee on Urban Conditions of Negroes merges with the National League for the Protection of Colored Women and becomes the National Urban League.

Touring California, Sarah M. Overton speaks out for the suffrage amendment and tries to rally black support.

The **Universal Negro Improvement Association** is founded by Marcus Garvey.

1913

The Supreme Court rules that the Civil Rights Act of 1875 is unconstitutional. The test case is that of Emma Butts, a black woman who sued a steamship company for denying her accommodations equal to those it provided for white passengers.

Illinois becomes the first state east of the Mississippi River to enfranchise women.

Ida B. Wells is asked not to march with the white Illinois delegation at a National American Woman Suffrage Association parade in Washington, D.C. She does anyway.

In Los Angeles, black women open the Sojourner Truth Industrial Club, a home for orphans and unwed mothers.

The Great Migration of Southern blacks to Northern industrial towns begins.

1915

Mary Burnett Talbert becomes president of the National Association of Colored Women.

1916

Thirty towns with largely black populations exist in Oklahoma Territory alone. The town of Boley, Oklahoma, has two banks, a sawmill, a cotton gin, three newspapers, two hotels, and a college.

1917

Forty African Americans are killed in the East St. Louis, Illinois, race riots.

Ten thousand African Americans march down New York City's Fifth Avenue in a NAACP-sponsored silent parade to protest racial discrimination and, especially, racial violence.

The Circle for Negro War Relief is created by black women to give black soldiers access to medical and other services not provided by the still-segregated U.S. Armed Forces.

Domestic workers, waitresses, and tobacco stemmers form a union and organize a strike for higher wages in Norfolk, Virginia.

Ella Pete organizes the Domestic Servants Union in New Orleans, with more than 1,000 members.

1918

The Women's Political Association of Harlem becomes one of the earliest black organizations to promote birth control.

The U.S. Congress is petitioned by the National Liberty Congress of Colored Americans to pass a law that would make lynching a federal offense.

The African Blood Brotherhood is founded, with Bertha DeBasco, Gertrude Hall, and Grace Campbell as members of this radical black nationalist organization.

1918 to 1927

Eleven black women are lynched, three of them were pregnant.

1919

The National Association for the Advancement of Colored People (NAACP) commits itself to lobbying against lynching.

At least 100 people die and more than 1,000 are injured during the "Red Summer," when race riots flash across the country.

Mary Burrill publishes her play "They That Sit in Darkness" in the periodical, *Birth Control Review.* The play presents the then radical position that all women deserve access to birth control.

1920

The Nineteenth Amendment is passed, granting women the right to vote.

In New York City, **Audley "Queen Mother" Moore** starts organizing domestic workers. She also works to assist black tenants when their white landlords try to evict them.

The **International Council of Women of the Darker Races** is formed, largely by black women.

When the Universal Negro Improvement Association (UNIA) holds its international convention in New York City, Henrietta Vinton Davis chairs the mass meeting in Madison Square Garden.

Jessie Fauset is a delegate to the Second Pan-African Congress, representing the NACW.

1922

Mary Talbert, president of the NACW, enlists other women's groups and forms a group called the Anti-Lynching Crusaders. Among other things, the Crusaders work to bring white women into the antilynching movement.

The **Universal Negro Improvement Association** is accused of sexism by some of its own delegates. The accusation results in the appointment of Henrietta Vinton Davis as the fourth Assistant President General.

1925

The first women's auxiliary of the black Pullman porter's union is formed. It is called the Hesperus Club of Harlem.

In Birmingham, Alabama, while registering to vote, a group of black women is attacked and beaten by election officials.

1930

An organization called the Association of Southern Women for the Prevention of Lynching is founded by white women.

Ella Josephine Baker becomes the first national director of the Young Negroes Cooperative League, in Harlem.

The **Housewives' League of Detroit**, founded by Fannie B. Peck, is created to promote consumer loyalty within the black community.

1931

The Share Croppers' Union is organized in Alabama.

1933

The St. Louis, Missouri, nut-pickers' strike involves more than 1,200 black women.

1934

A resolution to end discrimination is rejected at the AFL's national convention. The AFL instead promotes segregated unions for blacks and whites.

1935

The Congress of Industrial Organizations (CIO) separates from the AFL. The new group concentrates more on black workers and on unskilled workers in the South in general.

The **National Council of Negro Women** is founded. **Mary McCleod Bethune** is president and **Lucy Diggs Slowe** secretary.

1938

Louise "Mamma" Harris, a black tobacco stemmer, starts a series of walkouts at the I. N. Vaughn Company in Richmond, Virginia. The strikes that result are supported by white International Ladies Garment Workers Union (ILGWU) women.

The **International Ladies Auxiliary, Brotherhood of Sleeping Car Porters** is officially created.

1940

Ella Josephine Baker joins the NAACP and eventually becomes president of the New York branch, the first woman in that position.

1942

In Chicago, the Congress of Racial Equality (CORE), an organization committed to nonviolent direct action to end racial discrimination, is formed.

A Gallup poll shows that a great majority of white Americans favored anti-lynching laws.

1943

A major strike held at the R. J. Reynolds company in North Carolina involves several black women union organizers, including Theodosia Simpson, Velma Hopkins, Viola Brown, Ruby Jones, and Miranda Smith. Reynolds agrees to sit down and talk with Local No. 22 of the Food, Tobacco, Agricultural, and Allied Workers of America (FTA).

Detroit's United Auto Workers co-sponsor, with the NAACP, a rally at which 10,000 workers demand that war industry jobs be opened to black women.

The CIO forms the Committee to Abolish Racial Discrimination.

The first sit-in at a segregated restaurant is conducted by the Congress of Racial Equality (CORE), in Chicago, Illinois.

A series of race riots occurs in cities across the country, including Mobile, Alabama; Detroit, Michigan; Beaumont, Texas; and Harlem, New York.

1944

Viola White is arrested on a bus in Montgomery, Alabama, for violating the segregation code and then is beaten and jailed. She is released from jail, but when she dies ten years later, the appeal of her conviction has still not been heard.

1945

Black union membership has risen from 200,000 in 1940 to 1.25 million.

Maida Springer Kemp is the American Federation of Labor's delegate to the United States Division of Psychological Warfare to Observe Wartime Conditions among English Workers.

1946

Dr. **Mary Fair Burks,** head of the Alabama State College English Department in Montgomery, founds the Women's Political Council (WPC).

The Links, Inc., is founded by Margaret Roselle Hawkins and Sarah Strickland-Scott in Philadelphia.

CORE organizes an interracial bus trip through the South, which is called the Journey of Reconciliation. It is later used as a model for the Freedom Riders of the 1960s.

1950

The Universal Association of Ethiopian Women is created by **Audley Moore,** Mother Langley, and Dara Collins in order to obtain economic reparations and foster black pride and education.

Forty-one percent of laboring black women in America work as domestics.

1951

The National Negro Labor Council (NNLC) is founded to put pressure on industries to comply with the Fair Employment Practices Committee nondiscrimination policies in peacetime. One-third of its original delegates are black women.

Eslanda Goode Robeson and two other protestors fail to convince the United Nations postwar conference on genocide that violence against blacks in America should be part of the U.N. agenda.

1952

The NAACP goes to the U.S. Supreme Court with *Brown* v. *Board of Education of Topeka, Kansas.* A year after the cases are first presented, the court votes unanimously that, "in the field of public education the doctrine of 'separate but equal' has no place."

The NAACP asks **Daisy Bates** to become president of the Arkansas state conference of NAACP branches.

1953
The National Council of Negro Women elects **Vivian Carter Mason** president.

1954
School desegregation begins on a large scale, in Washington, D.C., and Baltimore, Maryland.

1955
Rosa Parks decides to remain seated on a bus in Montgomery, Alabama, and the Montgomery bus boycott is born.

Autherine Lucy [Foster] becomes the first black student to attend the University of Alabama after the NAACP spends more than three years in court pressing for her enrollment.

1957
Nine young people attempt to enter Central High School in Little Rock, Arkansas. Governor Orval Faubus orders out units of the Arkansas National Guard to prevent their entry. President Dwight D. Eisenhower sends 1,000 paratroopers from the 101st Airborne Division to protect the students as they enter the school.

The Southern Christian Leadership Conference (SCLC) is formed with Rev. Martin Luther King, Jr., at its head and **Ella Baker** as organizer of the central office.

The first Civil Rights Bill since 1875 is passed.

The Prayer Pilgrimage is held on the steps of the Lincoln Memorial, attracting a crowd of over thirty thousand people.

In Tuskegee, Alabama, black residents begin a boycott of white businesses.

The National Council of Negro Women elects **Dorothy L. Height** as president.

1960
Ella Baker calls a conference of sit-in leaders at Shaw University. Out of this conference comes the **Student Nonviolent Coordinating Committee** (SNCC).

Four black students from North Carolina A&T College inaugurate the sit-in protests of the civil rights movement by integrating a Woolworth's lunch counter in Greensboro, North Carolina.

The Civil Rights Act of 1960 is passed.

1961
The Freedom Riders begin their bus trips through the South to desegregate bus terminals.

1962
Four black mothers begin a sit-in at a Chicago elementary school, protesting de facto segregation, unequal facilities, double shifts, and mobile classrooms.

1963
Vivian Malone and James Hood succeed in enrolling at the University of Alabama after National Guardsmen and U.S. Deputy Attorney General Nicholas Katzenbach force Alabama governor George Wallace to step aside.

The "March on Washington" attracts more than 200,000 people in a protest for civil rights and equality for African Americans in the United States. Martin Luther King, Jr., delivers his "I have a Dream" speech.

Four little girls—Addie Mae Collins, Denise McNair, Carole Robertson, and Cynthia Wesley—are murdered when an unknown number of white men bomb the Sixteenth Street Baptist Church in Birmingham, Alabama.

Violence against the Cambridge, Maryland, Non-violent Action Committee, led by **Gloria Richardson** and Inez Grubb, prompts a conference in Washington, D.C., attended by Attorney General Robert Kennedy, among others.

1964

With Ella Baker's participation, SNCC members **Annie Devine,** Victoria Gray, and **Fannie Lou Hamer** are among the founders of the **Mississippi Freedom Democratic Party** (MFDP), which registers 80,000 voters in its first year alone.

Voters from the MFDP elect a delegation to the 1964 Democratic convention, an alternative to the regular delegation that was elected by white voters.

Martin Luther King, Jr., wins the Nobel Peace Prize. He divides the prize money among six groups, including the National Council of Negro Women.

The Civil Rights Act of 1964 prohibits discrimination in public accommodations and in employment.

1965

Members of MFDP, along with women and men from SCLC and CORE, start on a march from Selma to Montgomery, Alabama, only to be clubbed and teargassed by police on horseback. Two weeks later, they start out again.

Lyndon Johnson signs the Voting Rights Act into law.

The National Guard is called in to Los Angeles to try to regain control during the largest race riot in the history of the United States. The Watts riots end with at least thirty-four people dead, 900 injured, 3,500 arrested, and most of that section of the city burned to the ground.

1966

Huey P. Newton and Bobby Seale found the **Black Panther Party** (BPP) in Oakland, California. The three women nearest the top of the organization are **Kathleen Neal Cleaver, Elaine Brown,** and **Ericka Huggins. Angela Davis** is deeply involved in BPP programs with prison inmates.

Ruby Doris Smith-Robinson becomes the executive secretary of SNCC.

1967

The YWCA elects its first black woman president, **Helen Jackson Clayton.**

During the summer, race riots break out in major cities all over the United States.

1968

Martin Luther King, Jr., is assassinated in Memphis, Tennessee. Riots break out in 125 American cities.

A biracial coalition unsuccessfully challenges the all white Mississippi delegation at the Democratic National Convention.

The **National Domestic Workers Union** is formed by **Dorothy Lee Bolden.**

1969

Women in the Black Panther Party begin to speak out in the *Black Panther* newspaper and at party meetings. They also actively seek and win leadership roles.

In Atlanta, Georgia, **Coretta Scott King** starts developing the Martin Luther King, Jr., Center for Nonviolent Social Change.

1970

Activist and Black Panther Party member **Angela Davis** is charged with conspiracy, kidnapping, and murder and put on the FBI's Ten Most Wanted list. She is later cleared of all charges.

Clara McBride Hale and her daughter **Lorraine** open Hale House, a home for drug-addicted babies.

1971

Rev. Jesse Jackson forms Operation PUSH. The letters stand for People United to Serve Humanity.

The National Organization for Women elects **Aileen Hernandez,** their first black woman president.

1973

The National Black Feminist Organization (NBFO) is founded.

Marion Wright Edelman forms the Children's Defense Fund (CDF) in Washington, D.C.

1974

Elaine Brown is named chairperson of the Black Panther Party.

1975

Black feminists create the **Combahee River Collective.** Among other things, it discusses homophobia in the black community and is the first organization to do so.

The Girl Scouts U.S.A. elect **Gloria Randle Scott** to be their national president. She is the first black woman to hold the position.

1976

The Congressional Black Caucus Foundation is founded by spouses of black congressmen. The foundation promotes Congressional internships and legislative training.

1978

Faye Wattleton is the first African American, the first woman, and the youngest person to be named president of Planned Parenthood.

The Daughters of the American Revolution admit their first black member, Karen Farmer.

1981

The **National Coalition of 100 Black Women** is formed by **Jewel Jackson McCabe.**

1982

Romona H. Edelin becomes head of the National Urban Coalition.

1984

Mary Frances Berry, along with Walter Fauntroy and Randall Robinson, is arrested at the South African embassy while holding a sit-in to protest that country's policy of apartheid.

Mary Frances Berry successfully sues President Ronald Reagan to retain her position on the U.S. Commission on Human Rights.

1986

Coretta Scott King meets with Winnie Mandela and awards Bishop Desmond Tutu the Martin Luther King, Jr., Non-Violent Peace Prize.

1991

The National Conference of Christians and Jews elects Maryann Coffey co-chairperson. She is the first woman and the first African American to hold this position.

1993

Elaine Jones becomes head of the NAACP Legal Defense and Educational Fund, Inc., the first woman to hold this position.

Mary Frances Berry is made chair of the U.S. Commission on Civil Rights by President Bill Clinton.

1995

In Chicago, the Rev. **Willie Barrow** leads Operation PUSH to get guns out of the neighborhoods, to fight domestic violence, to take care of untended children, and to fight for higher education.

Bibliography

GENERAL BOOKS USEFUL TO THE STUDY OF BLACK WOMEN IN AMERICA

Reference Books

African-Americans: Voices of Triumph. Three volume set: *Perseverance, Leadership,* and *Creative Fire.* By the editors of Time-Life Books, Alexandria, Virginia, 1993.

Estell, Kenneth, ed., *The African-American Almanac.* Detroit, Mich., 1994.

Harley, Sharon. *The Timetables of African-American History: A Chronology of the Most Important People and Events in African-American History.* New York, 1995.

Hine, Darlene Clark. *Hine Sight: Black Women and The Reconstruction of American History.* Brooklyn, New York, 1994.

Hine, Darlene Clark, ed., Elsa Barkley Brown and Rosalyn Terborg-Penn, associate eds. *Black Women in America: An Historical Encyclopedia.* Brooklyn, New York, 1993.

Hornsby, Alton, Jr. *Chronology of African-American History: Significant Events and People from 1619 to the Present.* Detroit, Michigan, 1991.

Kranz, Rachel. *Biographical Dictionary of Black Americans.* New York, 1992.

Lanker, Brian. *I Dream a World: Portraits of Black Women Who Changed America.* New York, 1989.

Logan, Rayford W., and Michael R. Winston, eds. *Dictionary of American Negro Biography,* New York, 1982.

Low, W. Augustus, and Virgil A. Clift, eds. *Encyclopedia of Black America.* New York, 1981.

Salem, Dorothy C., ed. *African American Women: A Biographical Dictionary.* New York, 1993.

Salzman, Jack, David Lionel Smith, and Cornel West. *Encyclopedia of African-American Culture and History.* Five volumes. New York, 1996.

Smith, Jessie Carney, ed., *Notable Black American Women.* Two volumes. Detroit, Michigan, Book I, 1993; Book II, 1996.

General Books about Black Women

Giddings, Paula. *When and Where I Enter: The Impact of Black Women on Race and Sex in America,* New York, 1984.

Guy-Sheftall, Beverly. *Words of Fire: An Anthology of African-American Feminist Thought.* New York, 1995.

Hine, Darlene Clark, Wilma King, and Linda Reed, eds. *"We Specialize in the Wholly Impossible": A Reader in Black Women's History.* Brooklyn, New York, 1995.

Jones, Jacqueline. *Labor of Love, Labor of Sorrow: Black Women, Work, and the Family from Slavery to the Present.* New York, 1985.

Lerner, Gerda, ed. *Black Women in White America: A Documentary History.* New York, 1972.

Books Which Include Information on Black Women Activists

Branch, Taylor. *Parting the Waters: America in the King Years, 1954–63.* New York, 1988.

Carson, Clayborne. *In Struggle: SNCC and the Black Awakening of the 1960s.* Cambridge, Massachusetts, 1981.

Egerton, John. *Speak Now Against the Day: The Generation Before the Civil Rights Movement in the South.* Chapel Hill, North Carolina, 1995.

Kluger, Richard. *Simple Justice: The History of* Brown v. Board of Education *and Black America's Struggle for Equality.* New York, 1975.

Payne, Charles M. *I've Got the Light of Freedom: The Organizing Tradition and the Mississippi Freedom Struggle.* Berkeley, California, 1995.

Robinson, Jo Ann Gibson. *The Montgomery Bus Boycott and the Women Who Started It: The Memoir of Jo Ann Gibson Robinson.* Knoxville, Tennessee, 1987.

Williams, Juan. *Eyes on the Prize: America's Civil Rights Years, 1954–1965.* New York, 1987.

Contents of the Set

(ORGANIZED BY VOLUME)

Brooks, Gwendolyn
Brown, Linda Beatrice
Burroughs, Margaret
Butler, Octavia E.
Campbell, Bebe Moore
Cary, Lorene
Chase-Riboud, Barbara
Cleage, Pearl
Cliff, Michelle
Clifton, Lucille
Cooper, J. California
Cortez, Jayne
Danner, Margaret Essie
Davis, Thadious
Davis, Thulani
Delaney Sisters, The
DeVeaux, Alexis
Dove, Rita
Drumgold, Kate
Dunbar-Nelson, Alice
Dunlap, Ethel Trew
Fauset, Jessie Redmon
Giddings, Paula
Giovanni, Nikki
Golden, Marita
Greenfield, Eloise
Guy, Rosa
Hamilton, Virginia Esther
Harper, Frances Ellen Watkins
hooks, bell
Hopkins, Pauline Elizabeth
Hunter, Kristin
Hurston, Zora Neale
Johnson, Georgia Douglas
Jones, Gayl
Jordan, June
Kincaid, Jamaica
Larsen, Nella
Lorde, Audre
Madgett, Naomi Long
Marshall, Paule
McElroy, Colleen J.
McMillan, Terry
Meriwether, Louise
Morrison, Toni
Naylor, Gloria
Petry, Ann Lane
Polite, Carlene
Sanchez, Sonia

Sanders, Dori
Shockley, Ann Allen
Southerland, Ellease
Spencer, Anne
Taylor, Mildred
Thomas, Joyce Carol
Vroman, Mary Elizabeth
Walker, Alice
Walker, Margaret Abigail
Wallace, Michele
West, Dorothy
Williams, Sherley Anne
Wilson, Harriet E.

Dance, Sports, and Visual Arts

Dance
Asante, Kariamu Welsh
Baker, Josephine
Blunden, Jeraldyne
Brown, Joan Myers
Collins, Janet
DeLavallade, Carmen
Dunham, Katherine
Forsyne, Ida
Hinkson, Mary
Jamison, Judith
Johnson, Virginia
Primus, Pearl
Turney, Matt
Waters, Sylvia
Yarborough, Sara
Zollar, Jawole Willa Jo

Sports
Ashford, Evelyn
Bolden, Jeanette
Brisco-Hooks, Valerie
Brown, Alice
Brown, Earlene
Cheeseborough, Chandra
Coachman, Alice
Daniels, Isabel
Dawes, Dominique
DeFrantz, Anita
Devers, Gail
Edwards, Teresa

Faggs, Mae
Ferrell, Barbara
Franke, Nikki
Gallagher, Kim
Garrison, Zina
Gibson, Althea
Glenn, Lula Mae Hymes
Harris-Stewart, Lusia
Hudson, Martha
Hyman, Flora
Jacket, Barbara J.
Jackson, Nell Cecilia
Jones, Barbara
Jones, Leora "Sam"
Joyner, Florence Griffith
Joyner-Kersee, Jackie
Love, Lynette
Matthews, Margaret
McDaniel, Mildred
McGuire, Edith
Miller, Cheryl
Mims, Madeleine Manning
Murray, Lenda
Patterson-Tyler Audrey (Mickey)
Pickett, Tydie
Powell, Renee
Rudolph, Wilma
Stokes, Louise
Stone, Lyle (Toni)
Stringer, C. Vivian
Thomas, Debi
Thomas, Vanessa
Tyus, Wyomia
Washington, Ora
White, Willye B.
Williams, Lucinda
Woodard, Lynette

Visual Arts
Beasley, Phoebe
Blount, Mildred E.
Brandon, Barbara
Burke, Selma
Catlett, Elizabeth
Fuller, Meta
Gafford, Alice
Humphrey, Margo
Hunter, Clementine

Education

Religion and Community

Social Activism

Science, Health, and Medicine

Contents of the Set

(LISTED ALPHABETICALLY BY ENTRY)

Index

Page numbers in **boldface** indicate main entries. Page numbers in *italics* indicate illustrations.

Modjeska Simkins Scholarship
Award 165
Mondale, Walter 23
Montgomery bus boycott
16–20, 40
and Mary Fair Burks 56, 57
and Rosa Parks 16, 17, 18,
20, 57, 61, 96, 145, 146,
191, 203
and Jo Ann Gibson Robin-
son 17, 18, 19, 57, 159,
160
and Women's Political
Council 160, 190–192
*Montgomery Bus Boycott and
the Women Who Started It,
The* (Robinson) 160
Montgomery Improvement Asso-
ciation 19, 20, 40
and Jo Ann Gibson Robin-
son 160
and Women's Political
Council 191
Montgomery Women's Political
Council *see* Women's Political
Council, Montgomery, Ala-
bama
Moody, Anne E. **133**
and Annie Devine 73
Moon, Henry 118
Moore, Amzie 1
Moore, Audley **133–135**, 200,
202
Moore, Eloise 134
Moore, Fred 31
Moss, Thomas 184–185
Mossell, Gertrude 198
Mother Clubs 176, 177
Mothershed, Thelma 120
Motley, Constance Baker 80
Mott, Lucretia 6–7
Mountain View Hotel 11

N

NAACP *see* National Association for the Advancement of
Colored People
NAACP Legal Defense and Educational Fund 27, 206
NACW *see* National Association
of Colored Women

Nash, Diane **136–137**
and Freedom Riders 23,
136, 172
and Highlander Folk School
97
and Student Nonviolent Coordinating Committee
23, 136–137, 172, 173
Nashoba colony, Tennessee 195
Nashville movment
and Diane Nash 136
National Abortion Rights Action League 25
National Afro-American League
and Ida B. Wells-Barnett
187–188
National Alliance against Racism and Political Repression
and Angela Davis 71
National American Woman Suffrage Association
and Alpha Suffrage Club
29–30
and Ida B. Wells-Barnett
187, 199
National Association for the Advancement of Colored People
15–16, **137–141**
antilynching campaign 10,
200
and Ella Baker 16, 36, 39,
40, 201
and Daisy Bates 21, 45, 46,
140, 203
and Amelia Boynton 51–52
and Elizabeth Brooks 53
and *Brown* v. *Board of Education* 16, 65, 202–203
and Septima Clark 60, 61,
96
and Marian Wright Edel-
man 76
and Medgar Evers 78
and Myrlie Evers-Williams
27, 77, 79, *138*, 140–141
first woman president
129–130
founding of 15, 199
and Aileen Clarke Hernan-
dez 90
and Ruby Hurley 101–102
and Elaine Jones 206

and Kathryn Johnson 15,
107, 139–140, 199
and Daisy Lampkin 115,
116, 117–118, 140
and Little Rock Nine
45–46, 129
and Clara Lupe 123
and McMillan, Enola
129–130
and Montgomery bus boy-
cott 20
and Rosa and Raymond
Parks 145
and Bernice Robinson 158,
159
and Modjeska Simkins
163–164, 165
and Althea T. L. Simmons
165–166
and sit-ins 123
and Vada Watson
Somerville 171–172
and Mary Church Terrell
15, 137, 139
and teachers' salaries equalization 60
and University of Alabama
integration 80–81, 203
and Ida B. Wells-Barnett
15, 137, 139, 187
and Margaret Bush Wilson
189
Youth Council 17, 21
National Association of Colored
Women
and Elizabeth Brooks 53
founding of 9, 175, 186,
198
and Daisy Lampkin 115,
116, 117
and Audley Moore 135
and Mary Burnett Talbert
200
and Mary Church Terrell 9,
175–176, 198
National Black Feminist Organization 25–26, 63, 205
National Black Women's Health
Project
and Avery Byllye 32, 33
National Coalition of 100 Black
Women 205